Voicing Women

Voicing Women

Gender and sexuality in early modern writing

Edited by Kate Chedgzoy,
Melanie Hansen and Suzanne Trill

KEELEUNIVERSITY**PRESS**

First published in 1996 by
Keele University Press
Keele, Staffordshire

© respective contributors

Typeset by Carnegie Publishing Ltd
18 Maynard St, Preston
Printed by Hartnolls
Bodmin, Cornwall, England

ISBN 1 85331 108 1

Contents

Acknowledgements

The editors would like to thank the University of Liverpool for the financial and practical support which made it possible for us to organize the original conference, 'Voicing Women', in April 1992. We are grateful to Kelvin Everest for giving us his backing as Head of Department, and to all the other staff who helped us, especially Cathy Rees and Barbara Smith.

'Voicing Women' was the first major conference in this country to focus on women and writing in early modern Britain, and it was also the first major academic event any of us was involved in organizing. In its affirmation of the ideal of feminist collective scholarship, and of the significance of the chosen subject, it had a huge influence on us subsequently. It was also an exceptionally enjoyable event. We would therefore like to extend our warmest thanks to everyone who attended, contributed, and helped to make it such a memorable conference. Particular thanks must go to Elspeth Graham, Ann Thompson and Helen Wilcox, for encouraging us to take on the project and supporting us throughout; and to the women who were our contemporaries as postgraduates at Liverpool, and created the context in which 'Voicing Women' could happen.

Finally, for personal support we would like to thank Keith, Leslie and Peggy Osborne; John and Val Trill; Jennifer and Kelvin Chedgzoy; and Claire Stevens.

Notes on Contributors

Maureen Bell is Lecturer in English at the University of Birmingham. She has worked on the *History of the Book in Britain* project, and is joint author of *A Biographical Dictionary of English Women Writers, 1580–1720* (with George Parfitt and Simon Shepherd, 1990) and *The Early Seventeenth-century Book Trade and John Foster's Inventory of 1616* (with John Barnard, 1994).

Kate Chedgzoy is in the Department of English and Comparative Literary Studies at the University of Warwick. She is the author of *Shakespeare's Queer Children: Sexual Politics and Contemporary Culture* (Manchester University Press, 1995), and is working on an anthology of writings by and about early modern women with Melanie Hansen and Suzanne Trill (to be published by Edward Arnold).

Danielle Clarke is Lecturer in English at University College Dublin. She is currently editing the works of three Renaissance women poets for Penguin.

Helen Hackett is Lecturer in English at University College London. She is the author of *Virgin Mother, Maiden Queen: Elizabeth I and the Cult of the Virgin Mary* (Macmillan, 1995), and of articles on Mary Wroth's *Urania* and on courtly writing by Renaissance women. She is currently working on a book on women and romance in the Renaissance.

Melanie Hansen lectures in English at the University of Durham. Her research interests are English Renaissance antiquarianism and geography, as well as early modern women's writing.

Katharine Hodgkin is Lecturer in English at the University of Wales, Swansea. She has written articles on autobiographical and confessional writing in the seventeenth and twentieth centuries, and is currently editing Dionys Fitzherbert's manuscript for publication.

Jacqueline Pearson is Lecturer in English Literature at the University of Manchester. She is the author of two books, most recently *The Prostituted Muse: Images of Women and Women Dramatists 1642–1737* (Harvester, 1988), and a number of articles on seventeenth and eighteenth-century women writers, including Aphra Behn, Mary Pix, Margaret Cavendish and Jane Barker. She is currently completing *A Dangerous Recreation: A History of Women's Reading 1750–1824*.

Bronwen Price teaches Renaissance Literature and Critical Theory at the University of Portsmouth. She has published articles on seventeenth-century poetry, and is currently working on early women's poetry.

Tamsin Spargo is Lecturer in Literary and Historical Studies at Liverpool John Moores University and has published a number of articles on Bunyan and on critical and cultural theory. She is currently working on a book on Bunyan and authority.

Suzanne Trill lectures in English at The Queen's University of Belfast. Her current research centres on religious writing by women in the Renaissance.

Susan Wiseman is Lecturer in the Department of English and Comparative Literary Studies at the University of Warwick.

Stephanie Wright is Lecturer in English Studies at the University of Sunderland. She has edited Elizabeth Cary's *The Tragedy of Mariam* for Keele University Press and recently directed the première production of the play. She is currently co-ordinating a joint research project, 'Women and Dramatic Production 1570–1670', with Alison Findlay and Gweno Williams.

Introduction:
'Voice that is Mine'

Kate Chedgzoy

Amongst the many books housed in the Bodleian Library in Oxford, one of the more enigmatic is an anonymous, untitled folio volume containing nearly a thousand pages of religious poetry, mostly of an ecstatic, prophetic nature. Authorship of this volume has been attributed to the Fifth Monarchist Anna Trapnel, but although Trapnel's life and work are becoming matters of some interest to historians and literary critics, this text has remained marginal even to her emergent canon.[1] There are several possible reasons for this continuing neglect, all of which have wider implications for the study of early modern women's writing. The volume's anonymity and the insecurity of the attribution to Trapnel present an obstacle to potential readers, in so far as the reconstruction of the early modern canon which is currently in process has done little to destabilize the importance of the authorial signature as guarantor of a text's identity. Indeed, since for feminist literary history the gender of the author is often a crucial aspect of the text's interest, one effect of the project to revalorize women's writing and to reclaim forgotten or neglected texts has been a reaffirmation – against the grain, as several feminists have noted,[2] of some influential strands of literary theory – of the significance of the author as subject of her own writing. Anonymous texts, such as the Bodleian folio, thus sit uneasily with the feminist project in some respects; while we might bear in mind Virginia Woolf's guess that Anon was often a woman,[3] nevertheless our desire as feminist readers is often still – as Woolf suggested – to think back through literary foremothers (with) whom we can identify.

Moreover, since this collection of poetry has remained essentially unedited and unrepublished since its first appearance and is known to exist in only this one copy, it typifies rather dramatically the material restrictions which still limit access to much writing by women. In the last few years a handful of important and valuable anthologies, such as *Her Own Life* and *Kissing the Rod*,[4] as well as larger-scale projects like the Brown University Women Writers text database and the Pickering Women's Classics series, have begun to bring early modern women's

1

writing to a wider readership. But by their nature, anthologies can only offer a limited and partial glimpse of what is a very substantial body of texts; and surprisingly few women writers have so far been accorded the honour of adequate modern single-author editions of their works.[5] For many readers who do not have easy access to copyright libraries, then, access to texts such as this one attributed to Anna Trapnel, which have not been established as part of the tiny emergent canon of Renaissance women's writing, is a question of material as well as ideological restrictions.

Many of the essays in *Voicing Women* tackle this question of the cultural contexts for the production and reception of women's work, showing how it was written, circulated and published in the sixteenth and seventeenth centuries as well as considering the volatile circumstances in which it is now being retrieved, read and discussed. For instance, Katharine Hodgkin notes that Dionys Fitzherbert had her manuscript copied and prepared for circulation, clearly therefore intending to make her text available to a reading public in a form which has rather different social and cultural meanings from publication for sale. This suggests that in re-evaluating the nature and extent of early modern women's literary production, we should be wary of fetishizing women's access to a public print culture as the sole indicator of their participation in the literary domain. But it also means that Fitzherbert's text has long remained particularly inaccessible, since there are only two copies in existence; and the aspiring reader of those needs both to meet the criteria for admission to the Bodleian Library, and to possess the necessary skills in deciphering seventeenth-century handwriting. On the other hand, Hodgkin's essay also suggests that without the impetus provided by the feminist interest in the social construction and history of women's mental health and madness, as well as the privileged status given to female hysteria in certain strands of recent feminist theory, Dionys Fitzherbert's fascinating text might have continued to languish unread. The agenda set by feminist scholarship and activism in the late twentieth century thus plays an important part in stimulating the recovery of Renaissance women's writing. Similarly, Jacqueline Pearson's essay shows that although the initial retrieval of Aemilia Lanier's poetry may have stemmed from the cultural allure Lanier derived from A. L. Rowse's claim that she was Shakespeare's Dark Lady, it may actually be more relevant to place her in a female-centred literary context, in which the female author's dedication of her work to other women is important as both a textual and pragmatic strategy. Where Shakespeare's prestige once authorized Lanier's entry into print in a modern edition, her work is now, in the light of feminist preoccupations with women's relations with each other as well as with men, able to be read in the context of a network of women.

These and other essays in this volume establish the cultural conditions in which early modern women were writing; but as well as illustrating the material and ideological constraints upon women's voices – and this is true of the twentieth century as much as of the seventeenth – they also demonstrate women's capacity to resist or evade these constraints, and to negotiate with the contradictions of femininity. The important issue of women's position in relation to the material practices which enable texts to circulate in the world is addressed here by several contributors. Maureen Bell, in focusing on women as printers rather than writers, brings to view an important and often overlooked aspect of women's cultural agency, tracing the extraordinary commitment to the written word demonstrated by the courage in the face of persecution shown by women publishers of oppositional texts in the 1660s. Stephanie Wright takes the writing career of Elizabeth Cary as a case study in order to explore the processes by which multiple concerns – economic, educational and institutional, as much as intellectual or aesthetic – intersect to shape and reshape the canon of Renaissance literature, and warns that some strategies used by feminist critics to argue for the (re)instatement of women writers may, in the long run, prove counter-productive. At the same time, her own work on editing, interpreting and staging Cary's work constitutes an important intervention in the changing canon. Indeed, many of the contributors to *Voicing Women* are engaging directly with all these issues by working on editions of early modern women's texts, including some which are discussed in this volume. The union of textual scholarship and critical sophistication which characterizes the work of many of the scholars represented here is playing an important part in redrawing the literary map of early modern Britain.

I began this introduction by referring to the anonymous volume of poems which has come to be associated with the authorial signature of Anna Trapnel, and it may seem odd to open a collection of essays which centres on the complex, multi-faceted relations between gender, identity and writing by referring to a text which so flagrantly problematizes those concerns. But it is precisely by virtue of its anonymous, enigmatic status that the Bodleian folio brings its feminist readers face to face with a number of crucial questions: whose is the voice that is speaking in this text? Is there, indeed, only one voice, or is the text polyphonic, a site traversed by many voices rather than the articulation of a single one? What kind of evidence, about both material and stylistic issues, can we use to identify an anonymous text? Suzanne Trill's essay explores these issues in relation to the problematic attribution to a male author, Nicholas Breton, of a text which purports to represent a woman who was herself both a writer and an influential literary patron. Trill demonstrates that asking such questions enables us not only to deepen and extend our understanding of women's writing, but also to reconsider the place of masculine subjectivity in textual production.

Most fundamental, perhaps, is the question which many of the contributors to this volume pose in different ways to themselves and to the community of feminist Renaissance scholars: as we seek to retrieve the voices of early modern women, to create a space where they can be heard afresh, what desires are caught up in the process of looking for them, and how far do our feminist desires influence what it is that we hear? These questions echo throughout this book, and I will return to them later in the introduction. For the time being, though, I want to take the attribution of the Bodleian volume at face value, and allow that voice which may or may not belong to Anna Trapnel to articulate some of the concerns about voice, identity, authority and desire which are central to this volume:

> The voice it doth come down and cast
> All that is of self away;
> But what's of Christ it doth show forth;
> For it is that must bear sway.
> That voice which is mine, pass sentence on;
> But what is of the Lord,
> Do thou most sweetly utter forth,
> And O spread it abroad.
> That voice which is mine, is very dross,
> It is filthy dregs also:
> But what is of the Lord Christ, is that
> For which the Spirit do blow.
> Voice that is mine, throw to the pit,
> It's worthy to have no other place:
> But what is of the Lord shall be advanced
> In its most lovely grace.
> What is of me is mixed, and
> Its defilement is great:
> But what is of the Lord is pure,
> And cometh from his seat.
> Voice which is mine, bury under ground,
> And let it no more come:
> But what is of the Lord, let it run forth
> With a mighty discovering tongue.
> Voice that is mine, O do thou bury,
> And lay it in the grave;
> But what is thine, do thou raise up,
> A glorious resurrection to have.[6]

Trapnel here focuses our central questions of what it means for a woman to give voice, and of how a voice marked as feminine may be constructed, articulated and heard, and she does so in the context of concerns which will recur throughout this volume: politics, resistance and oppositionality, for example; the relation of spirituality to the subjective and social dimensions of life; and the body as a site where social meanings are produced and circulated.

This passage illustrates very vividly the ambiguity of Trapnel's position as a female prophet and the sense of self associated with it. She insists here on her own insignificance and passivity, representing herself as merely the transmitter of God's message; yet she is also empowered by the social status that being a prophet gives her. In what might appear an essentially conservative textual strategy, Trapnel affirms the conventional association of masculinity with what is high and exalted, femininity with the chthonic – what Bakhtin famously calls 'the lower bodily stratum'.[7] She contrasts the foulness and insignificance of her own voice with the purity and glory of 'the Lord Christ'. Yet there is a curious irony here; for it is her own poetic voice which encloses and oscillates between statements of her own supposed degradation and of the 'royal grace' of her divine master. Both the subterranean voice and the 'mighty discovering tongue' are in fact produced by Trapnel herself. It is the prophet's very self-abnegation which enables her to celebrate that which is holy and to give voice to the social and spiritual desires which prophetic texts typically articulate.

These lines thus illustrate the extent to which prophecy constructs an ambiguous position for women, in which weakness becomes a kind of strength, and a public voice with which to make pronouncements on the key social and religious issues of the day is attained, albeit at the cost of reaffirming conventional views of female weakness and irrationality. The poem returns us, then, to the question of the relation between female subjectivity and writing, a relation which Trapnel's prophetic texts both produce and disavow, in that they are presented as 'true relations' of her inspired utterances, yet the abnegation of self required in prophecy means that she remains unconscious of what she is supposed to have said; her words have to be returned to her by an amanuensis. The problematic nature of the relations between female subjectivity, writing and the inscription of a gendered textual persona is explored by several contributors. Stephanie Wright considers the problematic consequences of a critical strategy which appears to prioritize the authority of female experience over female authorship across a range of genres and forms. Susan Wiseman's essay on writings by Quaker women about their travels in Europe and the 'New World' shows that in their inscription of encounters with cultural diversity, these texts may resist our desire to find in them the traces either of the proto-abolitionist sentiments often attributed to Quakers, or of a sense on the part of the writers that their gender is a crucial determinant of their experience and of the means by which they choose to textualize it. She proposes that this recalcitrance might prompt us to reconsider the limitations of currently influential theories of alterity. Similarly, Helen Hackett addresses the uncomfortable disjunction between the kinds of expectations feminist readers may bring to bear on women's writing, and the textual strategies they actually employ. Employing feminist film theory to read Renaissance texts, and then using those texts to interrogate the insufficiently historicized and nuanced assumptions of theory, she argues that we need to develop ways of reading which can respond flexibly to the complex and volatile relations between gender, subjectivity and writing.

The relationship between language, the body and sexuality is a crucial aspect of Helen Hackett's essay, and these concerns are also explored by several other contributors. Danielle Clarke, Katharine Hodgkin and Jacqueline Pearson all show how the cultural construction of the female body offers a range of tropes which mediate women's concerns about, for example, religion and spirituality, and influence the perception of women's agency. Bronwen Price argues that Aphra Behn self-consciously negotiates with conventional poetic representations of the female body and female subjectivity in order to destabilize assumptions about the relationship between gender and writing, so that in her poems traditional tropes are rewritten to construct a site on which female desire can be articulated. Yet what enables this is precisely a kind of poetic dis-articulation – a difference of view or point of resistance within the text which problematizes the relationship between gendered identity and poetic voice.

I want at this point to return briefly to Anna Trapnel, for as Diane Purkiss has argued, such dis-articulations are characteristic of prophetic utterance, and may account for the particular appeal of that form to women; since 'prophetic utterance necessarily involves a radical dis-location of the voice from the body', the discourse of prophecy arguably offered women an opportunity 'to represent their own anomalous position in relation to language'.[8] Prophecy, then, foregrounds and makes explicit the problematic nature of women's place in discourse. As many of the essays in this collection will demonstrate, such contradictions and ambiguities are characteristic of women's relation both to literary production and to public discourses and practices – notably, as here, religion – in the early modern period. The passage quoted above from the Bodleian folio swiftly moves away from a sense that the woman's voice is located as straightforwardly oppositional, in order to centre it in its own discursive space. It is, to borrow Jean Franco's term, *ex-centric*,[9] in that it refuses to be constrained by its marginal location by asserting its centrality to a different scheme of things, while also relishing the persistence of what is undeniably a certain eccentricity. Melanie Hansen's essay opens the collection by challenging the habitual relegation of women to the cultural margins, and showing that it may be when women are most culturally central – located, symbolically and actually, 'in the middest of men' – that their voices become a site of contestation.

Like a number of contributors – especially Suzanne Trill, Danielle Clarke and Tamsin Spargo – Hansen is less concerned with women's writing than with textual constructions of femininity by male authors. *Voicing Women* differs from some of the other collections of essays which explore gender relations in Renaissance culture in that we have chosen to exclude studies of *canonical* male authors. The juxtaposition of women's writing which is being subjected, as a result of the impact of feminist scholarship, to such intense new scrutiny, with male writers who have always occupied a relatively minor status, or whose position appears unstable, creates a different view of the landscape of early modern writing and brings to light some unexpected and intriguing connections and differences, as well as foregrounding questions about the processes by which the canon is shaped. Writers like Nicholas Breton, Anthony Stafford, John Knox and John Bunyan all have, in different ways, somewhat uneasy relations to the canon: Breton and Stafford, for most purposes, are scarcely less marginal and neglected than, say, the Quaker women Susan Wiseman discusses, and it is arguable that the transformation of the canon initiated by feminist criticism means that they are now rather more obscure than increasingly prominent women such as Aemilia Lanier or Aphra Behn. Bunyan and Knox occupy intriguingly ambiguous positions, in that although they are well-known figures, their texts these days are relatively little read. It is arguable, indeed, that their fame is guaranteed by their status not as writers, but as cultural icons whose power derives largely from their association with, respectively, the history of nonconformity and debates about women and power. In her essay on Bunyan, Tamsin Spargo examines the disruptive presence of female figures in his narratives, showing how their 'contra-dictions' challenged the male authorities which sought to erase them, and thereby exposing the gendered nature of the strand of religious discourse and practice in which Bunyan is such an important figure. Danielle Clarke, in contrast, examines the work of male authors, now almost entirely obscure, who deploy an eroticized vocabulary and the tropes of neo-platonism to construct woman – in the particular form of the Virgin Mary – as a textual figure in which anxieties about politics, religion and female agency intersect. While writers like Henry Hawkins and Anthony Stafford are now largely forgotten, their work provides important

insights into the symbolic centrality of fantasies of female power in a
culture which hedged about the agency of actual women with innumerable restrictions.

I want finally to consider the place of another gendered voice – that
of the feminist critic, who constructs her own public identity as re-
searcher and writer by invoking the textual voices of women otherwise
silenced by time. Here, Suzanne Trill's warning, following Toril Moi,
that in taking it upon ourselves to speak for the other woman, we run
the risk of silencing her or appropriating her voice to serve our own
ends, is relevant. Our voices as critics are fashioned in dialogue with
each other, with the academy at large, and with the men and women
we write about, and the sexual politics of our own speaking becomes
intelligible within an overdetermined intellectual and institutional
matrix. As Helen Hackett and Susan Wiseman warn, if our motivation
for doing this work at all is a consequence of our feminism, it may be
that we bring with us to the study of early modern women a certain
desire to establish a kind of proto-feminist bond which will enable us
to transcend historical difference, but which can only result in the
falsification of the work of women who had other priorities and other
concerns.

The answer to the problem does not lie in denial of the motivating
power of this feminist political desire; again, as a number of these essays
demonstrate, a meditation on the nature of the problem may in itself
be a productive starting point for work which both addresses the
theoretical and historiographical questions which we need to engage
with, and also furthers our understanding of early modern culture and
texts. Moreover, in bringing this issue to view, we challenge that
pretence of disinterestedness in literary criticism which in practice has
always served the interests of the status quo. Stephanie Wright, for
instance, points out that in tackling the politics of canon formation, it
is not sufficient merely to import fresh texts into the canon, but that
a feminist re-evaluation of the criteria for admission is also necessary.
In this connection, I want to invoke Eve Kosofsky Sedgwick's remark
that the value of the feminist re-evaluation of the canon does not lie
merely in the retrieval of forgotten or marginalized works by women,
but also in its laying bare of the imbrication of the processes of canon
formation with power, by attacking:

> if not the empirical centrality, then the conceptual anonymity of the
> master-canon ... If it is still in important respects *the* master-canon
> it nevertheless cannot now escape naming itself with every syllable
> also *a* particular canon, a canon of mastery, in this case of men's
> mastery over, and over against, women.[10]

In many ways, the essays in this volume – and arguably, in some cases, the writers discussed – seek to challenge masculine cultural mastery; and to the extent that as Renaissance scholars we are all also teachers and administrators, such a challenge is by no means confined to the terrain of scholarship, but spills over into all aspects of our lives as feminists in the academy. In this context, the editors are intensely aware of the enabling impact of an earlier generation of feminist scholars' work on women in the Renaissance, and we would, indeed, like to record a special debt to Elspeth Graham, Ann Thompson and Helen Wilcox; without their example and support, we would never have contemplated either organizing the conference which gave rise to this volume, or bringing the book to completion. Similarly, the 'Voicing Women' conference confirmed that there is a community of men and women eager to sustain an engagement with Renaissance women's writing, and questions of gender in early modern culture more generally, in ways which are continuing to transform our discipline.

Meanwhile, the processes of expansion and change at institutional and intellectual levels which the academy has undergone in the last few years have opened up new spaces in which we can do the kind of work exemplified by *Voicing Women* and share it with students. But this work has also been undertaken in a context which sees increasing pressure on staff–student ratios, and increasing poverty among students who often simply cannot afford to buy editions of early women's writing – which are not, of course, available in any of the ranges of cheap paperback classics – and who are often too exhausted, as the result of undertaking paid work to finance themselves, to engage with the ideas we want to share with them.

I began this introduction by talking about the material and ideological constraints on women's cultural participation in the Renaissance; I want to end by invoking the political stakes of our own project. Maureen Bell's essay, which closes this volume, is the only one which still bears, in some respects, the traces of its origin as an occasional piece, a conference paper written for a particular moment. The conference took place a few days after the Conservative Party's unexpected victory in the 1992 General Election. I think it would be fair to say that few delegates to 'Voicing Women' had contributed to the Tory triumph, and the atmosphere of what was otherwise an exceptionally pleasurable event was undoubtedly tinged with a sense of what we had lost – and what we stood to lose over the following years. Anyone who has lived or worked in this country since 1992 will be able to produce their own narrative of that loss; but as Maureen Bell reminds us, although the sentimental appropriation of the past carries its own political dangers, attending to the many voices in which women spoke in early modern

Britain may also enable the production of narratives of resistance which do not foreclose on the possibility of an other understanding of the past, a different vision of the future.

Notes

1. For introductions to Trapnel, see Elspeth Graham, Hilary Hinds, Elaine Hobby and Helen Wilcox (eds), *Her Own Life: Autobiographical Writings by Seventeenth-Century Englishwomen* (London: Routledge, 1989), pp. 71–86; and Kate Chedgzoy, 'Female prophecy in the seventeenth century: the instance of Anna Trapnel', in Suzanne Trill and William Zunder (eds), *Writing the English Renaissance* (London: Longman, 1996). Portions of this introduction appear in that essay in a slightly different form.
2. See for example Nancy Miller, *Subject to Change* (New York: Columbia University Press, 1988).
3. *A Room of One's Own*, 1929 (London: Grafton, 1977), p. 48.
4. Graham *et al.* (eds), *Her Own Life*; Germaine Greer, Jeslyn Medoff, Melinda Sansone and Susan Hastings (eds), *Kissing the Rod: An Anthology of Seventeenth-Century Women's Verse* (London: Virago, 1988).
5. However, the new Northern Renaissance Seminar series of texts will include a number of works by women, while Penguin are beginning to commission editions of works by Renaissance women.
6. Quoted from a section headed 'From the 29th day of the 10th month, 1657', p. 257. I am very grateful to Peter Davidson for providing me with a transcript of this and other extracts from the Bodleian volume (shelfmark S. 1. 42 Th).
7. Mikhail Mikhailovich Bakhtin, trans. Hélène Iswolsky, *Rabelais and his World* (Cambridge, MA.: MIT Press, 1968), p. 240. For an excellent recent account of the gendering of 'high' and 'low', purity and filth etc., with particular reference to women's cultural agency, see Mary Russo, *The Female Grotesque: Risk, Excess and Modernity* (London: Routlege, 1995).
8. Diane Purkiss, 'Producing the voice, consuming the body: women prophets of the seventeenth century', in Isobel Grundy and Susan Wiseman (eds), *Women, Writing, History 1640–1740* (London: Batsford, 1992), pp. 139–58 (pp. 141, 142). See also Elaine Hobby's *Virtue of Necessity: English Women's Writing 1649–88* (London: Virago, 1988), which claims that in the years from 1649 to 1688, more than half the texts published by women were prophecies (p. 26).
9. Jean Franco, *Plotting Women: Gender and Representation in Mexico* (London: Verso, 1989), p. xi.
10. Eve Kosofsky Sedgwick, *The Epistemology of the Closet* (New York: Columbia University Press, 1991), p. 63.

The Word and the Throne: John Knox's *The First Blast of the Trumpet against the Monstrous Regiment of Women*

Melanie Hansen

The tumultuous career and fiery character of John Knox as a radical Protestant reformer have continued to attract the attention of scholars of Scottish and English political and religious history, as well as those interested in Knox's activities within European Protestant communities. A prolific writer of letters, tracts, sermons and the momentous history, The Reformation in Scotland, Knox's vociferous and frequently polemical outpourings constitute a crucial insight into the Reformation and counter-Reformation turmoils of the mid to late sixteenth century.[1] However, whilst Knox's career has retained this scholarly interest, it is for his Monstrous Regiment of Women that he is perhaps most popularly known. Written during his period of exile in the reign of the Catholic Mary Tudor, the tract's ferocious damning of female monarchy in general and its vicious character assassination of Mary Tudor in particular acquired instant notoriety following its publication, a notoriety that it retains to the present day.[2] As a piece of Protestant propaganda, the explicit purpose of the tract was to employ classical, Christian and sixteenth-century patriarchal commonplaces that asserted women's inability to govern as a powerful and conclusive means by which Knox could substantiate an attack on the Catholic reign of Mary Tudor at the same time as advancing evangelical Protestant faith.

Whilst the reputation of the Monstrous Regiment of Women has accrued primarily from the aggression of its tone and argument, the tract incurred further infamy owing to the unfortunate timing of its publication. Although written by Knox in Dieppe when there seemed to be no end to Mary's reign on the horizon, the tract eventually appeared in England just four months after her death. The undeniable allure of making easy recourse to patriarchal commonplaces about

11

women and government in order to vilify a Catholic female monarch evaporated instantly, of course, on the accession of a Protestant female monarch. Understandably, Elizabeth's response to Knox's tract was not a favourable one and as a consequence of this, its publication seriously damaged the influence and position of Protestant reformers in England, and, even worse, it implicated Calvin as sympathetic to its claims. In many ways, Knox's tract was plucked from potential obscurity to become one of his most well-known works not so much on the basis of its subject matter (the publication of misogynistic pamphlets was far from unusual during this period), but rather because of the unfortunate timing of its publication and the response which that mistiming subsequently engendered. Letters passed from Knox and Calvin to Cecil which, with varying degrees of desperation, attempted to pacify the female monarch in the hope of an appeasement that would attract her support for the Protestant reformers. And John Aylmer sought to contribute to this appeasement by countering Knox's *Monstrous Regiment of Women* with his publication *An Harborowe for Faithful and Trewe Subjectes, agaynst the late blowne Blaste, concerninge the Gouernment of Women* (1559), a text that sought (arguably less than successfully) to approve, legitimate and support the accession of a Protestant queen.[3]

Alongside these ironies surrounding the impact and reception of the *Monstrous Regiment of Women* in England, Knox's interweaving of Protestant and counter-Reformation ideologies with those of gender renders his tract particularly complex. This is because the tract specifically utilizes patriarchal commonplaces and discourses at the same time as the Protestant 'Word' in order to contest political legitimacy, albeit a female legitimacy. Throughout the tract, Knox seeks to affirm by the 'plaine' discourse of the evangelical writer the 'truth' of what he speaks, and he authorizes that 'truth' by citing God's 'plaine will reueled in his wordes' (*Monstrous Regiment*, 9r). And by corroborating his pronouncements by reference to the Scriptures, Knox treated the Old Testament as a source text of legal precedents delineating the subjection of women, legal precedents that, in his view, inevitably transcended any national law. Consequently, Knox's biblical literalism and his evangelical discourse served not just to attack female monarchy, but also to contest the political legitimacy of any monarch.

In fact, the political and gender ideologies encoded in this tract were not the product of a particular moment in Knox's evangelical career. Four years before the tract was written, Knox had formulated a set of questions concerning monarchical inheritance, obedience of subjects to the monarch and the validity of female government, and he had addressed these questions to Calvin and Bullinger. On the issue of 'whether a female can preside over, and rule a kingdom by divine right, and so transfer the right of sovereignty to her husband' Calvin had

answered that whilst government by a woman constituted a deviation
from her 'natural' subjection, if she inherited and governed by custom
and public consent, then it was not to be challenged by her subjects
since that government was ordained by God.[4] However, at precisely
the same time as Knox was failing to persuade Calvin and Bullinger to
concur with his perspective on the obedience of subjects to their
monarchs and on female government, Mary Tudor passed an Act of
Parliament that specifically sought to delineate the constitutional right
of a woman to accede to the throne and to carry out monarchical
dictate. This Act of Parliament of 1554 declared 'that the Regal Power
of this Realm, is in the Queen's Majesty as fully and absolutely as ever
it was in any of her most noble Progenitors, Kings of this Realm'.[5]
Contrary to Knox's position, Mary Tudor's Act illustrates that it was
legal discourse rather than reference to exceptional women in the
Scriptures (women such as Deborah, an individual whom Calvin cited
in his answer to Knox) that ratified her authority to govern. The purpose
of this essay is to situate Knox's tract in the context of Mary's Act of
Parliament of 1554 in order to examine the way in which each of these
figures negotiated with monarchical authority, a negotiation that was
articulated through recourse to different kinds of discourse, patriarchal
and Protestant, legal and gendered.

   There is, however, a further complexity to the orientation of Knox's
tract with Mary's Act of Parliament, and this complexity manifests itself
in relation to the positions from which both Knox and Mary speak.
Knox's subject position is profoundly enigmatic: he positions himself
as an authoritative speaker by means of his utilization of patriarchal
commonplaces that advocate female silence in contradistinction to
masculine speech, whilst also presenting himself as an anonymous
author. At the end of the Preface to the tract, Knox assures his readers
that he is concealing his name not because he fears any physical
retribution but instead, and rather strangely, because 'twise I intende
to do it without name, but at the last blast, to take the blame vpon my
selfe, that all others may be purged' (*Monstrous Regiment*, p. 9). Knox's
simultaneous elision of authorship and promise of future revelation, his
centring of himself as an authoritative masculine speaker, combine
peculiarly with his speaking from a marginal Protestant position and
as a Scottish exile writing in Dieppe about an English Catholic monarchy. In the case of Mary Tudor, however, her own marginal position
as a woman was countered by the legal discourse of the Act of Parliament, one that conferred legitimacy upon her. As the Act confirmed
that the throne could signify a queen as well as a king, Mary was able
to elide the 'natural' subjection and silence of women to position herself
instead as an authoritative speaker within the public realm. For both
Mary and Knox, it was the throne as a sign of monarchical power and

authority that became the site of conflict and ideological appropriation; and it was through recourse to the Word – Protestant or jurisdictional – that they both sought to express that appropriation.

Critical assessment of Knox's *Monstrous Regiment of Women* tends to fall into three distinct areas. In the first instance, scholarship on Knox's career as a whole either stresses that the misogyny of the tract can be explained in part by the prevailing attitudes expressed towards women during this period, or claims that there is little evidence from his writings to suggest that Knox hated women per se.[6] Geddes MacGregor notes that no doubt Knox 'was feeling tired of women in general' when he wrote the tract and that 'when a woman was set in a place of the highest authority in a nation, she could become, Knox felt, a positive evil'.[7] Whilst MacGregor's reading represents a rather simplistic approach, this scholarship invariably interprets the tract in relation to sixteenth-century Protestant prescriptions for female behaviour and definitions of female spirituality, misconceptions which Knox himself espoused. According to this view, the tract encodes ideologies of gendered spirituality, ideologies that are so violently articulated because they constitute a reaction to the immediate political situation of Mary's Catholic reign, and as a consequence of this, they represent the evangelical fervour of the exiled Protestants.

Historical analyses of Mary's reign, however, tend to contradict this approach, arguing that the publication of the *Monstrous Regiment of Women* provides demonstrable evidence of a popular and unanimous male response to the terrible vision of a woman acceding to a throne. Alan Smith in *The Emergence of a Nation State*, for example, introduces his discussion of Mary's reign by citing Knox's assertion that for women to govern confounded nature, God's law, civil law and justice, in order to claim that 'most men of the day would have agreed with these sentiments, if not necessarily with the violence with which Knox expressed them'.[8] Consequently, Knox's tract serves to substantiate Smith's observation that 'Mary's government, simply because it was government by a woman, had grave disadvantages', disadvantages which contributed to the alleged political 'weakness' of her reign as a whole. Whilst Smith's assessment of 'weakness' is shared by most historians of the period, the use of Knox's tract as a means to introduce the dimension of gender into historical analysis tends to be reductively employed: the specific problems encountered by a woman acceding to a throne that Knox's tract polemicizes are never fully confronted.[9]

An alternative approach to the significance of gender in relation to monarchy has been represented by the third critical response to Knox's *Monstrous Regiment of Women*. Feminist criticism of Renaissance literature and culture, and especially studies that address gender debates as articulated through the 'controversy' pamphlets, often include a brief examination of the tract. Because Knox's argument against female monarchy necessarily incorporated prescriptions for the silence and obedience of all women, the tract has been read as one of many formal attacks made against women during this period. In their introduction to the anthology *Half Humankind: Contexts and Texts of the Controversy about Women in England, 1540–1640*, for example, Katherine Usher Henderson and Barbara F. McManus describe the tract as a specific attack on female monarchs as well as on women in general.[10] And in her seminal account of 'controversy' literature, Linda Woodbridge situates Knox's tract in relation to her analysis of texts that respond to the representation of women as dominant and powerful figures, concluding that the tract 'reads more as a marriage sermon than a political treatise'.[11] In this context, Knox's tract can be understood as registering an extreme patriarchal anxiety; an anxiety that constitutes a response to a culture in which women were increasingly visible. From this perspective, the tract has been interpreted as sharing with other misogynistic pamphlets the attempt to constrain women's behaviour and identity; and its notoriety derives from its aggressive argument and discourse in comparison with similar formal attacks.

Whilst these different approaches have successfully registered the historical and cultural significance of Knox's *Monstrous Regiment of Women*, a more detailed analysis of the tract has yet to be offered. Furthermore, despite the fact that interpretation of the tract as a 'formal' attack or 'controversy' pamphlet greatly facilitates the analysis of gender identity in the Renaissance period, the specific gender politics of Knox's polemic have not been fully explored. Since Knox's tract was directed towards Mary Tudor and by implication towards other European female monarchs at this time, such as the Queen of France, Catherine de Medici, the Queen Regent of Scotland, Marie de Lorraine, and her daughter Mary, the *Monstrous Regiment of Women* necessarily considered the political ramifications of any female government. Knox's tract is significant not just because it reiterated popular arguments against women's participation in the public sphere, but also because it responded to the specific legal and religious situation of a female and a Catholic monarchy.

In fact, prior to the accession of Mary Tudor there had been no legal precedent for a female monarch, as there had not been an English queen since Maud or Matilda in 1127–35. It was this lack of legal precedent, together with the confirmation that regal authority was invested in the Queen following the signing of the marriage treaty at Westminster on 12 January 1554, that motivated Mary to pass an Act of Parliament, an Act that affirmed the constitutional right of a woman to accede to the throne in her own right. In expressing that

right, the Act explicitly negotiated with the meanings of the words
'queen' and 'king'. Acknowledging that all previous statutes had been
enacted in the name of king, the Act took issue with those who
subsequently inferred that the word 'King' and the dictates enacted
under that word, could not denote or refer to a 'queen'. The Act
described how:

> malicious and ignorant persons may be hereafter induced and per-
> suaded unto this error and folly, to think that her Highness could
> nor should have, enjoy, and use such like royal authority, power,
> preeminence, prerogative, and jurisdiction, nor do nor execute and
> use all things concerning the said statutes, and take the benefit and
> privilege of the same, nor correct and punish offenders against her
> most royal Person and the regality and dignity of the Crown of this
> realm and the dominions thereof, as the kings of this realm her
> most noble progenitors have heretofore done, enjoyed, used and
> exercised.[12]

Rebuking those 'malicious and ignorant persons' who contested the
investment of regal authority in Mary, the Act was passed for 'the
avoiding and clear extinguishment of which said error or doubt, and
for a plain declaration of the laws of this realm in that behalf'. The
fact that Mary passed this Act of Parliament, despite the existence of
Henry VIII's Third Succession Act of 1543, which specifically named
Mary and Elizabeth as legitimate heirs to the throne, suggests that
genealogy alone was not sufficient to assure the constitutional right of
Mary's accession as a woman. Consequently, despite the fact that Knox's
Monstrous Regiment of Women conforms to many sixteenth-century 'controversy' texts that attacked and prescribed women's behaviour, at the
same time the tract also engaged with and challenged the position
outlined in this Act of Parliament.

In the introduction to the tract, for example, Knox's claim that
women rulers usurped the proper place of men by situating themselves
within the 'middest of men' directly confronted the woman's relationship to power that Mary's Act of Parliament was so careful to delineate.
Knox wrote that 'What wolde this writer [Aristotle] (I pray you) haue
said to that realme or nation, where a woman sitteth crowned in
parliament amongest the middest of men' (*Monstrous Regiment*, 10v).
By the concept 'middest of men' Knox was alluding to the physical
presence of women within the public and the political arena, as well as
to the woman ruler's accession to the constitutional power of a monarch. But, Knox argued further, the ultimate consequence of a woman
being on the throne, and thus by necessity taking her place within
the 'middest of men', had a profound effect upon its signification.

He not only claimed that a woman on the throne subverted the natural and civil order – the 'monstrous regiment of women' – but also, that by acceding to the throne, a woman actually altered and perverted the signification of monarchy itself. Instead of signifying the power and preeminence of the male, a woman on the throne signified a monstrous misuse of power. Thus, whilst Mary's Act of Parliament sought to insert the Queen within the legal and linguistic boundaries of power, to place Mary constitutionally within 'the middest of men', Knox's *Monstrous Regiment of Women* sought to exclude her, an exclusion that was expressed by dissociating the 'true' signification of monarchy from that of a woman.

In order to demonstrate the way in which Knox contested the premises of Mary's Act, it is necessary to outline the gender ideologies that are invested in his tract. This is because it is precisely Knox's utilization of patriarchal commonplaces about women, however obvious they actually appear in the tract, that has encouraged us to understand it as, in essence, explicitly representative of pervasive and, therefore, dominant gender ideologies of sixteenth-century patriarchal culture. However, the tract's recourse to those very commonplaces about women illuminates the way in which attitudes towards women during this period could be encoded textually, and in popular pamphlet form. In addition, the tract's emphatic and lingering emphasis upon those commonplaces represents Knox's deliberate manipulation of popular prejudice and thus constitutes political propaganda. In this sense, the tract does not merely express a masculine anxiety in response to the increasing visibility of women in a variety of public spheres (although this remains an important strand, I think); it also illustrates Knox's attempt to appeal to popular prejudices and gender stereotypes as a means to make easily accessible the specific political point about female government with which he was primarily concerned. For example, Knox's claim that Mary's marriage to Philip prejudiced the English throne because that marriage, according to English marital law, automatically made her subject to the authority of her husband, is a claim that serves to undermine popular confidence in her regal authority and in England's autonomy; whereas in fact, this marital law and the relations between wife and husband encoded within it did not apply to Mary's position as a female monarch (and was preempted by the marriage treaty of 1554). Consequently, it was Knox's conscious manipulation of patriarchal commonplaces, and of popular understanding of marital law, that functioned to make a specific political point about female government; and in the case of Mary's marriage, it was a political point that was manifestly untrue.

So, Knox initiated his attack on Mary Tudor by means of employing classical, Christian and sixteenth-century commonplaces that defined

the identity of 'womankind', and in this respect the tract reads in the
first instance as a formal attack against women. In this reading, it
appears to share similar cultural preoccupations about female identity
that are expressed by sixteenth-century 'controversy' pamphlets, pamphlets that vigorously debated the 'question' of the nature of women.
Thus, Knox utilized the Scriptures, together with citations from classical
and patristic authors, as substantive evidence that women were manifestly unable to assume any kind of authority. For example, he cites
Aristotle, who asserted that women were unable to govern because by
doing so, they disturbed the social order and, furthermore, this disruption brought about the destruction of the people and the country. Thus,
Knox claims that Aristotle:

> doth plainlie affirm, that wher soeuer women beare dominion, there
> must needes the people be disordered, liuinge and abounding in all
> intemperancie, geuen to pride, excesse, and vanitie. And finallie in
> the end, that they must nedes come to confusion and ruine. (13r)

This belief in disruption of the social and political order caused by
women in power, a disruption that actually altered the character of the
people, was reflected in patristic writings. Knox cites Augustine, claiming that 'women ought to be repressed and brideled be times, if she
aspire to any dominion, alledging that dangerous and perilous it is to
suffer her to proceed'. And St John Chrysostome is quoted to suggest
that men became 'brutish' when unable to perceive the 'monstrous'
nature of women in power.

But by far the most influential argument against women possessing
any kind of authority is that of the story of the Fall of Adam and Eve.
In the tract, Knox argues that women are unable to govern because
they were created by God as helpmeets for Adam and that it was God's
law that:

> woman in her greatest perfection was made to serve and obey man,
> not to rule and command him: As Saint Paul doth reason in these
> wordes. Man is not of the woman but the woman of the man. And
> man was not created for the cause of woman, but the woman for the
> cause of man, and therfore ought the woman to have a power upon
> her head (that is a couerture in signe of subjection). (13r–13v)

The relationship between Adam and Eve revealed the way in which
women were specifically created to be subject to the authority of men.
Genealogy, and the importance of being born first, was an intrinsic
part of that argument. But Eve was also to be under the subjection of
Adam because of her role in the Fall. As Knox describes, her yielding

to Satan and her subsequent tempting of Adam culminated in 'two punishments [which] are laid upon her, a dolor, anguishe and payn, as oft as euer she shal be mother; and a subjection of her selfe, her appetites and will, to her husband and to his will' (p. 15). This clearly states that women's subjection to men was a punishment for Eve's part in the Fall; according to biblical commentators, Eve had revealed a character that was liable to be deceived by Satan as well as being capable of deceiving Adam. God's punishment and Eve's character combine to suggest the way in which future generations of women were to be perceived and were to behave. From the story in Genesis, then, Knox claimed that women were unable to govern because of Eve's part in the Fall and God's punishment. All women, regarded as daughters of Eve, were to be treated according to this punishment. But this biblical precept provided the basis from which women's actual identity was constructed. Women, Knox claims, are by their very nature weak and feeble and consequently unable to assume an authoritative role:

Nature I say, doth paynt [women] further to be weake, fraile, impacient, feble and foolishe: and experience hath declared them to be unconstant, variable, cruell and lacking the spirit of counsel and regiment. And these notable faultes have men in all ages espied in that kinde, for the whiche not onlie have they removed women from rule and authoritie, but also some have thought that men subject to the counsel or empire of their wyues were unworthy of all publike office. (10r)

According to Knox, women were naturally 'unconstant' and 'foolish' so that their characters would be manifestly unsuitable for any involvement with constitutional power. And for Knox to suggest that men themselves were unfit to rule if they listened to women, and particularly their wives, reflects the belief that women, like Eve, were capable of great deceit. For Knox, women's most effective role in the management of the state was to be silent.

So, what happened when women were not silent? What happened when, even worse, they gained power and became monarchs as Queen Mary had done? According to Knox, these women not only overruled God's punishment and law about female subjection to the male as described in Genesis but also subverted the nature and law of society itself. They became monstrous women, reigning over a disfigured and monstrous nation, a nation that was inhabited by people who became brutish, and by men who, through their lack of authority in favour of the women, became effeminate. In describing the effect of female monarchs, Knox uses the commonplace Renaissance trope of the world being turned upside down by subversive behaviour:

For who can denie but it be repugneth to nature, that the blind shal be appointed to leade and conduct such as do see? That the weake, the sicke, and impotent persones shall norishe and kepe the hole and strong, and finalie, that the foolishe, madde and phrenetike, shal gouerne the discrete, and give counsel to such as be sober of mind? And such be all women, compared unto men in bearing of authoritie. For their sight in ciuile regiment, is but blindnes: their strength, weaknes: their counsel, foolishenes: and judgement, phrenesie, if it be rightlie considered. (9v)

Female monarchs, Knox claims, lead the country with foolishness rather than with wisdom. Women are unable to govern because of their inherent 'natural' weaknesses which prevent them from ruling effectively. For women to enter the public domain, therefore, to place themselves within the 'middest of men', subverted the natural, political and social order. But even worse, according to Knox, was that women who assumed power actually subverted and polluted the sign of monarchy itself:

For this present, I say, that the erecting of a woman to that honour [of monarchy], is not onely to inuert the ordre, which God hath established: but also it is to defile, pollute and prophane ... the throne and seat of God, which he hath sanctified and apointed for man onlie. (34r)

The throne, which was to signify masculine power and authority, justified by God, became a polluted and a defiled sign when a female monarch was on the throne. It was no longer authority which was signified but rather, the polluted sign of the monarch signified the subversion of the natural and the political order. Consequently, women in power transformed the signification of themselves as women: women were prescribed to signify virtue and submission, and in Knox's terms to have upon their heads a 'coverture in signe of subjection', but instead, women in power signified a monstrous perversion of gender role. Furthermore, women in power also transformed the signification of men: instead of signifying masculine authority, men become effeminate. And finally, there is a transformation of the realm itself when a woman accedes to the throne. As Knox asserts:

I am assuredlie persuaded that if any of those men, which illuminated onelyie by the light of nature ... shuld this day liue and see a woman sitting in iudgement, or riding frome parliament in the middest of men, hauing the royall crowne upon her head, the sworde and sceptre borne before her, in signe that the administration of justice was in her power: I am assuredlie persuaded, I say, that suche a sight shule so astonishe them, that they shuld iudge the hole worlde to be transformed into Amazones. (10v–11r)

As a result, Knox's argument about female monarchy creates two major effects: 'a woman promoted to sit in the seat of God' and be a monarch is 'a monstre in nature'. And furthermore, Knox asserts, 'monstrouse is the body of that commonwelth, where a woman beareth empire'. The monstrous body of the woman and the monstrous body of the nation are articulated by Knox through the metaphor of the body itself. For the woman to assume authority, she was adopting the function of the superior head. Consequently, it is the reversal in the relationship between men and women, when women assume power, that creates a monstrous body. To quote Knox, 'For who wolde not judge that bodie to be a monstre, where there was no head eminent above the rest, but that the eyes were in the handes, the tonge and mouthe beneath the belie and the eares in the feate' (26v). And the arch monarchical monster reigning over a monstrous and disfigured nation was, for Knox, none other than Queen Mary herself.

Mary incorporated all the major sins associated with women: she was naturally capable of deceit and foolishness, being a daughter of Eve; by being a monarch, she overruled God's punishment meted out to Eve that women were to be subject to men; she possessed all the 'natural' characteristics of a woman, being 'weake, fraile, Impacient, feble and foolishe ... unconstant, variable, cruell and lacking the spirit of counsel and regiment'; and due to her necessary involvement in the public sphere of state, she failed to remain in the private sphere, silent and obedient. But for Knox, Mary was guilty of two further crimes: she was Catholic and she married Philip of Spain. That Mary was Catholic entailed for Knox 'the overthrow of true religion' and the entry of Satan into the counsel of England. But it was her marriage to Philip that actually altered the status of England as an English nation. Because she was a woman, Knox argued, all her inheritance and wealth, including the power of her government, would be transferred to her husband on marriage. Consequently, Knox lamented, the national status of England would be radically transformed – England would be translated into Spain:

England for satisfying of the inordinat appetites of that cruell monstre Marie (unworthie by reason of her bloodie tyrannie, of the name of woman) betrayed (alas) to the proude spandiarde ... Doth such translation of realms and nations pleasure the justice of God? (48r)

Using the commonplace of a female sexuality that betrays nationality, Knox claims that as a monstrous woman ruler, Mary was responsible for transfiguring the national status of England. Instead of signifying English power, the throne of Mary signified Catholic Spanish interest. And intrinsic to that national betrayal, Mary is finally denied even the name of woman.

By denying a woman's right to accede to the throne, Knox's argument rests upon the basic premise that women disfigure and pollute the God-given signs of monarchy and authority. And he uses the wealth of classical, biblical and patristic precepts excluding women from power to claim that women cannot enter the linguistic boundaries that determine authority, without radically transforming and disfiguring them. Furthermore, Knox argues that it is a woman's gendered role that also prevents her from participation in constitutional matters, and as a result, prevents her from taking a place within the 'middest of men'. It is Knox's polemical use of this argument that makes Mary Tudor's Act of Parliament so crucial for a woman's constitutional right to accede to the throne. As the Act makes clear:

> that what and whensoever statute or law doth limit and appoint that the King of this realm may or shall have, execute and do anything as King … The same the Queen … may by the same authority and power likewise have, exercise, execute, punish, correct, and do, to all intents, constructions and purposes, without doubt, ambiguity, scruple or question.[13]

Here, the Act not only included the name of Queen within the boundaries of signification prescribed by previous statutes that were enacted in the name of king; but also, it placed women rulers securely within the linguistic boundaries of power. It allowed Mary not just to take her place within the 'middest of men' but also to exercise jurisdictive control over those men, to have authority over them without transforming either the sign of monarchy or the national status of the country over which she reigned.

There are, however, further implications deriving from Mary's Act of Parliament in that it constituted in itself a unique challenge to the patriarchal commonplaces that asserted women's inability to govern; commonplaces which an individual like Knox could readily utilize to pander to popular prejudices and thereby acquire popular support. Unlike other women in sixteenth-century culture, who in countering the misogyny expressed by an individual such as Knox only had available to them the defence of their own virtue in terms of ideal stereotypes of femininity or exemplary women, and unlike men who emphasized those stereotypical ideals in constructing a defence of 'good' women, Mary Tudor could actively challenge that patriarchal misogyny by means of her unique recourse to law and to legal discourse. This

THE WORD AND THE THRONE

challenge could be expressed in the first instance because it was precisely Mary's position as a monarch that enabled her to avoid completely gender prescriptions that prevented women's active participation in all matters of law. In this way, the very existence of this Act of Parliament necessarily testified to the regal authority invested in Mary as a queen, an authority that allowed her to define – through the 'Word' of law – her own position in relation to previous 'kings of this realm', 'her noble progenitors', and thus to assert her constitutional and linguistic right to government. But at the same time that this Act functioned as a statutory testament to and signifier of her regal authority, it also affirmed that authority to all her subjects through its content and expression in legal discourse; and in particular, the Act affirmed it with crystal clarity to those 'malicious and ignorant persons' who had contested the validity of Mary's constitutional right to undertake monarchical dictate. Thus, other women could only challenge misogyny by defining both themselves and the position from which they spoke as virtuous or exemplary, a position that necessarily had to engage with and counter prescriptions for women's silence, textual or in the public sphere. In distinction to these women, Mary Tudor was able to construct a subject position through law that was central although not masculine; as invested with authority over all her subjects although a woman; as a speaker in the public realm – the 'middest of men' – although surrounded by patriarchal exhortations for women to be 'silent' and remain in the private sphere; and finally, she was able to position herself as a legitimate queen of England, sitting on an English throne, although married to Philip of Spain.

Thus, the force of the polemic of Knox's *Monstrous Regiment of Women* was preempted – in jurisdictional terms – by the passing of Mary's Act of Parliament. However, whilst the tract's function as an attack on Catholicism is evident, its effect as a piece of Protestant propaganda was profoundly diminished by the unfortunate timing of its publication, for it eventually appeared in England four months after the death of its key protagonist. Elizabeth's attitude towards Knox's *Monstrous Regiment of Women* was not a favourable one, not least because Knox's theology advocated and justified the removal of any monarch who was tyrannical or evil. The publication of the tract seriously damaged the cause of Genevan Protestant theology and even Calvin was implicated in the views propounded by Knox. The ironic outcome of the tract, for Knox at least, was that despite the accession of a Protestant monarchy, albeit female, he was as exiled from England as a result of the disfavour of Elizabeth as he had been under the Catholic reign of Mary. Consequently, it was Mary, and then Elizabeth, who remained within the 'middest of men', who embraced the regal authority and power of the throne and their position on it. Knox's position remained marginal as he remained outside England – even in Scotland, he found himself under the suspicious eye of Mary, Queen of Scots.

Notes

1. *The Works of John Knox*, ed. David Laing, 6 vols (Edinburgh: Thomas George Stevenson, 1864).

2. John Knox, *The First Blast of the Trumpet against the Monstrous Regiment of Women* (Geneva, 1558).

3. John Aylmer, *An Harborowe for Faithful and Trewe Subjectes, agaynst the late blowne blaste, concerninge the Gouernment of Women* (Strasbourg, 1559).

4. Henrich Bullinger, 'An answer given to a certain Scotsman, in reply to some questions concerning the kingdom of Scotland and England', in Knox, *Works*, III.

5. 'Act concerning the regal power, 1554', in J. R. Tanner, *Tudor Constitutional Documents 1485–1603, with an Historical Commentary* (Cambridge: Cambridge University Press, 1948), pp. 122–4.

6. Jasper Ridley, *John Knox* (Oxford: Clarendon Press, 1968), p. 226; W. Stanford Reid, *Trumpeter of God: A Biography of John Knox* (New York: Charles Scribner's Sons, 1974), pp. 146–8.

7. Geddes MacGregor, *The Thundering Scot: A Portrait of John Knox* (London: Macmillan, 1958), pp. 90–1. For further commentaries and particularly on Knox's religious beliefs see, for example, Hugh Watt, *John Knox in Controversy* (London: Thomas Nelson and Sons Ltd, 1950), Iain Murray, *John Knox* (Cheltenham: Taylor, Young Ltd, 1973), Duncan Shaw, *Knox and Mary, Queen of Scots* (Edinburgh: Saint Andrew Press, 1975), Henry R. Sefton, *John Knox: An Account of the Development of his Spirituality* (Edinburgh: Saint Andrew Press, 1993).

8. Alan G. R. Smith, *The Emergence of a Nation State: The Commonwealth of England 1529–1660* (Harlow: Longman, 1984), p. 78.

9. See, for example, John Guy, *Tudor England* (Oxford: Oxford University Press, 1988) or David Loades, *The Reign of Mary Tudor: Politics, Government and Religion in England, 1553–58* (Harlow: Longman, 1979). Loades' historical account continues to be the most comprehensive treatment of Mary's reign to date.

10. Katherine Usher Henderson and Barbara F. McManus, *Half Humankind: Contexts and Texts of the Controversy about Women in England, 1540–1640* (Chicago: University of Illinois Press, 1985), p. 12.

11. Linda Woodbridge, *Women and the English Renaissance: Literature and the Nature of Womankind, 1540–1620* (Brighton: Harvester, 1984), p. 197.

12. 'Act concerning the regal power, 1554', p. 122.

13. 'Act concerning the regal power, 1554', p. 123.

Engendering Penitence: Nicholas Breton and 'the Countesse of Penbrooke'

Suzanne Trill

Perhaps one of the most complex questions facing feminist literary criticism today is the knotty issue of how to ascribe gender to the 'voice' of a given text. The modern critic has to be aware of the problems that recent developments in critical theory have posed in relation to identifying such a voice: the logic of post-structuralism undermines a direct correlation between the author and the narrator of a text (in Foucault's phrase, 'what is an author?'); the insights of psychoanalysis and French feminism have highlighted the fact that the biological sex of the author may bear no relation to the gendered voice of the text (what does it mean to write 'as a woman' or 'as a man'?); and reader-response theories demand that we be aware of our own preconceptions in approaching a literary text (do we read texts by men and women differently?). Informing all of these approaches is a critique of liberal humanism and individualism, which results in an emphasis upon the social construction of subjectivity and an awareness that our expression is not simply the result of individual agency but is at least partially determined by external factors. At the heart of these problems is a central question, first posed by Foucault and rephrased here by Elizabeth D. Harvey, '[w]hat difference does it make who is speaking and who fashions a literary voice?'[1] This essay seeks to explore the difficulties involved in identifying a gendered voice in the work of a sixteenth-century writer, Nicholas Breton. More precisely, it will analyse why Breton appropriates an ostensibly female voice in many of his texts. Harvey has recently defined the practice of a male writer using a female voice 'in a way that appears to efface originary marks of gender' as 'transvestite ventriloquism'.[2] Acutely aware of the problems I have outlined above, she is careful to avoid an essentialist approach to this issue; thus, rather than questioning whether a male author can represent a female voice, she focuses upon the ethics of such an appropriation and asks '[w]hat are the theoretical and political implications of male authors ventriloquising the female voice?'[3] This

25

essay will address this question by examining what kinds of texts Breton produced in which gendered voice, focusing upon the way in which his depiction of 'the Countesse of Penbrooke' as a model of female penitence exposes anxieties about the limitations of gendered roles during the sixteenth century.[4]

While penitence has always played an important role in Christian belief, it is often suggested that its form and significance altered as Protestantism became England's dominant, institutionalized religion. For regular churchgoers, as all were required to be by law, confession and penitence played a significant part in the liturgy. However, the shift in penitential and confessional discourses is also associated with an increased emphasis upon secrecy and individuality; for, as well as being an institutionalized requirement, penitence was also a popular aspect of private devotional activity.[5] The act of penitence demands that the individual insert himself or herself into a discourse that requires self-scrutiny and self-abasement; in the Calvinist schema, it is founded upon the belief that the individual can do nothing that warrants or deserves God's favour, as 'the mind of man is so entirely alienated from the righteousness of God that he cannot conceive, desire, or design anything but what is wicked, distorted, foul, impure and iniquitous'.[6] This belief led to the need for everyone to acknowledge their sinfulness continually, and the consequent insistence upon the unworthiness of the individual in relation to God produced a conception of the self as self-negating and self-abasing. According to Calvin, the natural self or the natural will must be effaced or erased; it must supplanted by an awareness of God's spirit which facilitates the creation of a new will, a new being, a new self.

Somewhat paradoxically, however, this insistence upon self-denial can also be seen to have played a vital role in the production of subjectivity, as the development of autobiographical narratives during this period indicates.[7] The 'self' that is presented in these narratives is by no means a singular or unitary entity; it is at least a divided self and, more commonly, a fissured or fractured self. But, most importantly, these narratives illustrate the perceived need for an individual to interrogate his or her consciousness in order to be assured of salvation.[8] Strictly speaking, therefore, penitence is not specifically gendered; rather, it is a requirement of all believers. As Foucault observed, '[e]veryone in Christianity has the duty to explore who he is, what is happening within himself, the faults he may have committed, the temptations to which he is exposed'.[9] However, Renaissance attitudes to women suggest that they in particular needed to repent as 'Woman' was believed to be inherently more sinful than 'Man' due to her association with Eve. Additionally, this meant that 'Woman' should be subordinate to 'Man' and, ironically, given that one of the

issues that led to the break with the Roman Catholic church was a
resistance to the intercessionary or mediatory position of the priest,
women were to be subject to their husbands in matters spiritual.
According to William Gouge, the husband was 'the head of his wife,
that by his provident care he may be as a saviour to her', and in family
prayer 'the husband is as a priest unto his wife, and ought to be her
mouth to God when the two are together'.[10] This hierarchical relationship between the sexes is confirmed in numerous Renaissance texts
that promoted penitential or confessional discourses as an appropriate
form of expression for women. From this perspective confessional
discourses overtly upheld the patriarchal order of Renaissance society,
instructing women to maintain their subjected position.[11]

While on the one hand the emphasis upon 'Woman's' sinfulness was
undeniably negative and served to highlight her difference and separation from God, on the other hand it created a situation in which the
characteristics that were culturally defined as feminine were precisely
those that *any* individual needed to attain in order to achieve a reconciliation with God. The characteristic of self-abasement has been identified as being 'common to prayers by women' and has been endowed
with negative connotations as, for most modern feminist critics at least,
this is viewed as a mark of women's internalization of patriarchal
evaluations of their position.[12] But this is not simply a characteristic
that is identifiable in women's prayers. Moreover, some religious
women writers (for example, St Teresa of Avila and Julian of Norwich)
use this self-abasement in order to facilitate their self-presentation; as
Toril Moi explains, 'the mystic's often self-inflicted abjection', which
is 'modelled on the image of the suffering Christ', is paradoxically able
to open up 'a space where her own pleasure can unfold'.[13] Julian of
Norwich pays tribute to, and to a certain extent self-consciously models
herself upon, the figure of Mary Magdalene; the latter's intimacy with
and forgiveness by Christ, and 'self-abasing' tears, provided a significant
model for the penitent to imitate. Although the stress on women's
inherent sinfulness is problematic, crucially it also suggests that to
repent fully men need to place themselves in a position that is culturally
defined as 'feminine'.

The need to emulate 'feminine' characteristics is illustrated in a text
which focuses upon Mary Magdalene. This text, entitled *Marie Magdalens Loue*, has been attributed to Nicholas Breton and stresses her
significance as a model of penitence to be imitated by both male and
female readers.[14] The Magdalene's exemplary position is founded upon
her recognition of her own sins, her capacity to repent and her desire
to be with her Lord. The narrator demonstrates an awareness of the
potential cultural objections to placing a female penitent in such an
exemplary position in the following rhetorical question: 'Mary was a

woman, and shal men follow women?' This objection is swiftly deflected as cultural prejudice is subordinated to the desire for spiritual happiness: 'why her happines came from God, and shall not wee follow her to her happiness?' (A6v). Her example represents a pattern for all believers to emulate; in order to attain the 'blessings of the soule', the narrator instructs the readers: 'let vs watch with Mary, walke with Mary, and weepe with Mary' (B1v). The text is acutely aware of instructing both men and women, and it highlights issues that are gender specific by altering the pronouns accordingly. Significantly then, the male believer is told that if he desires to come to Christ, he must 'learne to imitate Mary in her course: [he w]ho hath many sinnes, and findeth much remission, let his loue bee great, and his sorrowe not little' (B1v). In addition to this the narrator emphasizes that 'I woulde wishe that all men and women woulde learne to imitate Mary in this manner of speaking' (B6r) and concludes, 'I beseech God to graunt vs all Grace, so to sorrow for our sinnes, and to long for his comming, that seeking him as Mary did with teares, wee may see him with ioy, and say with Mary, Master' (E6v–E7r).

Attribution of this text to Breton is supported by its important parallels with his other writing; for, in constructing different images of the countess of Pembroke, Nicholas Breton repeatedly associates her with the figure of Mary Magdalene. While his use of this association is not unique to him, I would argue that he alters its significance. Current criticism predominantly interprets the connections between these two female figures as confirming Pembroke's identification as her brother's 'chief mourner'. What troubles feminist critics about Breton's use of this connection is his awkward and 'impolitic' depiction of Pembroke as a sister who apparently holds her sins to be responsible for her brother's death.[15] While Pembroke's filial relation to Sir Philip Sidney is an incontrovertible fact, and Breton's identification of Pembroke as a Magdalene figure is undoubtedly at times intensely problematic, if one analyses his depiction of Pembroke within the context of his other writing his appropriation of her name and voice addresses larger issues than her relationship to her brother. For, despite the liturgical requirements for confession of sins and the private books of devotion which emphasized self-examination as a practice to be exercised by all, Breton's writing suggests that there is a peculiar association between the language of individual penitence and a female voice. Only two of his texts on this subject are dedicated to male patrons and are narrated in a male voice, whereas five are dedicated to female patrons and are narrated in a female voice.[16] What does this use of specifically gendered voices reveal? Are there any recognizable differences in the style and form of speech in these texts, and how might these distinctions be explained in gendered terms?

On one level, the fact that the sex of the speaker of Breton's texts corresponds to the sex of the addressed patron would suggest that he is attempting to relate his work carefully to the intended audience. It indicates that, like other writers, Breton was hoping to ensure that the content of his texts would be of interest to his patrons.[17] But his gendering of his speakers has more far-reaching implications with regard to contemporary expectations about the limits of gendered expression. It is a notable characteristic of Breton's writing that those texts written in a male voice are far more other-directed and impersonal than those he writes in a female voice, as they focus upon the audience's rather than the speaker's experience. Although the male speaker asserts the importance of repentance, these texts stop short of representing the male speaker in an act of repentance. In *An Excellent Poeme, Vpon the Longing of a Blessed Heart: which loathing the World, doth long to be With Christ*, dedicated to Lord North, the first-person narrator is identified with 'Breton' by the work's short title, *Bretons Longing*. The full title suggests that this text shares similar concerns to those articulated in texts addressed to and narrated by female figures, as the countess of Pembroke in particular is identified with female speakers who hate or loathe 'the World' and who 'long to be with Christ'. However, there are distinctions between these texts in both the degree of first-person narration and accompanying self-examination. In *Bretons Longing* the speaker attempts to define love and the role of male speakers in approaching God. The primary indicator by which these male characters are defined is by reference to their occupation or social position: prince, scholar, poet, lawyer, cosmographer, merchant, courtier, farmer, sailor, traveller, painter, and beggar. The speaker commences by representing ungodly characters who occupy these positions and proceeds to contrast them with more godly figures. By characterizing these figures in relation to their social position, the speaker deflects attention from his own sinfulness and instead provides a mirror of different men's experiences. The narrator is positioned as one whose main intent is correcting others as opposed to examining his own conscience. Despite the professed desire to represent a 'blessed heart' which longs 'to be with Christ', the speaker's 'longing' is not the central concern of this text. It is primarily other-directed, both in its depiction of a variety of male characters and in its use of biblical figures as examples of penitence. While the text acknowledges that all are sinners, the speaker does not – until the very end of the poem – focus upon his own sins. In this there is a crucial difference from the texts presented in a female voice; *Bretons Longing* does not focus upon 'Breton' as speaker, or 'Breton' as penitent, rather the need to repent is projected onto other characters. Consequently, there is little emphasis upon the 'self'. Although the speaker does refer to his unworthiness, the need to repent is only

referred to in the last five stanzas and even then the speaker does not
engage in the act of self-examination. In this representation of penitence
and confession, the speaker's 'self' has barely emerged.

The other-directed focus of the main narrative may seem to be
counterbalanced by the more personal accompanying poems, 'What is
Loue' and 'Solus in toto laudandus Deus'; however, even here the
speaker analyses love at a distance, as an observer and commentator,
rather than presenting his own experience or articulating his own desire.
Rather than actually expressing his own experience of divine love, the
speaker's main focus is upon berating those that seek to find love within
human or secular experience. When, at the end of the first poem, the
speaker finally turns his attention to attempting to articulate divine
love, it is presented as inexpressible: 'What shall I say? but 'tis beyond
my saying, / To tell you all may of this Loue be sayd ... Let me ... say
but this, as I haue said before, / That Loue is God, and I can say no
more'.[18] Although it is a convention of Renaissance writing that experiences related to God are ineffable, Breton's texts seem to indicate
that they are peculiarly inexpressible in a male voice. Whereas *Bretons
Longing* avoids self-examination and does not articulate the speaker's
desire for God, the texts he writes in a female voice do exactly the
opposite. In *The Soules Harmony*, dedicated to Lady Sara Hastings,
the speaker is primarily concerned with expressing 'her' feelings of
unworthiness, and bewails her sins:

> And when, againe, the act of sinne is past,
> And that thy grace doth call me backe againe:
> Then in my teares I runne to thee as fast,
> And of my sinnes, and of my selfe complayne.
>   What can I doe, but cry, Sweet Jesus saue me:
>   For I am nothing, but what thou wilt haue me.[19]

The focus in this poem is firmly upon the experiences of the female
speaker; there is an immediate emphasis upon the speaker's unworthiness and sense of sin. Furthermore, the speaker immediately engages
in an act of repentance, as she cries out to God, and her accompanying
tears signify the passion of her emotions upon this subject. Whereas
the male speaker in *Bretons Longing* deflects attention onto others, the
female speaker focuses upon herself. The impassioned nature of her
expression seemingly perpetuates Renaissance conceptions of women
as more uncontrollable than men; rather than being an indictment,
however, in this context it is actually vital. The self-abasement present
in the above quotation is necessary in order to obtain an intimate
relationship with God. These examples are indicative of the distinctions
that Breton's writing as a whole upholds; what interests me is what

these distinctions reveal about the relationship between 'feminine' characteristics and the articulation of penitence. In another context, Elizabeth D. Harvey has suggested that '[i]n male appropriations of feminine voices we can see what is most desired and most feared about women and why male authors might have wished to occupy that cultural space, however contingently and provisionally'.[20] But what does Breton fear and desire? What purpose or function does appropriating a female voice serve for him?

Although Breton's writing as a whole embodies gender difference in its representation of penitence, nowhere are these distinctions more apparent than in *The Pilgrimage to Paradise, ioyned with The Countesse of Penbrookes loue* (1592). This book was dedicated to the countess of Pembroke, and examines the way in which two characters overcome the trials and temptations of earthly existence in their desire for spiritual happiness. *The Pilgrimage to Paradise* relates the experiences of a male pilgrim and *The Countesse of Penbrookes loue*, as the title suggests, purports to portray Pembroke's experience. By comparatively analysing the two parts of this book, it is possible to examine what Breton can represent in a male voice and what he can articulate in a female voice, and from this to examine how sexual difference affects the representation of penitence.[21]

In *The Pilgrimage to Paradise* the male pilgrim embarks upon an actual physical journey which commences in a forest where his senses come under assault from various temptations, requiring him to overcome the seven deadly sins. On his travels this pilgrim meets a number of other characters at different stages of their own pilgrimages and often enters into debate with them; he travels across the sea, enters a university town, attends the court, and witnesses victorious battles and terrifying defeats. All of these experiences teach him the best way to approach God; having traversed the various terrains of the world, this pilgrim proves himself to be steadfast. As he keeps to the 'straight' path, the pilgrim finds the 'true church' and enters the 'heavenly court of the high King of Kings'.[22] When he finds the 'true church' the pilgrim discovers that:

> The gate, is Grace, Contrition, is the key,
> The locke, is loue, the porter, Penitence. (stanza 4)

However, although the male pilgrim acknowledges the need for penitence, he is not actually represented as engaging in it, either in public or in private. In order to reject or overcome the world's temptations, the male pilgrim has to experience them through a physical quest.

In contrast to this, *The Countesse of Penbrookes loue* emphasizes private penitence and enclosure within the 'closet'. It commences with a display of 'Penbrooke's' dissatisfaction with the world, which is represented by a variety of figures from different walks of life who approach her to try to find out what would make her happy, or what it is that she desires. Although the 'Countesse' experiences many of the same temptations as the male pilgrim, the context in which she encounters and overcomes them is distinct; she remains within her 'house' or court, and 'the world' comes to her – she is visited by women, soldiers, peasants, merchants, lawyers, courtiers, scholars, sailors and poets. Moreover, the *Loue* text stresses her personal relationship with Christ, and focuses upon repentance, grace and forgiveness. Christ is carefully constructed as her lover and he is portrayed in terms usually ascribed to the lady in Elizabethan sonnet sequences. In her closet 'Penbrooke' undergoes the process of self-examination. Unlike the male pilgrim, the female speaker engages in 'private' penitence, articulating in highly emotional terms her love for Christ and her dependence upon him. In this, 'Penbrooke' identifies herself with Mary Magdalene, saying 'Looke on thy Mary with her bitter teares, / That washt thy feete and wipte them with her heares' (p. 26, stanza 14). As in *Marie Magdalens Loue*, it is her tears and her desire for her 'Lord' that are the means by which she achieves her reconciliation with God through Christ.

The two halves of this book, then, on one level, perpetuate or reinforce distinct gender roles; the female penitent remains 'safely' within her 'house' (the private, 'domestic' sphere), whereas the male pilgrim is able to travel through the world and engage in public debate.[23] However, the intricacy of textual 'voice' and its association with gender is complicated by the three dedications that preface the book. Breton's dedications construct gender-specific audiences for both parts of this text. Insofar as the second half of the text seeks to represent the 'Countesse of Penbrooke' and her 'love' for Christ, it would seem that Breton is inviting her to take pleasure in his depiction of her, to read of herself. However, while 'Penbrooke' is portrayed as the speaking subject of this part of the text, Breton's dedicatory address does not explicitly invite her to read her 'own' meditations. On the contrary, his dedication attempts to focus her attention upon 'the poeticall discourse of a poore pilgrimes travaile' and entreats her to 'let the poore pilgrime, that seeketh Paradise, finde heauen the better by your fauour' (p. 4). Rather than inviting 'Penbrooke' to derive narcissistic pleasure by identifying herself with his depiction of 'her' meditations, Breton directs her toward the first part of the text and thus initially encourages her to adopt the position of spectator of another's pilgrimage. Specifically, he invites her to read about the male pilgrim's experience. Given Breton's self-representation in both this and other dedicatory addresses to Pembroke, this is simultaneously an invitation to view 'Breton's' experience and constitutes a intratextual reference to the patronage relationship between these two figures. Breton consistently positions himself as a 'poore' poet / pilgrim / beadman, who, in this instance, is 'the abject of fortune' in contradistinction to 'Penbrooke' who is identified as 'the object of honour'.[24] The countess is invited to read of the male pilgrim's experiences and, therefore, to watch the male protagonist's travels through the world and witness his avoidance of (female) obstacles and temptations.

Conversely, Breton's construction of the audience for *The Countesse of Penbrookes loue* designates that audience as male by two methods; firstly through the dedication 'To the Gentlemen students and Scholers of Oxforde' and, secondly, by the presence of an 'unseene' (male) narrator reporting her meditations within the poem itself. In both instances, the male audience is invited to derive voyeuristic pleasure in observing – or, more precisely, intruding upon – 'Penbrooke's' private meditations. The dedication to the Oxford students and scholars does not mention the first part of the text, but argues that Breton's purpose in presenting this text to public view 'was to acquaint the honest mindes of vertuous dispositions, with the heauenly Meditations, of an honourable Lady'. The narrator of the *Loue* section reports these meditations from an 'unseene' vantage point; he tells us that when she 'saw the worlde was gone indeede' and thought 'Her selfe alone', in fact he was present ('save but my selfe unseene'). Unaware of his observation, 'Penbrooke' proceeds in her private devotions and expresses her desire for Christ in a quasi-mystical discourse. While the subject matter is religious, the content is sexualized by the voyeurism of the narrator and the fact that the speaker's desire culminates in a rapturous union with Christ.[25] 'Penbrooke' is thus constructed as the object of a male gaze.

In his dedications to this text, then, Breton sets up a cross-gendered audience: the speaker of the text is of the opposite sex to that of the imagined reader. Not only is the construction of the audience at variance with the sex of the protagonist, a point which highlights an apparent necessity to 'see' the Other's experience rather than identify with one's 'own', but the content of the text and the manner of its telling are structured in such a way as to enhance potential differences between male and female experience. In *The Countesse of Penbrookes loue*, the narrator determines the action and the landscape and the reader's perception of events is focused through his ('unseene') eyes, which are 'unseene' in more than one sense; within the structure of the narrative, 'Penbrooke' is unaware of his presence, and secondly, as the narrator only interjects a comment at two points in the narrative, the majority of the text is presented as her 'own' words. Her meditations are presented 'before [our] eies', or more precisely, for male eyes, and she is therefore represented as 'spectacle to be looked at and object to be desired, investigated, pursued, controlled, and ultimately possessed by a subject who is masculine, that is, symbolically male'.[26] Depicting 'Penbrooke's' meditations for a male readership could certainly be seen in these terms, especially given the narrator's surreptitious presence in her closet, which places him as the narratorial equivalent of a 'peeping Tom' with all the connotations of scopophilia and fetishization that that position embodies. But Breton's 'literary' depiction also reveals some spaces in which the object of his spectatorship is not entirely within his control: it is these spaces which point up the boundary between male and female experience.

For, although 'Penbrooke' is unmistakably the object of the *Loue* section of this text, her experience exceeds or escapes Breton's representational endeavour in a variety of ways. Her objectification, her position as icon, image or spectacle perhaps marks out an anxiety in masculine discourse, particularly in relation to Christian experience. On the one hand, Breton's disclaimer in his dedication to the Oxford students and scholars that the 'weake discourse' of her meditations falls 'farre short of her worthiness' could be seen to be a convention of dedicatory address; on the other, it is an indication of Breton's inability to articulate her experience. For the most part of this text, the narrator absents himself and presents the text as if it were her 'own' words, but occasionally he reminds us of his presence by commenting on her physical reactions. As spectator, he attempts to interpret them, but because he is 'outside' of that experience he cannot represent it fully:

> And with that worde proceeeding from her hart,
> The trickeling teares distilled downe her eies:
> As if her sence possest in euery part,
> A secret ioie that did the soule surprise.[27]

Here, and at the end of the text, the narrator indicates that he does not know what the 'Countesse' is experiencing (and / or cannot put it into words). The tears become a sign, but the meaning of that sign has to be interpreted by the narrator by the use of a simile ('as if'). Later, the exclusion of the narrator from the experience (and his consequent inability to define its meaning) becomes even more apparent:

> And with that worde, she sweetly fetcht, a sigh,
> And then a sobbe, and then a bitter teare,
> As who should saie, that either death was nigh,
> Or else her hart, was stroken with a feare,
> Or else the spirit might be ouercome,
> That for the time her tongue was stroken dumme.

But, let it be, all blessed is the traunce,
When so the soule is ouercome with loue,
That vertues choice, doth finde it is no chaunce,
When humble faith doth heaunly fauour proue:
And when the sences from their sleepe arise,
The spirit findes the life that neuer dies.

So, when it seemede shee waked from her sleepe,
Or sodaine traunce, for so I tearme it right.
When such high care did so her sences keepe,
That shee awakt, with glory of the light:
Oh sacred loue, and sweetest life, quod shee,
What happy figure hath appearde to me?

(p. 28, stanzas 8–10)

Her experience cannot be fully captured by the external observer, thus her experience remains unknown. Breton presents the illusion of revealing her experience, but in the last instance he is unable to articulate it. This point is substantiated by John Case's prefatory address to Breton, which concludes as follows:

> Your wit, pen, and art therein sounde well together. The song is sweete, the ditty sweeter, but that rare Phoenix is the sweetest Phoenix, whom your wit, pen and art can but well shadow with all your Muses; for as an image is but an image, and the tincture of any thing is not the substance thereof, so the coulours of her honours are in your booke, but the life of her vertue is in her selfe. (p. 5)

Again, Case's argument can be partially explained with reference to the conventions of dedicatory address, but here it is also a recognition of a separation between male representation and female experience. This gap reveals a distinction between the experiences of the sexes in relation to Christian discourses that, although it might seem to perpetuate a sense of women's exclusion from discourse, marks out the limits of masculine expression.

'Penbrooke's' bewailing of her sins is perhaps an indication of negative self-abasement; certainly, it is just such a representation which prompts Lamb and Hannay to critique Breton's depiction of her. However, Breton represents this characteristic positively rather than negatively, as the self-abasing soul achieves its aims. Indeed, this complete self-abasement is necessary in order for her to find herself through finding the object of her desire. At the opening of the poem, 'Penbrooke' is represented as not knowing herself or her desires; through self-chastisement she realizes that it is her separation from

God which has caused this discontent. By the end of the text, she is taken up into heaven in a form of mystical trance that enables her to recognize her true desire:

> For, this is it, sweete Lorde, that I woulde haue,
> The world is short, in sounding my desire:
> It is thy mercy that I onlie craue,
> Thy vertues loue, that set my hart on fire;
> And in thy loue, that onely liuing blisse,
> That world may wish, but know not what it is.
>
>   (p.28, stanza 18)

The contents of this experience are then known solely to 'Penbrooke', but the effect that it has upon her is designed to encourage readers to emulate her self-abasement in order to obtain the happiness of an assured relationship with Christ. In order to achieve such union, the individual must be able to become self-abasing, self-denying; and it is precisely this self-abasement that Breton cannot even begin to represent when he writes in a male voice. For once the male concern with the public realm is a disadvantage, for by not reaching the same point of 'self-abasement' as women, the male believer also misses out on the ecstasy (ravishment) and corresponding 'happiness' or comfort that the female speaker can achieve. In order to articulate the self-abasement that is a prerequisite for an intimate relationship with God, Breton apparently has to appropriate a female voice. More specifically, he appropriates one particular woman's voice, that of the countess of Pembroke. But why is it Pembroke's voice that he appropriates? Why might her voice be peculiarly apposite for a male author writing about penitence?

On one level the answer to this question is material: Breton, following the footsteps of other poets, transferred his attempts to gain patronage from her brother to Pembroke at his death. In this process other writers also appropriated Pembroke's name for the titles of some of their texts, but unlike Breton they did not appropriate her voice.[28] This difference is, I think, integrally bound up with the subject matter of the texts and is crucially related to which aspects of Pembroke's writing these poets stress and why. Mary Ellen Lamb touches upon an important point when she suggests that Breton's repesentation of a wholly religious countess who distrusted 'fained' inventions 'might well have aroused considerable hostility towards him on the part of secular writers attempting to gain or to maintain Mary Sidney's support'.[29] Although this point is unsubstantiated, its significance lies in the way that it highlights Breton's insecure position as an individual poet who was competing with other (and generally better) writers for Pembroke's patronage and that, therefore, his emphasis upon her 'religious' interests should be read in this context. Lamb argues that Breton's representation of Pembroke obscures the variety of writing that she produced and effectively neutralized her 'threat to masculine dominance' because 'as a religious muse she served in the conventionally female role of providing inspiration to the male writer'.[30] Consequently, she suggests that in Breton's representation any authority wielded by Pembroke 'is securely contained within a religious model of patronage, through which she moves followers to conform to God's will, not her own'.[31] While in many senses this is accurate, the difficulty with this reading is that although Pembroke did produce secular texts her major literary work was her translation of the *Psalmes*, and those songs, sonnets and prayers indicate that following God's will as articulated in 'his' word actually was important to her. Furthermore, it seems to me that it is precisely this connection that explains why Breton specifically appropriated Pembroke's voice to articulate penitence.

For the psalms were central to the articulation of penitence during the sixteenth century. Not only did they play an important role in the church liturgy, but they were recommended for daily reading and became a crucial discourse in the construction of autobiographical writing. Most obviously the penitential psalms were central to this practice, but the psalms as a book were perceived to be able to anatomize the individual, laying him or her bare before God and enabling the individual to repent for his or her sins and cry out to God for forgiveness.[32] I would suggest that Breton's consistently positive evaluation of the psalms is an implicit recognition of Pembroke's literary achievements, of which all critics agree he was aware. His texts betray an acute concern with the contemporary debate about the proper nature of poetry – 'Let me not listen to sinners songes, / But to the Psalmes thy holy saints doe sing' – and reveal a desire to prioritize spiritual poetry.[33] Whereas Lamb suggests that Breton's emphasis upon the spiritual aspects of Pembroke's writing denies the significance of her other writing, I think it is also important to recognize that Breton's inability to represent the heights of spiritual ravishment in a male voice betrays an anxiety about the value of both poetry per se and his own writing in particular. This anxiety is emphasized by his choice of patron, as the contemporary debate about the efficacy of sacred and secular forms of poetic endeavour is a vital factor in explaining why Breton dedicates four of his texts to Pembroke. Breton's emphasis upon sacred writing places him in alignment with the position outlined by Sir Philip Sidney, at least in his theoretical work *The Defence of Poesy*.[34] While other critics have suggested that Breton does not acknowledge Pembroke's *Psalmes*, underlying his representation of her voice is an anxiety about his ability as a poet, and his consistent references to the need for

poetry to have a spiritual direction indicates this. The poetry that
Breton, like Sidney, most consistently refers to as a model of 'right'
poetry is the book of psalms. This is an important point because whereas
other critics argue that Breton's depiction of Pembroke mistakenly
situates her as one who denies poetry and explicitly abjures the practice
of writing for herself, I would suggest that Breton's position is
rather more complex. Margaret P. Hannay, for example, argues that
Breton makes a mistake in 'attributing to [Pembroke] an inappropriate
asceticism that denied poetry', but Breton does not represent Pembroke
as denying poetry per se, rather he shows her denying secular poetry
specifically.[35] In this way Breton does indeed emphasize Pembroke's
spiritual position, but his ability to do this (rather than denying her
literary skills) is firmly grounded upon her translation of the psalms,
themselves the highest form of poetry. Moreover, the depiction of
Pembroke as one who 'denied poetry' is contradicted by Breton's own
writing as, except for *Auspicante Iehoua*, the texts that he addresses to
the countess are themselves *poetic*.

Breton's discussion of poetry focuses upon the right subject matter
of this form of writing; a point which is perhaps most forcibly expressed
in *Bretons Longing*, where the narrator contrasts the characteristics of
the 'wayward' and the 'godly' poet. The former is characterized thus:

> The Poet with his fictions and his fancies,
> Pleaseth himselfe with humorous inuentions;
> Which well considered are a kinde of franzies,
> That carie little truth in their intentions:
> While Wit and reason falling at contentions,
>   Make Wisedome finde that Follie's strong illusion
>   Bringes Wit and Senses wholly to confusion.[36]

However, the latter is depicted far more positively, and in such a way
as to justify Breton's (and Pembroke's) own literary endeavour:

> And such a Poet as the Psalmist was,
> Who had no minde but on his maister's loue,
> Whose Muses did the world in musique passe,
> That only soong but of the soule's behoue,
> In giuing glorie to the God ahoue,
>   Would all worlde's fictions wholly laye aside,
>   And onely long but with the Lord to bide.
>
>   (p. 9, stanza 5)

As in the *Loue* text, this speaker expresses the desire to 'laye aside'
worldly pleasures, or the 'worlde's fictions', and focus upon the truth

of God. And the way to achieve that, at least in poetic terms, is through the psalms.

In *A Solemne Passion of the Sovles Loue* the speaker (who is increasingly associated with 'Breton') attempts to instruct poets in the right way to write, positioning himself as an example for others to emulate:

> Come poets, ye that fill the world with fancies,
> Whose faining Muses shew but madding fits,
> Which all too soone doe fall into those franzies
> That are begotten by mistaking wits:
>> Lay downe your lines, compare your loue with mine,
>> And say whose vertue is the true diuine.[37]

This is continued in the next stanza where the speaker instructs other poets to 'adde a truth unto your idle stories' with which they deceive the world. 'Breton' here claims that 'when you see where sweetest sights are showne, / Looke on my Loue, and blush to see your owne' (p.6, stanza 1). In contrast to a secular writer's false comparisons, 'Breton' attempts to write 'truly' and plainly, even though 'his wits are short of such a worth' (p.6, stanza 16) as God's 'smallest praise is for my pen too much' (p.7, stanza 7). It is 'Breton' who is anxious about his inability to articulate God's praises. In this poem, the speaker is estranged from God's love. Although the speaker seeks to represent his love of God, this is outweighed by his expressions of his poetic incapacity to do so: 'And I (alas) of many thousand soules, / Vnworthy most of His high worth to write'; 'my wit as short to pen His praise, / As darkest nights in light of clearest days' (p.8, stanzas 15 and 16). While this inability to articulate God's praises is, on one level, a conventional stance for sixteenth- and seventeenth-century writers, there seems to me to be no small degree of irony in the fact that 'Breton' is acknowledging that he has not been able to achieve what Pembroke did in her translations of the psalms. The stress upon the psalms underlines Breton's inability either to articulate Pembroke's experience or to match her skill as a poet. And his representation of penitential discourses suggests that men in their inability to cry, or to interrogate themselves, or abase themselves, are unable to achieve such intimacy with God.

As Toril Moi's reading of Irigaray suggests, 'God, even in theology, exceeds all representation; the human incarnation of the Son is the "most feminine of all men" (*Speculum*, p.259). Christ undoes specular logic, and the mystic's self-abasement re-enacts his passion'.[38] Whilst in her own writing Pembroke cannot truly be described as a mystic, this is the position allocated to her in Breton's writing. In *The Countesse of Penbrookes loue* and other texts dedicated to her by Breton, she is represented as desiring and, to a certain extent, achieving the 'loss of subjecthood' or the 'disappearance of the subject/object opposition' which Irigaray argues is at the core of mysticism and which explains its appeal for women.[39] As I illustrated at the beginning of this essay, this 'loss of subjecthood' was a requirement of both men and women within the structures of Christianity, but it seems that Breton can only achieve the ecstasy of this 'denial' by appropriating a female voice. Interestingly, the discourse of penitence seems to prioritize 'female' desire. Christ, the 'most feminine of all men', is positioned as the 'loved object', equating him with the 'Lady' in Elizabethan sonnet sequences. Correspondingly, the female lover is, like the male speaker in those sequences, the true centre of attention. The poems focus on her desires, her separation from her lover and her eventual attainment of her desires. The feminization of Christ creates the possibility of a 'female' homoerotic desire, but importantly Christ was also male, as he was the head of the church and legitimized the husband's position of authority over his wife. But what is absent from this is a recognition of the feminization of all believers through their identification as 'the Bride of Christ', and perhaps this is partially responsible for the particular association of penitence with female figures. The need to maintain patriarchal order facilitated the focus on female penitence to obscure the feminization of men in relation to Christ. But this also disrupts Elizabethan hierarchies, for in representing female penitents Breton situates them as speaking directly to Christ, without the requisite 'covering' of their husbands. Another important consequence of his representation is that women are placed in a position from which they can instruct men, in direct contravention to Pauline doctrine. Specifically with regard to Pembroke, this has an added significance, for she was not only a model of female penitence in her association with Mary Magdalene, but also an exemplar of the highest form of Christian poetry. Whilst the psalms may not seem to be an 'authentic' female discourse, they did have a particular association with women and were central to Protestant confessional requirements.[40] From this perspective we can view Breton's writing not simply as a reflection of the controlling mechanisms of 'patriarchal ventriloquism', but rather as an acknowledgment of the significance of the 'feminine' in Christianity and his recognition of his exclusion from the privileged intimacy with Christ that both Mary Magdalene and the countess of Pembroke, by different means, were able to obtain.

As Elizabeth D. Harvey has suggested, male ventriloquism of female voices can on one level be seen to reinforce the 'norm' of silence for women and can be viewed as an example of the further silencing and marginalizing of women's 'own' voices and experiences. But this problematic aspect of ventriloquism is not simply related to sexual difference. As Toril Moi points out, feminist critics can also 'silence'

other women by taking up the 'masculine position' of speaking '*for*
women, or in the name of women'.[41] Moreover, it is important to
recognize that Breton's attempt to ventriloquize 'Penbrooke's' experiences does not only mark the limits of female expression; it
simultaneously reveals the limitations of male expression in the realm
of spiritual experience. While in their socio-cultural identification as
'Woman', women were excluded from public forms of articulating their
faith, texts like Breton's point toward the uncomfortable conclusion
(for men, at least) that in many ways women were in a better position
to express their desire for Christ and could therefore achieve a closer
union with him than their male contemporaries. Perhaps somewhat
paradoxically, and uncomfortably (for modern feminist critics), the
'negative' characteristics attributed to cultural definitions of 'femininity'
were precisely those which facilitated their closer relationship with
God. Appropriating a female voice facilitates the articulation of desire
for God within the 'normative' discourses of heterosexual desire. Adopting a female voice, therefore, enables Breton to articulate such a desire
without confronting its homosocial implications. The gendered distinctions in Breton's articulation of religious desire suggest that 'feminine'
characteristics are vital and enviable qualities in the pursuit of an
intimate relationship with Christ. In seeking to represent *The Countesse
of Penbrookes loue*, Breton aspires to record the bliss of spiritual union,
which when writing in his 'own' voice or in a male persona he can
only desire, not obtain. Perhaps the fact that women could express such
a desire for Christ explains why men sought to exclude them from
public ministry; for such exclusion is arguably founded upon an anxiety
that women might be able to reach greater spiritual heights than men.
Although 'Breton' can get closer to articulating penitence by appropriating a female voice, he cannot fully represent Pembroke's experience;
like God, the woman's penitential experience is ineffable or it is, at least,
beyond the reach of a man's pen. It is, therefore, significant that Breton
refers to Pembroke as 'Penbrooke'. Although, as Lamb points out, this
could be a conventional form of address, the consistency of Breton's
use of this spelling indicates a more deliberate usage.[42] Lamb suggests
that it illustrates Breton's repression of Pembroke's secular writing, but
it could be read as an implicit recognition of her spiritual writing, as
the appropriateness of Pembroke's voice for the articulation of penitential discourses is heightened by her own translations of the psalms.
Moreover, Breton's claim in his dedication to *The Pilgrimage to Paradise*
that the text contains 'the heavenly Meditations, of an honourable Lady'
is problematic precisely because Pembroke has written her own
meditations. Breton's admiration of the psalms and anxiety about the
worth of his own writing could suggest that he realized that Pembroke's
meditations demonstrated her ability – as a woman writer – to express

that which for him was inexpressible. While Breton's writing highlights a broad gender distinction in relation to penitence, in this instance Pembroke's superior literary talent bears witness to the fact that she achieved what Breton could only desire.[43]

Notes

1. Elizabeth D. Harvey, *Ventriloquized Voices: Feminist Theory and English Renaissance Texts* (London: Routledge, 1992), p. 16.
2. Harvey, *Ventriloquized Voices*, p. 16.
3. Harvey, *Ventriloquized Voices*, p. 16.
4. It is arguably significant that Breton refers to the countess of Pembroke as 'Penbrooke', as I shall go on to discuss. In order to make a distinction between Breton's representation of the countess and references to Pembroke's own life and writing I shall maintain the distinct spellings.
5. See 'Protestant Confession and the genesis of secrecy' in Jeremy Tambling, *Confession: Sexuality, Sin, the Subject* (Manchester: Manchester University Press, 1990), pp. 87–102; Helen C. White, *The Tudor Books of Private Devotion* (Westport, CT: Greenwood Press, 1979); and John Bossy, 'The social history of confession in the age of the reformation', *Royal Historical Society Transactions*, 5th series, 25 (1975), pp. 21–38.
6. John Calvin, *Institutes of Christian Religion*, trans. Henry Beveridge, 2 vols (Grand Rapids, 1962), II, v, p. 19, cited Paul Delany, *British Autobiography in the Seventeenth Century* (London: Routledge & Kegan Paul, 1969), p. 35.
7. See Delany, *British Autobiography*; Stephen Greenblatt, *Renaissance Self-Fashioning: From More to Shakespeare* (Chicago: University of Chicago Press, 1980).
8. However, this is not, strictly speaking, a Calvinist notion; see R. T. Kendall, *Calvin and English Calvinism to 1649* (Oxford: Oxford University Press, 1969), especially p. 24.
9. Michel Foucault, *London Review of Books*, 21 May–3 June 1981, cited by Tambling, *Confession* (1990), p. 3.
10. William Gouge, *Of Domesticall Duties* (1622), cited by Margaret Olofson Thickstun, *Fictions of the Feminine: Puritan Doctrine and the Representation of Women* (Ithaca, NY: Cornell University Press, 1988), pp. 18–19.
11. The subjugating force of confession and penitence as a general rule is examined by Tambling, *Confession* (1990); Michel Foucault, *The History of Sexuality*, I, *An Introduction* (Harmondsworth: Penguin, 1990); and Dennis A. Foster, *Confession and Complicity in Narrative* (Cambridge: Cambridge University Press, 1987).
12. See Margaret P. Hannay's summary of Elaine Beilin's argument in *Philip's Phoenix: Mary Sidney, Countess of Pembroke* (Oxford: Oxford University Press, 1990), p. 137.
13. This reading of Irigaray is Toril Moi's in *Sexual / Textual Politics: Feminist Literary Theory* (London: Methuen, 1985), p. 137.
14. *Marie Magdalens Loue* (London: John Danter, 1595). The authorship of this text is uncertain: Alexander B. Grosart maintains it is not by Breton;

however, it is attributed to him by S. A. and D. R. Tannenbaum *in Eliza-*
bethan Bibliographies, vol. 1 (New York: Kennikat Press, 1967), p. 2.

15. Breton's depiction of Pembroke as a Magdalene figure is especially promi-
    nent in *A Diuine Poeme, diuided into two Partes. The Rauisht Soule & The*
    Blessed Weeper (1601) and *Auspicante Iehoua. Maries Exercise* (1597). Other
    writers who depict Pembroke in this manner include Samuel Daniel and
    Edmund Spenser. See also Margaret P. Hannay's discussion of Breton's
    poem in *Philip's Phoenix,* p. 138.

16. The texts that Breton addresses to male patrons in a 'male' voice are *Divine*
    Considerations of the Soule (1608), dedicated to Sir Thomas Lake and *Bretons*
    Longing (1601), dedicated to Lord North; those addressed to female patrons
    in a 'female' voice are *The Pilgrimage to Paradise, ioyned with the Countesse*
    of Penbrookes loue (1592), *A Diuine Poeme, diuided into two Partes. The Rauisht*
    Soule & The Blessed Weeper (1601), *Auspicante Iehoua. Maries Exercise* (1597),
    all of which were dedicated to the countess of Pembroke; *The Soules*
    Harmony (1602), dedicated to Lady Sara Hastings; and *The Countesse of*
    Penbrookes Passion (n.d.). This last text was dedicated to the countess of
    Pembroke in manuscript but was dedicated to Lady Mary Houghton when
    the text was published under the title, *The Passions of the Spirit.* For more
    detail about textual history, see Michael Brennan, *Literary Patronage in the*
    Renaissance: The Pembroke Family (London: Routledge, 1988), p. 65, and
    Mary Ellen Lamb, *Gender and Authorship in the Sidney Circle* (Madison,
    WI: University of Wisconsin Press, 1990), p. 51. There is one other text
    specifically concerned with penitence, *A Solemne Passion of the Sovles Loue*
    (1623), which does not have a dedicatee, but is very similar in style and
    subject matter to both *The Soules Harmony* and *The Countesse of Penbrookes*
    Passion.

17. See the introduction to Guy Fitch Lytle and Stephen Orgel (eds), *Patronage*
    in the Renaissance (Princeton: Princeton University Press, 1981), especially
    p. 19.

18. *Bretons Longing* (1601), in Alexander B. Grosart, *The Works in Verse and*
    Prose of Nicholas Breton, 2 vols (privately published, 1879), I, p. 13, stanza
    15. For ease of reference, I have numbered the stanzas on each page rather
    than continuously through the text.

19. *The Soules Harmony* (1602), in Grosart, *Works,* I, p. 4, stanza 12.

20. *Ventriloquized Voices,* p. 32.

21. According to Elizabeth D. Harvey, such an analysis enables us to see 'where
    and how the boundaries between the sexes have been set', *Ventriloquized*
    Voices, p. 53.

22. *The Pilgrimage to Paradise, ioyned with the Countesse of Penbrookes loue* (1592),
    in Grosart, *Works,* I, p. 20, stanza 16.

23. See Teresa de Lauretis's explication of Jurij Lotman's work on mythic
    narratives in *Technologies of Gender: Essays on Theory, Film, and Fiction*
    (Bloomington: Indiana University Press, 1989), p. 43.

24. In addition to *The Pilgrimage to Paradise, ioyned with the Countesse of*
    Penbrookes loue, see the conclusion of the dedication to *Auspicante Iehoua,*
    'Your La: sometime vnworthy Poet, and now and euer poore beadman',
    in Grosart, *Works,* II, p. 4; and *Wits Trenchmour, In a conference had betwixt*

a Scholler & an Angler (1597), the Angler advises the scholar ('Breton'), 'be her bead-man in thy prayers, till she make imployment of thy further service'; in Grosart, *Works*, II, p. 20. See also the reference to the (unnamed) female patron in the dedication to *The Praise of vertuous Ladies* (1599) in Grosart, *Works*, II.

25. Lamb, *Gender and Authorship*, p. 49.
26. De Lauretis, *Technologies of Gender*, p. 99.
27. Grosart, *Works*, I, p. 24, stanza 14.
28. See, for example, Abraham Fraunce, *The Countesse of Pembrokes Iuychurch* (1591) and *The Countesse of Pembrokes Emmanuel* (1591).
29. *Gender and Authorship*, p. 50.
30. *Gender and Authorship*, p. 47.
31. *Gender and Authorship*, p. 48.
32. The importance of the psalms in this process is explored in depth by Calvin in his commentaries on the psalms; see also Paul Delany's discussion of Donne, *British Autobiography*, p. 28. For a discussion of the role of the psalms in the production of subjectivity, see Alan Sinfield, *Faultlines: Cultural Materialism and the Politics of Dissident Reading* (Oxford: Oxford University Press, 1992), p. 166.
33. *A Solemne Passion of the Sovles Loue* (1623), in Grosart, *Works*, I, p. 8, stanza 10.
34. *Sir Philip Sidney: An Apology for Poetry or The Defence of Poesy*, ed. Geoffrey Shepherd (Manchester: Manchester University Press, 1973), especially pp. 98–9.
35. Hannay, *Philip's Phoenix*, p. 136.
36. Grosart, *Works*, I, p. 7, stanza 7.
37. Grosart, *Works*, I, p. 5, stanza 18.
38. Moi, *Sexual Textual Politics*, p. 137. The internal quote is from Luce Irigaray, *Speculum of the Other Woman*, trans. Gillian C. Gill (Ithaca, NY: Cornell University Press, 1985).
39. Quoted in Moi, *Sexual Textual Politics*, p. 136.
40. For further details about women's association with the psalms, see Suzanne Trill, '"Patterns of piety and faith": the role of the psalms in the construction of the exemplary renaissance woman', unpublished Ph.D. dissertation, University of Liverpool, 1993.
41. Moi, *Sexual Textual Politics*, p. 68. See also Hannay, *Philip's Phoenix*, p. 139, and Lamb, *Gender and Authorship*, pp. 51–2.
42. Lamb, *Gender and Authorship*, p. 50. All four of the texts that Breton dedicates to Pembroke (including *The Countesse of Penbrookes Passion*) use this spelling.
43. In addition to my co-editors, I would like to thank Elspeth Graham and Peter Stoneley for their constructive comments on earlier drafts of this essay.

Women Writers and Women Readers: The Case of Aemilia Lanier

Jacqueline Pearson

Women's literacy was deeply controversial in early modern England. It is not only that women's writing was viewed with deep suspicion by male contemporaries, and often with ambivalence by the women themselves: even women's access to literature as readers seemed problematic. A central purpose of Aemilia Lanier's *Salve Deus Rex Judaeorum*, first published in 1611, is to celebrate and legitimize women's roles as both writers and readers, and this task is performed with remarkable vigour and imagination. I propose to examine this strand in the poem, but first to make some general points about its treatment of gender.

Salve Deus Rex Judaeorum is a remarkable work, 'densely packed and intensely written'.[1] Its overt subject is, of course, the passion of Christ. Its four-word title consists of a verb and three masculine nouns: and yet it works to emphasize and empower the female at every level, literary, political and spiritual. The poem begins with the apotheosis of Queen Elizabeth I ('Saints and Angells do attend her Throne'),[2] and ends with the apotheosis of the Countess of Cumberland. It incorporates a range of female voices and female viewpoints, emphasizing the sex of the poet and focusing on the role in the passion narrative of the women of Jerusalem, Pilate's wife, and the Virgin and the other Maries. It also stresses more generally the importance of women in Christ's life. Although he was not the son of a human male he was 'begotten of a woman, born of a woman, nourished of a woman, obedient to a woman; and ... he healed women, pardoned women, comforted women' (p. 78). Indeed, the poem centres on a speech by Pilate's wife urging him not to execute Christ, which itself includes 'Eves Apologie', in which the first woman is defended for her loving generosity, while Adam is attacked for failing to use his greater strength to resist temptation. *Salve Deus* also has appended to it what is possibly the earliest of English country house poems, 'The Description of Cooke-ham', in which the Countess of Cumberland's Berkshire estate is seen as an Eden inhabited by unfallen females. Moreover, the poem uses what

Linda Woodbridge has identified as one of the key techniques of proto-feminist argument in the period, the accumulation of examples of famous, virtuous, wronged or powerful women of the past to make points about women's capacity and / or male oppression:[3] Deborah, Jael, Esther, Judith, Susannah (p. 78), Helen, Lucrece, Cleopatra, Octavia, Rosamund, Matilda (pp. 85–6), and others feature in Lanier's poem.

In addition, *Salve Deus* presents a Christ who is emphatically feminized – born 'without the assistance of man' (p. 78) – and who is praised for traditionally female virtues, 'Humility' (p. 94), 'Obedience', 'Patience' (p. 95), 'chast behaviour', 'meekenesse' (p. 71), even beauty (p. 120). Moreover, his silence (another specifically feminine virtue in contemporary ideologies of gender) is vigorously emphasized (e.g. pp. 100, 106, 115), especially in contrast with the corrupt uses of language consistently attributed to the poem's other males. Peter makes presumptuous claims but denies Christ when he is put to the test (pp. 89–90), Judas betrays his lord (p. 102), Pilate's lips are 'polluted' (p. 105), and the high priest Caiaphas utters not holiness but blasphemy (p. 101). Christ's vulnerability to slander and his silence in the face of it even identifies him with one of the poem's female heroes, Susannah.

If Christ is feminized in the poem, women conversely become masculinized through a religious commitment, allowed to take on male roles which are saintly and even divine. 'Vertuous Ladies' become priests anointed with '*Aarons* pretious oyle' (p. 49) and the Queen of Sheba is seen as a female magus who 'came from farre, / To reverence this new appearing starre' (p. 128). Both the Countess of Cumberland and her daughter Anne Clifford become female St Peters, able with 'those Keyes saint *Peter* did possesse' to use 'spirituall powre' to 'heale the Soules of those that doe transgresse' (p. 122). Even the address to Clifford as 'Faire Shepheardesse' is less a conventional pastoral compliment than an identification of her with the saint, with the power and duty 'To feed his flocke' (p. 76). Finally the Countess of Cumberland is even a kind of female God, 'Directing all by her immortal light ...' (p. 61).

The poem naturally asserts God's benevolent fatherhood: but in fact its central image for this is the bond between mothers and daughters. The poem functions as a network of maternities literal and metaphorical. Its 'dedications continually emphasize the descent of virtue in the female line, from virtuous mothers to daughters'[4] – Margaret and Anne Clifford, the Duchess of Suffolk and her daughter Susan Bertie, Countess of Kent, Anne of Denmark and Elizabeth of Bohemia, Katherine Howard and her daughters. 'A Description of Cooke-ham' describes 'a lost female paradise'[5] presided over by Margaret and Anne Clifford, who paraphrase the primal, fallen, heterosexual couple into a perfected, unfallen relationship between mother and daughter. The mothering role of the Virgin Mary is emphasized, and women in general are vindicated as 'Our Mother *Eve*' is praised.

Nurturing and positive relationships of all kinds, poetic, spiritual and political, are imaged as maternity. Queen Elizabeth I is described as a political Madonna, virgin 'Mother of our Common-weale' (p. 47), and the emphasis on the resurrection of the soul as a 'second berth' (p. 50) defines the divine as maternal as well as paternal. Finally, Lanier derives her poems from 'Nature', not from 'Learning' or 'Art', and Nature is supremely the great 'Mother of perfection' (p. 46). One could even argue, in an Irigarayan sense, that the narrative functions as a series of enfoldings themselves modelled on pregnancy, so that the appeal to female patrons contains the passion story, which contains the speech of Pilate's wife, which contains the vindication of Eve, and that Eve herself contains the maternal potential for all future generations. Wombs within wombs, and within the innermost womb the potential for all human beings. Lanier not only rewrites the passion story to emphasize the roles of women: she creates a poetic form modelled on pregnancy which depicts a world structured as a web of maternities. In this world women consequently have a central, not a marginal, role.

Lanier's poem emphasizes one of the key images of Christianity, the reversal of hierarchies embodied in Christ and also offered to believers: he makes 'the powerfull judged of the weak' (p. 127). Jesus, although the 'all-commaunding King' (p. 118), submits to be 'counted of so meane a berth' (p. 94) as 'A seeming Trades-mans sonne' (p. 132). His death leads to his glorification, and the same is true of the saints, as Stephen 'was humbled and cast downe, / To winne in heaven an ever-lasting crowne' (p. 153). This emphasis on the reversal of hierarchies is, of course, very profitable for those removed from the sources of power on grounds of class and / or gender. The Christian reversal of hierarchies thus particularly benefits the female poet whose own class status is so ambiguous, for it will to some extent work to equalize her with her great female patrons: and it must also benefit her female readers, for women's weakness will, in the new order, be transformed into extraordinary images of female power. Indeed, if in the new Jerusalem 'he that is the greatest may be least' (p. 72), then the weaker and more oppressed the poet and her Muse might seem now, the more they have to gain: 'But yet the Weaker thou doest seeme to be / In Sexe, or Sence, the more his Glory shines' (p. 88). This is a seductive argument for women to whom the social structure offers no official kinds of power, and Lanier uses it very effectively.

However, I want to concentrate not on the poem itself but on its dedications, and on the images of women readers as well as the woman writer that it suggests. I am not at present concerned with what we

can deduce about the reading of the poet herself, though there is I think
interesting work to be done here. If A. L. Rowse was right to identify
Lanier with the Dark Lady of the Sonnets, then there is a particular
piquancy in her apparent memories of Shakespearean heroines, like
Lucrece and Cleopatra, and even a few of what sound to me like echoes
of *The Rape of Lucrece*.[6] Pilate washing his hands may even raise the
spectre of Lady Macbeth. But at the moment I am interested in Lanier's
dedications to women she hopes to recruit as readers. Elaine V. Beilin
is certainly right to see Lanier writing 'specifically to praise women,
and ... to place women at the heart of Christianity'.[7] But Lanier is also
taking part in the contemporary controversy about women's access to
literacy, as she argues not only for the propriety of female reading and
writing, but that these can be intensely empowering without transgressing the limits of Christian virtue.

Professional Renaissance poets – and here of course I mean male
poets – needed patrons; but at the same time they were likely to feel
anxious, even ambivalent, when confronting the class superiority of
these patrons. In addition, the reader's power over the literary text
certainly disturbed some poets. An extreme case, Marston's *The Scourge
of Villainy* (1599), displays a deep hostility, anxiety and envy about the
active power of the reader, who is seen as competing with the poet for
the right to construct and assert meanings for the poem. Thus the
reader is capable of 'quite altering the sense' (p. 3), imposing meanings
that the author would seek to deny, 'that which I never meant' (p. 6).
This poem enacts a bitter battle between the author and the reader
over who shall have control over its meanings and establishes a confrontational model for poetry.

The usual anxieties about class inferiority or loss of authority over
meanings are, however, likely to be exacerbated, if the poet is male
and the patron is female, by gender anxieties: even the term 'female
patron' offers a grammatical contradiction. These anxieties can surface
in the form of bizarre and contradictory treatments of female characters
and female sexuality. To take a single, though by no means unique,
example: William Barksted's *Hiren: or the Fair Greek* (1611: the same
year as Lanier's poem) is in two parts, the first dedicated to the Earl
of Oxford, the second to Elizabeth Stanley, Countess of Derby, who
is praised for possessing all the virtues, 'the Perfection of Perfection'.
However, that this is not as simple as it looks is suggested by the fact
that the change of patronage from male to female comes at exactly that
point in the poem when Hiren breaks her vow of chastity, an act which
demonstrates female frailty and lust and which ultimately leads to her
own death. Despite the overt and conventional rhetoric of praise for
the female dedicatee, a disturbing subtext works to identify her with
transgressive, death-bringing female sexuality.

While Marston presents a confrontational model for poetry, and Barksted reveals deep anxiety about female sexuality even while celebrating the perfection of his female dedicatee, Lanier offers a cooperative, even a collaborative, model. 'The Authors Dreame' of the Countess of Pembroke specifically shows competitiveness between women giving way to friendly and supportive cooperation. Such collaboration is implied by the extraordinary dedication of her poem to *nine* named women patrons.[8] Some of these Lanier knows personally, and especially Susan Bertie Grey, Countess of Kent, 'the Mistris of my youth' (p. 53), and the Countess of Cumberland, who is regularly addressed throughout the course of the poem. These nine women form a group identified both with the nine Muses and with a feminized version of the 'nine Worthies' (p. 49). In addition there are dedications 'To all vertuous Ladies in generall' (p. 48) and 'To the Vertuous Reader', also envisaged as female, since this prose dedication names its intended audience, 'all vertuous Ladies and Gentlewomen of this kingdome' (p. 77). Where Marston is anxious and resentful of the reader's control over the text, Lanier actively solicits it. Her 'rude unpolished lines', read by Anne of Denmark, will 'seem the more divine' (p. 42), and the female dedicatees, like the Countess of Kent, are seen as the subject and, indeed, the very medium of the poem, 'the ground I write upon' (p. 54).

In the dedications, women are repeatedly described reading the poem, and the physical materiality of 'this little Booke' (p. 50) is emphasized'.[9] Even Lanier's proto-feminist parade of famous women is embedded within a world of female writing and reading, and especially the reading and writing of her dedicatees. Elaine Beilin finds Cleopatra's participation in the poem's praise of virtuous women problematic:[10] but surely she figures so largely because the Countess of Pembroke had written a translation of Garnier's *Antonie* and commissioned Daniel's *Cleopatra*, so that the repeated references to Cleopatra suggest and participate in a counter-Shakespearian tradition in which women writers and readers were central. Rosamond is relevant because Daniel's *Complaint of Rosamond* was also dedicated to the Countess, and Matilda because Drayton's *Matilda* is dedicated to the Countess of Bedford. It is not only that Lanier's poem praises virtuous and powerful women: these women, powerful and with a vital place within literary traditions, are actually seen, like their mythological counterparts the Muses, to generate literary texts.

To direct the poem so forcefully to a female readership is an emphatic political statement. (The dedication to Arbella Stuart, which does not appear in all versions of the poem, was particularly risky, especially in offering her the suffering Christ, 'this humbled King' [p. 52], in a phrase which could well have sounded threatening to James I.) *Salve Deus* is not an isolated case of a work with multiple dedications to women, though it utilizes images of its female readers in a way markedly different from male-authored texts, which helps to emphasize its gender politics. Most works dedicated to women are religious, but none seem to emphasize female power as Lanier does. Joshua Sylvester's translation of du Bartas, an epic poem about Judith, *Bethulias Rescue*, is dedicated to Anne of Denmark and to an additional *sixteen* named noblewomen. His treatment of Judith (and indeed of his female patrons) is however basically repressive, praising her for traditional female virtues like modesty and domesticity. He emphasizes Judith's timorousness and her ability to function only because God is acting through her, so that far from being a courageous heroine she in fact becomes the apotheosis of female passivity, quite unlike Lanier's Judith, a woman of 'invincible courage, rare wisdome, and confident carriage' (p. 78). While Sylvester emphasizes Judith's unique difference from other women, and fills the poem with negative feminine images, Lanier regards her female dedicatees and subjects as representative women and creates a strong sense not only of female power but of female solidarity.

Lanier's female patrons are, of course, encouraged to 'read' her work (e.g. pp. 41, 69, 87). But books and the acts of reading and writing are symbolically crucial throughout the poem. Virtue, 'this faire Queene' (p. 48) carries 'in hir hand the Booke where she inroules' the virtuous; the 'worth' of 'famous women' is written 'in lines of blood and fire' (p. 125); and the Queen of Sheba, Susannah and the Countess of Pembroke deserve to be 'Writ' and 'read' by 'after-comming ages' (pp. 61, 127, 133). The Countess of Pembroke is encouraged to read this poem, but her literary competence goes further than this since it also enables her to 'reade' the semiotics of salvation in Christ's wounds (p. 45). And if reading is assimilated to salvation, there can no longer be any argument about the propriety of reading and writing as activities for good women.

Lanier adopts the conventional rhetorical pose of the writer before powerful patrons, a pose of self-conscious humility – 'that which is seldome seene, / A Womans writing ...' (p. 41): to do otherwise would be almost unthinkable in the prevalent tradition within which she writes. But at the same time the activities of reading and writing, the generation of literary texts, which she shares with her patrons work to equalize them and to begin to obliterate the rift of class that separates them. As writer, Lanier shares at least one key image with her female readers, the recurrent image of the mirror (e.g. pp. 42, 44, 48, 63, 72). This proves rhetorically extremely useful for the poet, for 'mirror' is a common Elizabethan image for a work of literature (the *Mirror for Magistrates* for instance), but it is also a conventional female symbol, so that the mirror forcefully combines ideas of literary creativity and femaleness usually kept separate. While the poem is a 'Glasse ... full of spotlesse truth' (p. 42) created by the poet, her female dedicatees also write themselves as the poet writes the poem, producing lives which are texts, mirrors of their virtues – Susan Bertie Grey's 'Perfections', for instance, are a 'Glasse' (p. 53), and Margaret Russell Clifford has, like the poet, produced a 'mirrour' of her 'minde' (p. 67), though the product in her case is not a poem but her daughter Anne Clifford. While Marston needs to stress his superiority to his readers, Aemilia Lanier depicts herself, and her female readers, as involved in similar processes of self-mirroring and self-fashioning. Distinctions between reader and writer, high status and low, usually so important in the rhetoric of patronage, are – partially at least – erased.

Women read and write texts: in addition, women *are* texts to be read. This is a common, and usually a repressive, concept in male writing of the period, in which a woman is figured as a book to be read or a *tabula rasa* to be written on by men. So Desdemona is a 'fair paper, this most goodly book' on which Cassio has allegedly written 'whore', Sidney's Stella is a 'fair text' into which the poet will 'pry', Alexander Craig's Erantina can be 'read' like a 'sheet / Of paper fair', and in Shakespeare's *The Rape of Lucrece* women are 'books' in which their faults can be read, texts so malleable that women cannot be held the 'authors' of their own actions, but only the paper on which these are written by men.[11] Lanier, though, reclaims these oppressive images of women as books. Men 'boast of Knowledge', although this was originally obtained by Adam 'From *Eves* faire hand, as from a learned Booke' (p. 104). The text / woman is no longer passive, unable even to author her self, but is the active generatrix of male learning. Again, as in the case of the mirror, a potentially repressive image of literacy is broken open and reused to express female power.

Images of books, reading and writing are, however, not only import-ant for renegotiating the relation between poet and patron, or the relation between women and literacy. Throughout the dedications, the central tenets of the Christian religion, incarnation, atonement, re-demption and judgment, are persistently imaged as acts of reading and writing. Christ is both a reader and a writer, able to 'reade the earthly storie / Of fraile Humanity' (p. 65), and also '(w)riting the Covenant with his pretious blood' (p. 69). He has written the virtuous 'in the booke of Life' (p. 72), 'in th'eternall booke of heaven' (p. 108), and has cancelled the 'blacke infernall booke' of 'due punishment' (p. 70). At the last judgment, when the heavens 'shall depart, as when a skrowle is rolde' (p. 81), Christ will open 'the Booke, and undoe the Seales' of human sins (p. 131), and will enter the names of the virtuous 'In deep Characters, writ with blood and teares' (p. 133). Moreover, like a woman, Christ is not only a writer and a reader but also a text, the

'Booke / Whereon thine eyes continually may looke' (p. 121). And, like
a woman, he is also a Muse, the inspiration of the poet, whose 'powre
hath given me powre to write' (p. 68). Christ's example as writer, reader,
Muse and text works to authorize the roles of the poet and her dedicatees (at least two of whom, the Countess of Pembroke and the
Countess of Bedford, were themselves poets) as writers and readers.
Images of books, reading and writing are used to equalize the relation
of poet and patron, to show these women as deeply divided in terms
of class but as sharing in literature cooperatively, not competitively,
women's literacy is justified by no less an example than that of Christ;
and women are placed 'at the heart of Christianity' since they share
with Christ activities of reading, writing and textuality.

When in the seventeenth century a woman dedicates a text to other
women, the meaning is likely to be different from a male poet's address
to a patron, female or male. Since the language of dedications is often
sexualized,[12] a woman avoided potentially awkward situations by addressing only women readers: but this apparent limitation could be
turned to her advantage. A female writer could subvert the rhetoric of
patronage by implying her similarity to, not her difference from, her
female patron, since both are engaged in the same battle for access to
literacy, and both are marginalized in cultural history. It does seem to
be the case, to answer a question posed by Franklin B. Williams Jr,[13]
that women writers were more likely to dedicate their work to women
patrons.[14] As female readers and writers themselves, they are naturally
concerned with the reading experiences of other women. But it also
goes, I think, further than this. A Jacobean woman who published
original literary work emerged dangerously from the private domestic
world which traditional ideologies still prescribed for her: the term
'public' when used of women tended to suggest prostitution.[15] Aemilia
Lanier was doubly endangered. As a woman who published, and as a
woman who had also been the acknowledged mistress of the Lord
Chancellor and mother of his illegitimate daughter,[16] Lanier needed to
appeal to the full weight of the virtuous reputations of her nine dedicatees, whose implied similarity to herself she might have hoped would
counteract her own notoriety. There might thus be a special personal
need behind Lanier's extraordinary strategies of dedication. But the
dedications to *Salve Deus Rex Judaeorum* teach lessons beyond the
personal, and present an extraordinary defence of women's writing and
women's reading in which disparities of power and class are abolished,
and women's writing and reading become not only virtuous but literally
God-like activities.

Notes

1. Elaine V. Beilin, 'The feminization of praise: Aemilia Lanyer', in her
   Redeeming Eve: Women Writers of the English Renaissance (Princeton, NJ:
   Princeton University Press, 1987), p. 196. In addition to works referred
   to below, useful recent criticism of Lanier includes Tina Krontiris, 'Aemilia
   Lanyer: criticizing men via religion', in her *Oppositional Voices: Women as
   Writers and Translators of Literature in the English Renaissance* (London:
   Routledge, 1992), pp. 103–20; and Lorna Hutson, 'Why the lady's eyes
   are nothing like the sun', in Clare Brant and Diane Purkiss (eds), *Women,
   Texts and Histories 1575–1760* (London: Routledge, 1992), pp. 13–38.

2. References to Lanier are from A. L. Rowse (ed.), *The Poems of Shakespeare's
   Dark Lady* (London: Jonathan Cape, 1978).

3. Linda Woodbridge, *Women and the English Renaissance: Literature and the
   Nature of Womankind, 1540–1620* (Brighton: Harvester, 1984), pp. 14–16.

4. Barbara K. Lewalski, 'Of God and good women: the poems of Aemilia
   Lanier', in Margaret Hannay (ed.), *Silent but for the Word: Tudor Women
   as Patrons, Translators and Writers of Religious Works* (Kent, OH: Kent State
   University Press, 1985), pp. 207–8.

5. Lewalski, 'Of God and good women', p. 204.

6. There is a reference to Lucrece on p. 85. And compare, e.g., 'that he [i.e.
   Christ] might be the Booke / Whereon thine eyes continually may look'
   (Lanier, p. 121) with 'princes are the glass, the school, the book / Where
   subjects' eyes do learn, do read, do look' (Shakespeare, *The Rape of Lucrece*,
   lines 615–16).

7. Beilin, 'The feminization of praise', p. 179.

8. They are Queen Anne of Denmark; her daughter Princess Elizabeth;
   Arbella Stuart; Susan Bertie Grey, Countess of Kent; Mary Sidney Herbert,
   Countess of Pembroke; Lucy Harington Russell, Countess of Bedford;
   Margaret Russell Clifford, Countess of Cumberland and her daughter
   Anne Clifford, Countess of Dorset; and Katherine Knyvett Howard,
   Countess of Suffolk.

9. e.g. 'Reade it faire Queene' (p. 41), 'Desiring that this Booke Her hands
   may kisse' (p. 45), 'Though your faire eyes farre better Bookes have seen'
   (p. 47).

10. Beilin, 'The feminization of praise', p. 200.

11. Shakespeare, *Othello* IV. 2. 73–4; Sidney, *Astrophell and Stella*, Sonnet
    LXVII; Alexander Craig, *Amorous Songes and Sonets* (1606) in *The Poetical
    Works of Alexander Craig of Rose-Craig 1603–31* (Glasgow: privately printed
    for the Hunterian Club, 1873), p. 49; Shakespeare, *The Rape of Lucrece*,
    lines 1253, 1244.

12. See Fred Whigham, 'The rhetoric of Elizabethan suitors' letters', *PMLA*
    96 (1981), p. 865.

13. Franklin B. Williams, Jr, 'The literary patronesses of Renaissance England',
    Notes and Queries 207 (1962), p. 366.

14. e.g. Mary Sidney Herbert's *Psalmes* are dedicated to Queen Elizabeth;
    Dorothy Leigh's *The Mothers Blessing* (1614) to Elizabeth of Bohemia;
    Rachel Speght dedicated her poem *Mortalities Memorandum* (1621) to

her godmother Mary Moundford; Elizabeth Cooke Russell's translation of Poynet's *A Way of Reconciliation* (1605) is addressed to her daughter, Anne Russell Herbert; Diana Primrose's poems *A Chaine of Pearle. or a Memoriall of Queen Elizabeth* (1630) is addressed to 'All noble Ladies and Gentlewomen', Anne Wheathill dedicates her collection of prayers and meditations, *A Handfull of Holesome (though Homelie) Herbes* (1584) 'to all Ladies'.

15. See, e.g., Shakespeare, *Othello* IV. 2. 75.
16. For Lanier's life, see Rowse, *Shakespeare's Dark Lady*, pp. 1–37.

The Canonization of Elizabeth Cary

Stephanie Wright

The struggle to recover the work of women writers, particularly those of the Renaissance, has been so great that the sole issue of recognition appears to have dominated at the expense of a thoroughly worked out strategy for (re)instatement. Annette Kolodny identifies two of the major problems in (re)instating women writers into the literary canon. She argues that current acquired reading strategies, which focus on the appreciation of established canonical texts, may be at the root of the absence of women writers from the major canons. She emphasizes that this is:

> due not to any lack of merit in the work but, instead, to an incapacity of predominantly male readers to properly interpret and appreciate women's texts – due, in a large part, to a lack of prior acquaintance.[1]

These are crucial issues, but Kolodny does not take account of the politics of acquaintance. It is certainly impossible to (re)instate a woman writer into the canon if her works are unknown and unavailable, but even when women writers are granted some recognition, the terms upon which their texts are accepted is as political an issue as the question of (re)instatement itself.

The process of creating the Renaissance canon is subject to a variety of political agenda; what actually constitutes the Renaissance canon may range from the plays chosen for performance by the Royal Shakespeare Company, to the texts published by the major academic publishing houses, to those texts chosen for teaching at undergraduate level. This final category probably provides the most telling evidence of the status of Renaissance women writers because, due to limited time and resources, the inclusion of one text leads, inevitably, to the exclusion of another. Whilst it is feasible to extend the Renaissance canon (in its widest sense) indefinitely, this means that texts by women constitute little threat to established texts by men. But, were the situation to arise where a choice was to be made between teaching *The Courtier* or pamphlets by women;[2] 'To Penshurst' or 'The Description of

Cooke-ham';[3] *Othello* or *The Tragedy of Mariam*, then the proposition to (re)instate women writers into the Renaissance canon would be rather more serious and threatening.

This threat can, however, be contained to a certain extent by bestowing an 'exceptional' status on texts by women, rendering them worthy of interest, but not worthy of widespread academic study, because they are not seen to be (or are not allowed to be) part of the mainstream cultural milieu of the Renaissance. Ironically, this image of the woman writer in the Renaissance as a historical phenomenon can be seen to pervade works which otherwise make a positive contribution to the fight to gain recognition for Renaissance literature by women. For example Betty Travitsky, in her invaluable anthology of women's writing in the Renaissance, *The Paradise of Women*, comments on Lady Mary Wroth:

> Lady Wroth has true facility and grace; she is lacking in the ability to make her materials moving. Therefore, her achievement must be qualified finally as historical rather than literary ... The [*Urania*] itself must be considered derivative, since it adds nothing original to her uncle's contribution to the genre.[4]

Similarly, Simon Shepherd's edition of five Renaissance pamphlets written in defence of women, by women, and another invaluable source of Renaissance women's writing, ends with this conclusion:

> We are left with a handful of texts, all *limited intellectually and politically* by their being produced in an age before feminism, but all nevertheless pre-eminently remarkable for their intellectual bravery and adventure; *remarkable, in short, that they exist*.[5]

The case of Elizabeth Cary exemplifies the counterproductive results of a critical emphasis upon historical significance and exceptional status. Three texts have presided over the canonization of Elizabeth Cary: *The Tragedy of Mariam*, c. 1604, published 1613, *The History of the Life, Reign and Death of Edward II*, 1627, published 1680 (with its shorter manifestation, *The History of the Most Unfortunate Prince, King Edward II*, also published in 1680) and a manuscript biography, c. 1650 by one of Cary's four daughters (who were all nuns in the French convent of Cambrai), edited by Richard Simpson in 1861 and entitled *The Lady Falkland: Her Life*.[6] In the recent feminist work on Cary this trinity has reigned supreme for nearly two decades; and rightly so, it would seem. For these texts constitute the first extant play and the first major historical work by an Englishwoman, together with a remarkably detailed biography of the author. We who seek the (re)instatement of

women writers into the Renaissance canon should be thankful that
Cary provides us with such a wealth of pioneering literary and historical
primary source material. And yet these texts have caused more than
a few problems in the development of feminist, indeed any, scholarship concerning Cary's literary texts. What this article seeks to argue
is that the last two decades of feminist work on Cary, whilst ostensibly
struggling for her right to canonical status, have, somewhat counter-
productively, effected a canonization of the rather more venerative
kind.

Nancy Cotton, in one of the earliest articles calling for recognition
of Elizabeth Cary, takes a line which is predominantly historical and
consequently devalues the very text which it is trying to promote, *The
Tragedy of Mariam*. The article makes excuses for the literary standard
of *The Tragedy of Mariam*, by invoking biographical detail – Elizabeth
Cary suffered from excessive childbearing and religious mania. Whatever the questionable validity of such a claim (in fact Elizabeth Cary
did not suffer excessive childbearing until well after she wrote *The
Tragedy of Mariam* and it is questionable whether her inner religious
conflict was fully developed so early in her life), the real point is that
the article deems it necessary to make such excuses. Cotton's final
conclusion is similar to that of Betty Travitsky's comment on Lady
Mary Wroth: 'Elizabeth Cary, Lady Falkland, must still be remembered
as the first Englishwoman to write an original play'.[7]

The alternatives to this view, however, seem equally unsatisfactory.
Nancy Cotton's historical claim for Cary's text constitutes a strategy
to ensure and justify its place in the canon. When *The Tragedy of
Mariam* has been denied such a justification, it has not experienced
such supportive treatment:

> [T]he dramatist is no mean workman as far as construction is con-
> cerned, but is no poet.[8]

> [T]he play as a whole is singularly uninspired and deficient in
> interest.[9]

> *The Tragedie of Mariam* is certainly not to be numbered among the
> outstanding Mariamne [sic] tragedies.[10]

> As the plotting and characterisation of Lady Cary's *Mariam* are almost
> identical with that of Massinger's far greater fictionalized version of
> the story, it will not require separate analysis.[11]

In the face of such literary hostility, how are Elizabeth Cary's texts
to be brought to the fore as worthwhile texts for study? Nancy Cotton's
1977 article provided a strategy which has been generally approved and
adopted, most notably by Elaine Beilin, Margaret Ferguson, Sandra

K. Fischer, Tina Krontiris and Betty Travitsky.[12] Credit certainly has to be given to the critics listed above because they attempt the initial stage of the battle for (re)instatement, in that they create the necessary awareness of Cary and her works. Yet the manner in which they do so also creates new critical problems. All of these critics impose a version of biographical criticism upon *The Tragedy of Mariam*, justifying its place in the canon via the 'authority of experience' approach.[13] However, it is important to stress the extent to which an 'authority of experience' reading is determined by the (otherwise fortunate) fact that the life of Elizabeth Cary is apparently well documented due to the survival of her daughter's biography.[14]

The increasing reliance upon this biography as the major critical tool has become all too apparent. Whilst it is certainly true that disseminating information about a woman author can only improve her prospects of canonical (re)instatement, the opportunity to reclaim more information about Cary, and about the contexts in which she produced her works, has been largely overlooked. There are numerous documents in the Public Record Office (SP Dom., 1601–40; SP Irel., 1625–32) and the dedications which preface both her literary works and her translations[15] and six works dedicated to her by male writers[16] are particularly valuable because they offer an insight into how she perceived herself and how she was perceived by others. Doubtless due to a lack of awareness of the availability of these sources, Cotton, Beilin, Fischer, Travitsky, Ferguson and Krontiris make scant use of them. Rather, they explain the literary fiction of *The Tragedy of Mariam* by counterbalancing it with what they present as the literal truth of the daughter's biography. Despite Elaine Beilin's description of it as a 'spiritual history verging on hagiography',[17] neither she nor the other critics take much account of this, nor of the fact that the biography itself belongs to a separate and distinct literary genre.

It is, however, easy to understand why reading the daughter's biography as literally true is such a tempting prospect for the feminist scholar. For, if the biography could reasonably be accorded such trust, Elizabeth Cary's place in the Renaissance canon is guaranteed. We are presented with a literary and linguistic prodigy. Our attention is specifically drawn to the works which Elizabeth Cary wrote (the majority of which are, sadly, lost), to the numerous volumes which she read and also to her aptitude for languages. Furthermore, her independence and appetite for learning as a child are conveyed in the descriptions of how she bribed the servants to bring her materials to read and write at night, running up debts of £300; how she sent away her French tutor and learnt the language by herself in a matter of weeks; and how she saved an old woman from being condemned as a witch because of her precocious insight into the corrupt practices of local courts.[18] It is very difficult to resist the appeal of such a heroine – unless of course, this heroine puts an end to the efficacy of her own work.

It is therefore a matter of some concern that the daughter's biography has gained considerable critical strength in recent years. Whilst Cotton's earliest work bestows token status upon Cary as the first woman playwright, it is significant that the later works of Cotton, Beilin, Fischer and Ferguson emphasize the religious content of *The Tragedy of Mariam*. The daughter's biography is for the most part concerned with Elizabeth Cary's progress to Catholicism, and this begins to inform the reading of her mother's play; the more the biography becomes used as a decoding device, the more 'religious' the reading of the play:

> Like Cary, Mariam is unsuccessful in escaping the tragedy of personal and political tyranny; however, her death asserts the integrity of her conscience and apotheosizes her as a victim whose suffering and sacrifice affect the tyrant and open the way for change. This was perhaps more than Lady Falkland could hope for personally, and she used the marginal genre as a forum for the philosophical investigation of the subject closest to her heart.[19]

> On the one hand, Mariam's death punishes her outspokenness, so warning women to be silent; on the other hand, it makes her a martyr. Mariam's Christian triumph may well reflect Cary's optimism for her own art by detaching her surrogate from earthly oppression. By affirming Christian values, Cary modified the challenge her writing posed to traditional feminine boundaries.[20]

Margaret Ferguson seeks to 'show how, and to begin to show why, the play's ideological statement is so mixed', and goes part way to achieving this end by ascribing the 'culturally constructed censoring power' to 'the Chorus, and, at certain moments, to the heroine herself, speaking, evidently, for an aspect of the author's own conscience or superego'.[21] She also agrees with Beilin's Christian interpretation, further emphasising the religious significance of Mariam's death by drawing historical and scriptural links:

> [T]here is considerable emphasis on the 'fact' that she is beheaded. This detail, unremarked by Cary's critics so far as I know, seems an overdetermined and historically volatile allusion: it conjures up the ghost of Mary Queen of Scots, whose son ruled England when Cary wrote her play and who was in the eyes of many English Catholics a victim of Protestant tyranny; it also links Mariam with the figure of Christ's harbinger John the Baptist, beheaded by Herod's servants at Salome's request.[22]

Ferguson does not seem to have taken account of the fact that the
Salome who requested the head of John the Baptist was Herod's
stepdaughter by a later marriage, and not his sister, who is the Salome
of the play. And, following on from Nancy Cotton's anachronistic use
of Elizabeth Cary's conversion to Catholicism, Ferguson talks of
the 'aura of sanctification' which surrounds Mariam's death as an
'uncannily proleptic justification of the rebellious path Cary herself
would follow when she converted publically [sic] to Catholicism in the
mid-1620s'.[23]

These critical works unquestioningly reflect the focus of their major
critical tool. Furthermore, they present the heroine of the play and the
heroine of the biography as one and the same; the Mariam of the play
is viewed as a literary manifestation of the 'real' Elizabeth Cary of the
biography. Thus, *The Tragedy of Mariam* earns its place in the canon
because of who wrote it, not because of its value as a Renaissance text;
it becomes a phenomenon to be understood only in terms of its author
and thus denied vital interplay with other texts of the period. Elizabeth
Cary and *The Tragedy of Mariam* are in serious danger of becoming
inextricably fused together and 'canonized' as a feminist cultural icon,
revered, yet impotent, in the fight to redress the balance.

The invalidity of sealing off the text in such a way is irrevocably
exposed by the fact that it relates, on a purely textual level, to many
other works. For example, the play is part of the European tradition
of dramas concerning Herod and Mariam, upon whom two other
English Renaissance plays were based[24] and there is a clearly discernible
similarity between *The Tragedy of Mariam* and Shakespeare's *Othello*.
Two recent articles suggest that *The Tragedy of Mariam* may have been
a source for Middleton and Rowley's *A Fair Quarrel* and for the
anonymous *Second Maiden's Tragedy*,[25] and the hyperbolic misogynistic
discourse which is deconstructed so effectively by the pamphlets of
Esther Sowernam, Rachel Speght and Constantia Munda is given
similar treatment in *The Tragedy of Mariam*.

The extent to which the fusion of Cary and text has taken place is
evidenced by a recent publication on Cary, a volume which combines
an edition of *The Tragedy of Mariam* with an edition of the daughter's
biography. The editors, Margaret Ferguson and Barry Weller, justify
the production of this hybrid text thus: 'Although we believe that *The
Lady Falkland: Her Life* has independent value as an historical document,
we suspect that for most readers it will be an ancillary text to Mariam'.[26]
Despite their acknowledgment of many of the points made in the
previous paragraph, Weller and Ferguson have confirmed the biography
as the supreme critical tool by this very publication. The reader of this
publication is drawn into reading *The Tragedy of Mariam* in terms of
Cary's daughter's biography. Whilst one can choose to dismiss the

argument of a critical work, it is much more difficult to resist the temptation to draw parallels between these two works when they are presented together in a single binding. We do not have to read Weller and Ferguson's introduction to be seduced into a biographical reading of *The Tragedy of Mariam*; the nature of the volume demands it from us.[27]

The History of the Life Reign and Death of Edward II, and the shorter version *The History of the Most Unfortunate Prince, King Edward II*, would appear to be similarly attached to Cary's biography. The recent controversy over the authorship of the two texts would appear only to reinforce the symbiotic relationship between Cary and text. The most recent edition of Wing attributes both texts to Elizabeth's husband, Henry Cary, based on the fact that the later, shorter text makes the claim 'Found among the Papers of and supposed to be writ by the Right Honourable Henry Viscount Falkland, Sometime Lord Deputy of Ireland' (sig. A1r). However, the initials which appear at the foot of the preface 'To the Reader' in the earlier, longer text are 'E. F.' (sig. A2r). Elizabeth Cary, as 1st Viscountess Falkland, signed her letters 'E. Falkland', and it is this fact which led Donald A. Stauffer to suggest that she, rather than her husband, was the author.[28] His evidence has been accepted by many scholars since, such as Betty Travitsky, Elizabeth Hageman and Barbara Lewalski.[29] However, there has been some doubt cast on Elizabeth Cary's authorship. D. R. Woolf claims that both versions of the text were in fact written in 1679–80,[30] and so could not have been written by Henry Cary, as Wing claims, or by Elizabeth, as Stauffer claims. Woolf takes no account of the evidence brought by Stauffer and completely overlooks the possibility of Elizabeth Cary being the author. There has been little attempt by feminist scholars to supplement the evidence of Stauffer, even after the appearance of such an adverse article.[31] Tina Krontiris writes extensively about both texts of *Edward II*. In *Oppositional Voices*, her chapter on Elizabeth Cary merely retells the story of Cary's work, without any apparent theoretical perspective. Whilst she acknowledges the existence of other works on Edward II, she does not take the opportunity to place Elizabeth Cary's text in its literary context. In her earlier article 'Style and gender in Elizabeth Cary's Edward II' Krontiris relies heavily on the biography, in much the same vein as the critics of *The Tragedy of Mariam* discussed above, although this article is charged with a different motivation. Instead of trying to justify Elizabeth Cary's place in the canon like Cotton, Fischer and Beilin, Krontiris is trying to justify Elizabeth Cary's claim to the authorship of the *Edward II* texts. The principle is, however, the same. Krontiris says that she will introduce new evidence which will point to Cary as the author. What she does, in fact, is to draw parallels between the plight of Queen Isabel and that of Elizabeth Cary after she had converted to Catholicism. The eventual effect of this kind of reading is the closure of the text, the same effect imposed by Cotton, Fischer, Beilin and Ferguson upon *The Tragedy of Mariam*. Moreover, this kind of reading is, paradoxically, complicit with the preservation of the canon. It is rather difficult to deny Elizabeth Cary's *Edward II* a place amongst the political writings of the period, but closing the text by reading it as a pseudo-biography of Cary helps to effect precisely this denial.

The critical history to date, then, suggests that the only means by which to validate *The Tragedy of Mariam* as a text and Elizabeth Cary as the author of *Edward II* is by reference, not simply to her life, but to her life as conveyed by her daughter, resulting in the situation complained of concisely by Christiane Rochefort in 1975: 'A man's book is a book. A woman's book is a woman's book.'[32] At present, *The Tragedy of Mariam* exists as 'a woman's book'; it is known only as part of the myth of Elizabeth Cary, rather than as one of the group of literary texts known collectively as Renaissance drama. Similarly, the *Edward II* texts, if Cary is to be accepted as their author, must be seen to reflect her personal situation at the time of writing. This emphasis obscures the fact that the text are also part of the 'long tradition of didactic, cautionary tales such as the popular Elizabethan work, the *Mirror for Magistrates*'.[33] The Weller and Ferguson edition perhaps epitomizes (and, of course, will only perpetuate) these problems. They show cautious support for reading 'The Author's Preface to the Reader' from *The History of the Life, Reign and Death of Edward II* as indicative of Cary's personal plight at the time of writing, and progress to a more general approval of the biographical approach:

> [I]t is nonetheless tempting to consider 'E.F.''s preface in connection with Cary's traumatic separation from her husband in 1626, a separation occasioned, as we have seen, by an conversion to Catholicism that became public ... A biographical reading of the preface to the text of Edward is further encouraged by the obvious auto-biographical dimensions of Cary's Mariam. If Cary twice relied on her pen to console herself for troubles engendered by her marriage, in both cases she turned to history for her material, or rather, to a historical narrative that other writers had already worked into various shapes and meanings. Thus she teases us to find her literary 'identity' in the shadowy terrain between authorship, translation, and revision.[34]

This desperate desire to find Cary's literary 'voice' can perhaps be seen to have a causal relationship with the prevalence of biographical criticism. Much critical anxiety seems to have resulted from the diversity and scarcity of Cary's works. What is left of Elizabeth Cary's works is: a manuscript translation of Abraham Ortelius's *Le Miroir du Monde* (probably 1598–9); *The Tragedy of Mariam* (c. 1604, published 1613); *The History of the Life, Reign and Death of Edward II* (c. 1627, published 1680); and a translation of *The Reply of the Most Illustrious Cardinall of Perron* (1630).[35] In other words, a translation of a geographical work, a Senecan tragedy, an historical biography mixing prose and dramatic poetry and a translation of a religious work. This is certainly a very diverse set of texts, the production of which is spread thinly over a period of 34 years. This fact has bestowed an importance on the daughter's biography in that it simultaneously draws together and expands the Cary oeuvre. It tells of a verse 'Life of Tamberlaine', in addition to *The Tragedy of Mariam*; other translations, including Seneca's epistles; religious and biographical works – verses to the Virgin and the lives of St Agnes the Martyr and St Elizabeth of Portugal.[36] There is, as Weller and Ferguson say, no poetic voice by which to identify Elizabeth Cary; evidently this was viewed as a problem by previous critics and the biography was brought in to alleviate the situation.

One has to consider whether the situation has entirely benefited from such 'alleviation'. The result has been the emergence of a separate and distinct sub-canon, containing the daughter's biography, *The Tragedy of Mariam* and the *Edward II* texts. Defining the texts by their author's biography also problematizes the application of other critical approaches and compromises the possibility of the texts, being subject to any new developments in literary criticism. Chris Weedon defines the situation:

> The study of women's writing as a feminist project can take many forms depending on the assumptions and perspectives of the reader. It is possible, for example, to look at it in both essentialist and poststructuralist ways and the key difference in these approaches is the significance given to women as authors. Essentialist approaches assume that female authorship of texts is their most crucial aspect and that they are the product of a specifically female experience and aesthetic. In poststructuralist theory authorship does not guarantee meaning, though the historical context in which the author is located will produce the discourses of the text. The forms of gendered subjectivity offered by texts are also the product of the social discourses on gender in circulation at the time of writing.[37]

In the particular case of the cited criticism on Elizabeth Cary, not only does authorship guarantee meaning, but meaning guarantees authorship and the two live in a hermetically sealed symbiotic harmony – immune, but also harmless.

It would surely be more productive to make positive use of the
diversity of Elizabeth Cary's works and treat the difficulty in defining
her poetic voice as an advantage. Quite simply, each text must be taken
separately and read in its own literary context, without Cary, as patron
saint, presiding over its fortunes. Thanks to much of the pioneering
work executed by the critics mentioned in this article, the pompous
dismissal of Elizabeth Cary as a writer is no longer tenable. But precisely
because this dismissal is no longer tenable, the anxious biographical
validation of Cary's works is no longer necessary and is, in many ways,
regressive and harmful. Any feminist re-creation of Cary from her
daughter's biography constitutes a barely-refracted version of the Elizabeth Cary appropriated and celebrated by English Catholics as a recu-
sant heroine. The latter appropriation is, however, much more credible.
The veneration of saints is an integral part of Catholic doctrine; if
Elizabeth Cary is similarly venerated by feminist literary critics, the
resultant canonization will mean that her texts remain permanently
excommunicated from the rest of the Renaissance canon.

Notes

1. Annette Kolodny, 'Dancing through the minefield: some observations on
   the theory, practice, and politics of a feminist literary criticism', in Elaine
   Showalter (ed.), *The New Feminist Criticism* (London: Virago, 1986), p. 156.
2. For example, Rachel Speght, *A Mouzell for Melastomus* (1617); Esther
   Sowernam, *Ester Hath Hang'd Haman* (1617); Constantia Munda, *The
   Worming of a Mad Dog* (1617). These were responses to Joseph Swetnam's
   derogatory pamphlet, *The Arraignment of Lewd, Idle, Froward and Unconstant Women* (1615).
3. From Aemilia Lanyer, *Salve Deus Rex Judaeorum* (1611).'The Description
   of Cooke-ham' is a poem of the country house genre, written in honour
   of Margaret Clifford, Countess of Cumberland (1560?–1616). The un-
   deserved obscurity of this and the women's pamphlets is evidenced by the
   fact that they require an explanatory footnote, whilst *The Courtier* and 'To
   Penshurst' do not.
4. Betty Travitsky (ed.), *The Paradise of Women: Writings by Englishwomen of
   the Renaissance* (London: Greenwood Press, 1981), pp. 135–6.
5. Simon Shepherd (ed.), *The Women's Sharp Revenge: Five Pamphlets of the
   Renaissance* (London: Fourth Estate, 1985), p. 23, my italics. In his conclusion, Shepherd also refers to the second major problem which emerges
   when dealing with women's writing of the Renaissance: the role of feminism. This issue is raised, with much the same effect, by Katherine Usher
   Henderson and Barbara F. McManus, in their *Half Humankind: The Texts
   and Contexts of the Controversy about Women in England 1540–1640* (Chicago:
   University of Chicago Press, 1985). They go further than Shepherd,
   however, in citing the role of religion in limiting the degree of 'feminism'

to which Renaissance women writers could hope to aspire, and judging the texts with which they deal according to how successfully they overcome these 'limitations' (p. 27). Whilst it is quite true to say that Renaissance women writers operated in a society which did not give a name or an identity to female resistance against patriarchal oppression, this did not mean that the texts produced by women were intellectually and politically limited as a result. One could just as feasibly argue the opposite – that finding a means to articulate resistance, without the support of a distinct and recognisable group actually indicates the greater political and intellectual skill of the women who wrote under such circumstances.

6. Richard Simpson (ed.), *The Lady Falkland: Her Life* (London: Catholic Publishing and Bookselling Co., 1861). I should like to acknowledge the kind assistance of M. Claude Lannette, the Directeur des Archives départementales du Nord, who arranged for a photocopy of the original manuscript to be sent to me, in order that I could compare it with Simpson's edition. In his edition Simpson reinserts the sections of the text which have been crossed out (though fortunately not obliterated) by another hand and also includes the marginal notes which are made in the same hand. Simpson suggests that this hand could be that of Patrick Cary, Elizabeth's youngest son (p. vi).

   It is this edition upon which the critics tend to rely. However, they do make use of another edition, *The Life of Elisabeth, Lady Falkland*, edited by Lady Georgiana Fullerton (London: Burns & Oates, 1883). This substantially rewrites the manuscript, and incorporates many of Elizabeth Cary's letters. Fullerton obviously used the manuscript independently of Simpson, as there are points in her book which offer differing readings, e.g. where Simpson reads 'a little beer with a toast' (p. 17), Fullerton reads 'a little beer with a tart' (p. 29). However, the usefulness of Fullerton's edition is compromised by the fact that it is completely lacking in scholarly citation.

7. Nancy Cotton, 'Elizabeth Cary, Renaissance playwright', *Texas Studies in Language and Literature* 18 (1977), pp. 601–8 (p. 608).

8. A. C. Dunstan, 'An examination of two English tragedies', unpublished doctoral dissertation (Königsberg: Albertus-Universität, 1908), p. 43.

9. A. M. Witherspoon, *The Influence of Robert Garnier on Elizabethan Drama* (New Haven: Yale University Press, 1924), p. 154.

10. M. J. Valency, *Tragedies of Herod and Mariamne* (New York: Columbia University Press, 1940), p. 87.

11. L. Brodwin, *Elizabethan Love Tragedy* (London: University of London Press, 1977), p. 389. Even Catherine Belsey, whilst at least taking the play seriously in the context of other plays of the period, disappointingly fails to give it anything other than a conservative reading, unquestioningly casting Salome as the villainess, the 'spiritual sister of Vittoria and Lady Macbeth', without accounting for the fact that these two meet the death demanded by Renaissance poetic justice, whilst Salome does not. See her *The Subject of Tragedy: Identity and Difference in Renaissance Drama* (London: Methuen, 1985), pp. 174–5.

12. See Elaine Beilin, 'Elizabeth Cary and The Tragedie of Mariam', *Papers on Language and Literature*, vol. 16, (1980), pp. 45–64, and *Redeeming Eve: Women Writers of the Renaissance* (Guildford: Princeton University Press, 1987); Margaret Ferguson, 'The spectre of resistance' in David Scott Kastan and Peter Stallybrass (eds), *Staging the Renaissance: Reinterpretations of Elizabethan and Jacobean Drama* (London: Routledge, 1992), pp. 233–50; Sandra K. Fischer, 'Elizabeth Cary and tyranny, religious and domestic', in Margaret P. Hannay (ed.), *Silent But for the Word: Tudor Women as Patrons, Translators and Writers of Religious Works* (Kent, OH: Kent State University Press, 1985), pp. 225–37; Tina Krontiris, 'Style and Gender in Elizabeth Cary's *Edward II*', in Ann M. Haselkorn and Betty S. Travitsky (eds), *The Renaissance Englishwoman in Print: Counterbalancing the Canon* (Amherst: University of Massachusetts Press, 1990), pp. 137–53, and *Oppositional Voices: Women as Writers and Translators of Literature in the English Renaissance* (London: Routledge, 1992); and Betty S. Travitsky, 'The *Feme Covert* in Elizabeth Cary's *Mariam*', in Carole Levin and Jeanie Watson (eds), *Ambiguous Realities: Women in the Middle Ages and the Renaissance* (Detroit: Wayne State University Press, 1987), pp. 184–96. I should like to acknowledge Barbara Kiefer Lewalski's chapter 'Resisting Tyrants' in *Writing Women in Jacobean England* (London: Harvard University Press, 1993) as the kind of progression for which this article originally called. Lewalski sets *The Tragedy of Mariam* in the context of other drama of the period and focuses upon its political rather than its biographical connotations (pp. 191–201). Similarly, she treats *The History of the Life, Reign and Death of Edward II* as a political tract rather than as a psychomachia, setting it in the context of other histories of Edward II (pp. 210–11).

13. Far from wishing to devalue the 'authority of experience' per se, I merely wish to suggest that, as it is only one critical strategy amongst many, in the case of Elizabeth Cary it should be used with extreme caution and perhaps, at this stage, abandoned altogether.

14. There is also a short chapter in K. B. Murdock's *Sun at Noon: Three Biographical Sketches* (New York: Macmillan, 1939), which provides additional material.

15. 'The Mirror of the Worlde translated Out of French into Englishe', c. 1598, MS Bodleian Library, Dep. d. 817 is prefaced by a dedication 'To the righte honorable my singular good unckle Sr Henry Lee, knighte of the most noble order of the garter'; *The Tragedy of Mariam*, c. 1604, published 1613, is prefaced by a dedicatory poem to her sister-in-law, 'To Dianae's Earthlie Deputesse and my worthy sister, mistris Elizabeth Carye'; *The History of the Life, Reign and Death of Edward II*, c. 1627, published 1680, includes 'The Author's Preface to the Reader'; *The Reply of the Most Illustrious Cardinall of Perron*, 1630, is prefaced by a dedication to Queen Henrietta Maria and an epistle to the reader. There are also two manuscript poems, namely a sonnet to Henrietta Maria and a quatrain to Jacques Davy, Cardinall du Perron, which appear only in the copies in the Beinecke Collection at Yale University Library, shelfmark Me65 D925 +R4G; the Houghton Library at Harvard University, shelfmark fSTC 6385 and in the Bodleian Library, shelfmark P5. 7 Th.

16. Michael Drayton, *Englands Heroicall Epistles* (1597); John Davies, *The Muses Sacrifice* (1612); Richard More (ed.), *Englands Helicon* (1614); William Basse, *Poetical Works 1602–1653*, ed. R. Warwick Bond (London, 1893); Richard Beling, *A Sixthe Booke to the Countesse of Pembroke's Arcadia* (1624); William Sheares (ed.), *The Workes of Mr John Marston* (1633).

17. *Redeeming Eve*, p. 158.

18. Simpson (ed.), *The Lady Falkland*, pp. 4–7.

19. Fischer, 'Elizabeth Cary and tyranny', p. 237.

20. Beilin, *Redeeming Eve*, p. 185.

21. 'The spectre of resistance', pp. 236, 240.

22. 'The spectre of resistance', p. 245.

23. 'The spectre of resistance', p. 245.

24. Gervase Markham and William Sampson, *The True Tragedy of Herod and Antipater: With the Death of Faire Mariam* (1622); Philip Massinger, *The Duke of Millaine* (1623).

25. Richard Levin, 'A Possible Source of *A Fair Quarrel*', *Notes & Queries* 228 (1983), pp. 152–3; R. V. Holdsworth, 'Middleton and *The Tragedy of Mariam*', *Notes & Queries* 231 (1986), pp. 379–80.

26. Barry Weller and Margaret W. Ferguson (eds), *The Tragedy of Mariam, with The Lady Falkland: Her Life* (London: University of California Press, 1994), p. 50.

27. Nevertheless, this edition is a useful addition to the scholarship on Elizabeth Cary. It adds to the now growing editorial interest in *The Tragedy of Mariam*, and provides an accessible edition of the MS biography, the Simpson edition being a rather rare volume.

28. Donald A. Stauffer, 'A deep and sad passion' in Hardin Craig (ed.), *The Parrot Presentation Volume* (Princeton: Princeton University Press, 1935), pp. 289–314. It is my opinion that Elizabeth Cary is, in fact the author of *The History of the Life, Reign and Death of Edward II*, but that the shorter version, *The History of the Most Unfortunate Prince, King Edward II*, is not only an edited down, but substantially rewritten, version which owes more to the editor than to Elizabeth Cary. However, as none of the critics I discuss makes a distinction between the two and the issue of authorship is by no means resolved, I shall continue to refer to both texts here.

29. Travitsky, *The Paradise of Women*, pp. 216–20; Elizabeth H. Hageman, 'Recent Studies in Women Writers of the English Seventeenth Century', *English Literary Renaissance* 18, 1 (1988), pp. 138–67; Elaine V. Beilin, 'Current Bibliography of English Women Writers, 1500–1640', in Anne H. Haselkorn and Betty S. Travitsky (eds), *The Renaissance Englishwoman in Print: Counterbalancing the Canon* (Amherst: University of Massachusetts Press, 1990), pp. 347–60; Lewalski, 'Resisting tyrants', p. 201 and pp. 317–20.

30. D. R. Woolf, 'The true date and authorship of Henry, Viscount Falkland's *History of the Life, Reign and Death of King Edward II*', *Bodleian Library Record* 12 (1985–8), pp. 440–52.

31. Diane Purkiss's recent edition *Renaissance Women: The Plays of Elizabeth Cary and the Poems of Aemilia Lanyer* (London: Pickering and Chatto, 1994) does, in fact, give a comprehensive overview of the evidence which has

been presented to date and adds some new arguments in favour of Cary
(pp. xxi–xxx). Purkiss shares my opinion that Elizabeth Cary is the author
of the longer text, but not the shorter one.

32. Christiane Rochefort, 'Are women writers still monsters?', repr. in Elaine
Marks and Isabelle de Courtivron (eds), *New French Feminisms* (Brighton:
Harvester, 1981), p. 183.
33. Woolf, 'The true date and authorship of Henry, Viscount Falkland's
History', p. 441.
34. Weller and Ferguson (eds), *The Tragedy of Mariam*, p. 17.
35. The manuscript 'An Epitaph upon the death of the Duke of Buckingham'
and the verse on the tomb of her parents at Burford Parish Church are
also attributed to her, but I have not included them in the above list
because attribution is by no means certain.
36. Simpson (ed.), *The Lady Falkland*, pp. 4, 8–9, 39.
37. Chris Weedon, *Feminist Practice and Poststructuralist Theory* (Oxford: Oxford University Press, 1987), p. 153.

Dionys Fitzherbert and the Anatomy of Madness

Katharine Hodgkin

'The melancholie passion', according to Bright's *Treatise of Melancholie* of 1586, 'is a doting of reason through vaine feare procured by fault of the melancholie humour'.[1] Unreason – reason's doting – and anxiety – groundless fear – come together, as a result of physiological disorder: this basic understanding of melancholy as illness remains more or less constant over the next century. But the symptoms developing around that physiological core are far more elaborately varied. Melancholy, as many scholars have observed, is at this period an extraordinarily protean malady, whose characteristics are almost impossible to pin down, illustrated and epitomized in the endlessly ramifying explorations of Burton's *Anatomy of Melancholy* (1621); from mild depression to raving delirium, melancholy is everyone's disorder, its causes as innumerable as its symptoms.[2]

This imprecision may in part be traced to contradictions in the source ideas. The concept of melancholy as it developed in the early modern period brings together two separate traditions, commonly identified as Galenic (medical) and Aristotelian (philosophical and literary); it is also closely tied to a third tradition, that of religious doubt, and inherits to some extent the mantle of the medieval concept of accidia, spiritual sloth. With these disparate origins, melancholy had become by the late sixteenth century a highly mobile and unfixed condition, which might imply a slightly over-delicate sensibility, raving insanity, or sluggishness and torpor; a condition whose symptoms, causes and treatments were subject to almost endless variation.

An economical concept, available to account for many forms of madness in a single diagnosis, melancholy is thus central in discussions of mental disorder at this period. For some it was an aspirational affliction, a genteel sort of problem denoting the finer constitutions of the upper classes; for others it was a shame and an insult, the sign of someone only fit for Bedlam; for women in particular, it was shadowed by the suggestion of excessive and unseemly sexual desire. The recurrent anguishes of religious doubt also bring it to bear on spiritual terrors, and on the interpretation of strange behaviour amongst religious

enthusiasts. The distinction between the organic illness of melancholy and the spiritual suffering of religious despair is unstable and
shifting, and the ability to distinguish between the two a matter at once
of grave importance and of insuperable difficulty. Class, gender and
religious orientation all have a part to play in determining both the
diagnosis of melancholy and the patient's response to that diagnosis;
and given the uncertainty of the symptoms, diagnosis seems inevitably
unreliable and subjective, and in consequence contestable.

The subject of this essay is one such contestation. At the beginning
of the seventeenth century, Dionys Fitzherbert, a woman in her late
twenties from a gentry family, suffered a mental crisis of some kind;
on her recovery some months later, she wrote a lengthy and detailed
manuscript account of her affliction, and also of her own previous
history. Her aim in this narrative is to explain and to give reasons for
the catastrophe that had come upon her. Those about her at the time,
she claims, attributed it to 'melancholly or I know not what turning of
the braine'; in writing the fullest possible account of her sufferings she
hopes to rectify this misapprehension, placing her sufferings instead in
the framework of a religious calling and a subsequent fall from grace,
duly punished by God.[3] It is the contention of Dionys Fitzherbert's
narrative that to read her experiences as insanity is an error; that in
fact what had happened to her was a special trial by God, a testing of
her faith, which for God's hidden purposes happened to take on the
appearance of madness. Her decision to 'lay open to the world [her]
owne infirmities' (154, sig. 10r) is explained by the need for dialogue
and contestation, to admonish the many observers who fail to understand the truth of such experiences, and although it was never printed,
the manuscript was copied and prepared for circulation; it is clearly a
laying open, a public text.

Fitzherbert's account thus addresses directly the problem of the
construction and definition of insanity, and locates it as the product of
an unequal dialogue between the 'mad' and the 'sane'. The history of
madness and its discursive production, since the appearance of Foucault's *Madness and Civilization*, has been of considerable interest to
scholars working on the early modern period; histories written by the
mad, however, remain rarities.[4] Once an individual has been classed as
insane, she (or he) is silenced. There is no value to the words of the
raving, no point in recording or preserving them; for madness is the
condition in which speech loses significance. By recovering and writing
about her affliction (as well as in the survival of her manuscript), Dionys
Fitzherbert is an exception to this rule, even though hers is a madness
which disputes and denies that classification, which necessarily speaks
from outside, having escaped the condition which gives rise to the
diagnosis.

In Foucauldian terms, indeed, Fitzherbert's text can be read as a moment in that dialogue between madness and sanity. It is at once an attempt to traverse the distance between reason and non-reason, declaring that the division is not absolute; and on the other hand the expression of a desire herself to wrest a different truth from unreason, a truth which is not madness, but something else, something unnamed. As once perhaps insane, she writes between reason and madness, one moment in a process of distinguishing between the two and allocating to each its separate truth. Her text asserts the victory of reason both in plot and in principle, and yet retrospectively gives a provisional and hesitant voice to the silence which Foucault attempts to archaeologize, the silence of the mad denied speech.

To assert the centrality of God and sin to her mental collapse, for Fitzherbert, is an attempt to recuperate an experience which lacking that framework would be meaningless to her, without reason or justification, mere common madness. Instead, as she formulates it, the difference between her and a character like Job is one of outward forms only. Whether God's trials are internal or external, the central demands remain the same: patience under affliction, holding on to faith no matter how dim and hopeless the future seems, resisting the temptation to blaspheme, protest, cry out against God; and it is in terms of these trials and her responses to them that Fitzherbert constructs her narrative. Spirituality is thus for her a discourse precisely of reason, not its opposite; it offers a language in which she can attempt to come to terms with reason's collapse in her. In contrast to the ecstasy of the mystic, she aspires to a textually grounded rationality: her eventual recovery is attributed in part to her reading, and the act of writing itself seems to confirm this desire for an internal and explicable logic. The idea that the collapse of the self might itself be regarded as a route to mystical wisdom is not one she is prepared to acknowledge – a point I return to at the end of this essay. She attaches herself instead to the empirical, and demands that the science of medicine be brought to confirm the meaning which she gives to her affliction in the name of faith.

But if her spiritual challenge to medical definitions is concerned with both identification and treatment of those 'in her case', as this expression would suggest she is notably hampered by the want of a word to describe the specificity of what she wants to define as not mad. There is no language outside the medical that will fully name and account for her symptoms, and the medical is what she is concerned to reject. Inevitably, then, her account of her own disorder is marked by uncertainty and instability. The distinction she wishes to draw between the organic and the spiritual is crucial to her, but also difficult to sustain – a problem faced by other writers on the subject, but for her more momentous,

since on this distinction she must establish at once her sanity and her
salvation.

The central question for Fitzherbert, then, is one of the relation
betwen flesh and spirit, a question which comes into focus around three
areas in particular: melancholy, femininity and religion. Melancholy, a
disorder which Fitzherbert mentions only in denial, was at this period
itself attributed to organic causes; women were held to be peculiarly
subject to the ebb and flow of ungovernable humours, owing to their
unruly physiology; and the boundary between religious transport and
lunacy, once again the result of organic disorder, was a contested area,
disputed throughout the century and beyond. In this essay, then, I
begin with an exploration of the links and tensions between these three
areas in Renaissance accounts of melancholy, to provide a context for
the vehemence with which Fitzherbert opposed the characterization of
her affliction as mental disorder; subsequently I turn to her text and
examine that opposition in some detail, looking at the alternative
accounts she constructs to explain what had happened to her, and at
the problems generated in this attempt to redefine the meanings of her
experience.

The melancholy passion

Melancholy is of course only one figure, not always very clearly distinguished, on a map of unreason which depicts many shapes and many
routes to them – hysteria, possession, derangement, for example. The
importance of the body, however, of the physiological dimension in all
forms of mental disorder, is more or less constant in early modern
theory and practice. For the hysteric as for the melancholic, medical
treatment will attempt to remedy a physical disruption by means of
drugs and purges to restore the body's internal balances. To remove a
mental affliction from the sphere of the organic into that of the spiritual,
as Fitzherbert aims to do, is thus a more complicated undertaking than
it might appear; for even the spiritual can participate in the disorder
of the body.

Both organic causes and organic remedies are fundamental in the
aetiology of melancholy. Physiologically, melancholy was explained as
an excess of cold and moist humours, and any treatment attempted to
restore the balance of humours, in part by getting rid of the substance
of the melancholy humour itself, black bile clogging the body. Substantial portions of texts such as Bright's *Treatise of Melancholie* and Burton's
Anatomy are accordingly devoted to explanations and recommendations
concerning diet, exercise and other forms of bodily government;
and lists of the provocative causes of different types of melancholy

mingle the organic and the emotional without hesitation: 'Bad diet, suppression of hemrods, &c. and such evacuations, passions, cares, &c.'.[5] Haemorrhoids and passions here form part of the same system, in which problems are caused by irregularities in flow, the improper balance of incorporation and evacuation, and similar curative principles should therefore be applied.

Passion and madness are of course closely allied: passion is the temporary madness of the sane, and the problem for the insane is that the (impassioned) loss of reason is permanent. The common ground is the implied loss of control. The person carried away by anger or any other passion is – even if only temporarily – not under the government of reason, and thus not sane; self-government, it might almost be said, defines sanity, and along with it humanity. '[T]hat which crucifies us most,' declared Burton, 'is our own folly, madness … weakness, want of government, our facility and proneness in yielding to several lusts, in giving way to every passion and perturbation of the mind: by which means we metamorphose ourselves, and degenerate into beasts' (*Anatomy* I, p. 156). To yield to passion, to lose control, is bestial, less than human, and by the same token less than sane; the defining human characteristic is the capacity for reason.

But if reason, and the correlative capacity for self-control, differentiate the human and the animal, they do so unequally for men and for women. The ideal of manliness for the Renaissance gentleman invoked the notion of mastery – mastery of others but also crucially of oneself. The feminine at this period, by contrast, is constructed as fundamentally lacking in both reason and self-control: women are represented as governed by irresistible passions, physiologically less able to keep their lower instincts in check.[6] A woman's body was in its very fabric peculiarly liable to drive her out of control. The notorious wandering womb led women into hysteria; the corrupt fumes arising from menstrual blood drove them mad; greensickness marked the single woman with the sign of her physiological dependence on men to keep her in sound health and spirits, continually at risk from 'lovesickness, melancholia, listlessness and irrational behaviour'.[7] Even if a woman could overcome her lusts by an effort of will, the womb lurked in wait, ready to sabotage the most virtuous – and in that act of sabotage to prove that her virtue had never been more than a façade. Presented on the one hand with an ideal of governance over mind and passions similar to that of the gentleman, the early modern gentlewoman was thus at the same time given to understand that – due to her unruly physiology if nothing else – it was an ideal she could not hope to achieve more than provisionally. The sanity of woman, in this construction, can only be an unstable and precarious structure, a continual struggle to keep the forces of her lower nature in check.

This problematic relation to the rebellious forces of the flesh, it seems, is one of the factors inflecting women's relation to the melancholy passion. For if the Elizabethan era indeed saw a craze for the identity of the melancholic, it was in fact a craze largely confined to men. It seems that for women, even of the upper classes, the type of melancholy denoting the sensitive and creative soul was less readily attainable than that denoting some form of madness, apt to be read in specifically bodily and sexual terms – as Juliana Schiesari puts it, 'as a debilitating disease and certainly not as an enabling ethos'.[8] For women in the Renaissance, melancholy is a term likely to align them at best with gloom and ludicrous delusions, and all too often with an underlying suggestion of uncontrollable and indecent appetite. Women's melancholy, in effect, is not quite the same as men's: less intellectual, less interesting. Women in their disorders are thus emblems of the disorders of their ungovernable bodies and unruly passions, rather than of any idea that genius might be close to madness.[9]

The point to be emphasized is that mental disorder was not so much gendered, as sexualized; not that all women all the time were seen to be imminently at risk of madness, but that once afflicted, their disorders were liable to be interpreted in relation to their sexuality – and this was particularly true for certain categories of women.[10] If women's melancholy was liable to be read in terms of their specific physiology, the distinction was not purely between women and men, but additionally between single women and the rest. Thus when Burton writes about melancholy women, he does so in a chapter on 'Maids', Nuns' and Widows' Melancholy'; and he explains that this is a 'peculiar species', which 'much differs from that which commonly befalls men and other women, as having only one cause proper to women alone' (*Anatomy*, I, p. 476).[11] 'Women alone' are indeed, in his eyes, the problem; the lack of male company is the proximate cause of melancholy in women, for physiological reasons. The melancholy which plagues women in particular is generally attributable to lack of either childbearing (barren women are included in the category) or regular sex: 'vicious vapours which come from menstruous blood', and 'corrupt seed' (i.e. seed not finding its proper course of development in pregnancy), trouble brain, heart and mind, and 'the whole malady proceeds from that inflammation, putridity, black smoky vapours, &c. from thence comes care, sorrow and anxiety'. Widows, he explains, are subject to it 'by reason of a sudden alteration of their accustomed course of life, &c.', and the coy *et cetera* is elucidated by the recommended cure: 'the best and surest remedy is to see them well placed, & married to good husbands in due time' (*Anatomy*, I, pp. 476, 477, 479).

Thus, on the one hand, women in their right position, married (and preferably with children); and on the other, women at risk of going mad. Renaissance writers on melancholy, it may be suggested, invoke subterranean connections between femininity, sexuality and madness, which, if entangled, are deeply rooted and hard to escape; and they make it far less likely that a Renaissance woman suffering mental torment would happily accept the label of melancholy (any more than any other madness) to describe a suffering which would thereby be located in her restless and greedy body rather than her restless and creative mind. For a religious woman, such as Dionys Fitzherbert, this was perhaps especially true.

Private enthusiasms and revelations

The complex and contested links between religion and melancholy in early modern England provided the ground for a long-running debate between secular and spiritual tendencies in both church and medical profession.[12] The similarity between the symptoms of religious transport and mental disorder was generally acknowledged by enthusiasts as well as sceptics; and if rapture looked like insanity, its opposite, despair, was hardly better. Despair of salvation could signify either a necessary moment in the conversion process, or a delusion brought about by illness; the problems lay in the attempt to specify precise distinctions between the different phenomena. At what point – following what eccentricities of speech or conduct – should a sorrowful and penitent meditation on one's own sinfulness be renamed melancholy, and treated as such? And if religious despair was in some degree the consequence of humoral imbalance, was the despair discredited, or should it be recognized as valid in itself whether organic or spiritual in origin? Should sufferers be given medicine, or consoling books and counsel?

The distinction was generally felt to be important, yet it was near-impossible to pin down. Perkins, in his *Treatise of Conscience*, poses the question, 'whether there be any difference betweene the trouble of Conscience, and Melancholy? for many hold, that they are all one', and answers these sceptics with great decision, 'They are not all one, but differ much. Affliction of Conscience is one thing, trouble by Melancholy is an other'; but his brief and sketchy account of the difference would hardly have satisfied sufferers such as Dionys Fitz-herbert.[13] Bright, devoting several substantial chapters of his *Treatise on Melancholy* to the specific characteristics of affliction of conscience for sin (as opposed to ordinary melancholy) reproaches 'the error of some, and the prophanes of othersome, who ... accompt the cause naturall, melancholy, or madnes', insisting, 'in whatsoever respect these unreverent and prophane persons list to match them, they shall be of diverse nature, never to be coupled in one fellowship' (*Treatise*, pp. 187–8); but in his discussion they show a constant tendency to merge. However much one might want to separate the two, they were continually liable to become entangled; Dionys Fitzherbert, as will become apparent, had similar difficulties.

Orthodox distrust of religious excess in all its forms also fed into this debate. Burton, although not necessarily unsympathetic to the sufferer from spiritual doubt or despair, is generally more inclined than Bright to regard religious excess with suspicion; those afflicted are too often the zealous, who have spent too long inquiring into divine mysteries such as election and free will, 'with a deal of foolish presumption, curiosity, needless speculation', or who have come under the influence of 'thundering Ministers' who terrify them with hell-fire (*Anatomy*, III, p. 456). And significantly, the ignorance and weakness that may lead the heretic's victim astray are particularly characteristic of the low, the poor and the feminine – 'silly, rude, ignorant people … weak women, or some poor rude illiterate persons, that are apt to be wrought on' (*Anatomy*, III, p. 389). Women here figure both as uneducated and as naturally credulous. Women, the poor and the ignorant are united, in the eyes of the scholarly Burton, in their inability to make balanced judgments, and their susceptibility to religious extravagance verging on madness.[14] Nor was he alone in making such associations. Religious enthusiasm can be linked with insanity and femininity, to converge on the idea of unreason.

Insanity was always a haunting and contested presence for seventeenth-century religious enthusiasts; one person's visionary was all too liable to be someone else's lunatic. The language of the soul in spiritual torment comes dangerously close to that of insanity, and is frequently identified by the unsympathetic as a consequence or a symptom of excessive (unreasonable) emotion; for the relation to God is the focus of most intense emotionality in the writings of seventeenth-century sectarians. Despair, misery, fear, pride: those who recount their spiritual experiences tell stories in which they suffer from these, worry about them, are driven by them to desperation. Such pain may indeed be regarded as a necessary part of the spiritual pilgrimage in which the soul must recognize with anguish its worthlessness before repenting and turning to God – a process accepted also by writers such as Bright and Burton. But at an uncertain and shifting point, some lurch over a hidden boundary and become in the eyes of those about them – even their fellow-believers – distracted: their misery and terror are excessive, they are bereft of sense and reason, surrounded by devils and delusions; and this happened often enough and flagrantly enough for insanity to be readily available as an explanation for religious eccentricity or extremism. The accusation of madness thus could be used to devalue insights and prophecies, to turn the turbulence of God's power working in the soul into a simple matter of imbalanced humours, amenable to medication or marriage. The task for Dionys Fitzherbert is thus a delicate one, requiring not only the delineation of an affliction which will be spiritual to the exclusion of the organic, but also the repetition of a narrative of spiritual transformation which will remain, in spite of appearances, on the right side of reason: despair and terror may signify a spiritual trial, but they must not signify madness.

The miserable imputation of madness

By the mid-century, the flowering of the dissenting sects provided for many of the spiritually afflicted a sympathetic environment within which their excesses would be accepted and given meaning. For Dionys Fitzherbert, no such community of faith was available. As the daughter of a secular-minded gentry family at the beginning of the century, she was isolated both by class and by chronology. Her family, as she represents it, is large and close-knit, and at the time of her illness, brothers, sisters and parents variously rally round to give support, escort and encouragement. It is also the focus of a great deal of tension and anxiety in her account; her father and brothers in particular are trans-muted in her delirium into figures of alien menace, in ways which cast a different light on the loving family which she is ostensibly describ-ing, and her status as a member of her own family becomes both doubtful and life-threatening, as she fails to recognize her brother, and offers her neck to the swords of her kinsmen. Most striking, perhaps, is her emphasis on the extent to which her religious profession cut her off from the worldly pastimes of her relatives, and implicitly led to her departure from home to serve in the households of a succession of aristocratic ladies. Her spiritual commitment is described as self-generated, against the grain of her environment.

In the absence of immediate external support for her spiritual crisis, if there is to be any alternative explanation of the catastrophe, she must provide it herself. She is not, of course, entirely solitary in this enterprise, even if she has no gathered church. The existence of her manuscript in fair copy and with confirmatory and commendatory prefacing shows that, notwithstanding her spiritual alienation from her family, she succeeds in finding moral and religious support elsewhere – and in socially respectable circles, given that it is the Dean of Bristol who is backing her. Puritanism, of one sort or another, was after all a powerful if minority movement amongst the Jacobean aristocracy. Nonetheless, an insistent positioning of the self as isolated is one of the defining features of her narrative. Not only does her account lack the structural resolution which for many later narratives is provided by an eventual coming to rest in a specified church; it also emphasizes throughout a sense of being set apart by choice, of a narrator alienated by her spiritual commitment from her unchristian surroundings, whether her family or the great households she lived in.

Madness in women was in general liable to be interpreted in relation to the body and to sexuality; if mental imbalance is a consequence of imbalance in the humours, to be interpreted in a language of deficit and excess, the woman's body – which is defined by deficit and excess in any case – seeks to rectify the imbalance through sexual contact. In seeking to explain Fitzherbert's symptoms as the effect of melancholy or madness, those resorting to such accounts could have been taken to imply that she was suffering in a way peculiar to single maids – indeed, it is hard to imagine any form of distress in an unmarried woman which could not be in one way or another identified as sexual. For Fitzherbert, who never married (and who probably took a decision quite early in her life to stay single), her committed virginity and dedication to God would be likely to make her particularly resistant to any sexual inter-pretation of her disorder.[15] But whether she was refusing the specifically sexual associations of melancholy in an unmarried woman, or simply demonstrating a general and perhaps religiously motivated resistance to an identification with the flesh as opposed to the spirit, her objection to being classified as mad in any form is vehement and consistent. What her narrative attempts is a reading of her malady which moves it away from the body and into the realm of the spirit, one which contradicts the interpretations on offer from those around her. But as the discussion of melancholy so far should indicate, she is immediately confronted with difficulties both conceptual and terminological; in particular, the inappropriateness to contemporary medical and theological discourse of the categorical oppositions between organic, mental and spiritual which she seems anxious to establish.

The sympathetic prefacing letter written by the Dean of Bristol, as it turns out, exemplifies the problem she faces: in his analysis the distinction she wishes to draw is simply not significant. When he tells her that God on first afflicting her saw her 'grown cold and careless through prosperitie ... puffed upp with vanity; In a word ... too full of blood', he is addressing her simultaneously in metaphor and in literal description, and the two together lead directly to the metaphorical terms in which to continue: 'his resolution was to lett yow be lett bloud in the veine to make yow sound; and hereto Satan offered his service in hope to make yow bleed unto death, when God that could stopp the veine when he saw good, meant no such matter'.[16] The idea of blood signifies both worldly desires – to say she is 'too full of blood' implies metaphorically a commitment to the flesh and to fleshly desires – and physiological imbalance – an excess of blood, literally understood, implies an excess of passion and heat.[17] The divine bloodletting which he uses as a metaphor for her crisis would thus resolve both conditions simultaneously (as well as being the actual treatment many contemporary physicians might have prescribed, although apparently not in this case). Similarly, when he says that she should not hold herself responsible for what was spoken in her raving, because it 'came all from Satan and the humors that oppressed you', he is demonstrating a lack of interest in which of the two it came from *ultimately*: Satan and humours, religion and physiology, morals and medicine, blend into one another. Throughout his letter Dr Chetwynd shifts casually between the humours that oppressed her and the pride of heart which distempered her body 'and bred melancholy'. This, however, is precisely the type of interpretation which Fitzherbert wishes to challenge, despite its sympathetic standpoint – one which attributes her suffering to the body, even if she is thereby exonerated of blame. Against such explanations, she mobilizes medical and religious arguments to produce a theoretical account of her 'case' which will clearly distinguish it from melancholy or madness in any form.

Dionys and diagnosis

Her first move is to address the medical classification of melancholy, setting up a series of explicit contrasts between melancholy as it is constituted in medical discourse, and her own experience. The bodies of those suffering from melancholy, she explains, are oppressed by 'thick or dull humors' which accumulate to oppress the heart and spirit – a disorder, therefore, whose primary cause is located in the body, in the accumulation of humours, however its *symptoms* may subsequently affect mind or spirit (as they inevitably do). Those in her case, on the contrary, are first smitten in the heart and distracted in the spirit, 'then noe mervaile if all the rest goe out of frame' – body follows mind, not the other way about.[18]

A similar order of priorities informs Fitzherbert's discussion of possible courses of treatment. She does not discount the use of medicine, but claims that if physic is useful to sufferers such as herself, it is because 'uppon theis violent and strong passions of the mynd, the whole body is much disordered', still repeating her insistence that 'melancholly or any other distemperature of the body' are not 'the first Cause thereof' (154, sig. 11r). The physic, it seems, may ease the body, which is useful, but will be unable to quell the 'violent and strong passions'. Bright, by contrast, claims that medicine is of no use – 'no purgation, no cordiall, no tryacle or balme are able to assure the afflicted soule and trembling heart', he asserts (*Treatise*, p. 189); Perkins takes the same line.[19] Fitzherbert in fact goes so far as to acknowledge that in some cases of religious affliction the physical condition of melancholy may be a primary cause, bringing about as a consequence spiritual distress. Nonetheless, she insists, this was not her own case; and the two will remain distinguishable in the manner of their onset. If the disordered body moves the spirit to despair it does so by degrees, and is not on the whole violent. When the despair is of supernatural origin, however, it arrives with such suddenness and inexplicability as to leave its victim bemused, 'as when by some occasion it comes suddenly like lightning into a house, as an excellent divine truely compares ytt' (154, sig. 10r).

But for Dionys Fitzherbert as for other writers on the topic, the boundaries between mind and body, spiritual and physical, are not as stable as she would like them to be, and her causal structure is built on shifting ground. This instability is enacted by the word 'conceit', which crosses the boundary between the two fields, disrupting the distinction by its physiological ambiguity; a conceit is both the product of the disordered brain, in the shape of delusion (sufferers 'fall into Conceits' in which they think they cannot eat, 154, sig. 11r), and its cause, as if delusion itself were generative (she refers to 'those pestiferys humers which came of so many deadly concaits', 169, sig. 8v). The elucidation of the inside of the body, like that of the inside of the mind, is misleading. Trapped by an imprecise and ambiguous terminology which will not permit her to establish the desired separation of mental and physical disorder, then, she turns her attention instead to the visible sign, or the symptom.

In drawing attention to the differences in character of the two types of affliction, Fitzherbert is moving from a direct engagement with the terms of the medical debate over the relation of religion and melancholy towards another line of argument, which attempts to transform the grounds of the discussion. To shift the emphasis away from the narrowly physiological, and towards the spiritual, she moves the focus of attention from internal balances (of humours or passions) to external signs – in particular by identifying contrasts in behaviour – and constructs a typology of perceptible difference which will obviously distinguish the two contrasting 'cases', the mad and the spiritually afflicted. It is by watching and listening to the sufferers, she claims, that the differences will become apparent:

in all other distemperatures, their anger rages and accusations are bent more against others then them selves, in this it is wholly or for the most part directed against them selves ... Their often Complaints deep sighes, hearty wishes to be as they have been, with their exceeding tendernes of Conscience in every respect, and their humbling them selves lower then can be imagyned, and immeasurable the like passages doth more then distinguish their Case from all others in the Judgment of any well seeing eyes. (154, sig. 10v)

Self-abasement – abjection – appears here to be the crucially distinctive marker of religious affliction; the mad, by contrast, can be known by the way they direct their anger outwards, and are without humility. The mad are inclined to attack and reproach others; those afflicted by God turn all their accusations against themselves.

The moral weighting here is obvious: God's elect, even when distracted, are inclined to exhibit the characteristic features of virtue, especially humility. But the particular markers selected to indicate one or the other affliction are in a sense less significant than the location of distinction in the sphere of the visible, of common knowledge. As Roy Porter observes, discussing seventeenth-century notions of insanity, 'All agreed that it was of the essence of lunacy to be visible, and known by its appearance'.[20] If lunacy is held to be somehow legible on the body of the insane, however, it is a legibility that is perversely subject to misinterpretation. The general opinion, in Fitzherbert's case, appears to have read her symptoms and agreed that they signified insanity. But for her, this is precisely the problem: reading from the inside, she saw it differently; and as far as she was concerned what had happened to her (both the initial assumption of madness and the subsequent treatment) could be attributed in some sense to errors of perception on the part of others, to a failure to read her symptoms correctly.

By conceding anxiously that her symptoms are of a kind which 'may in some sort seme rediculus' (169, sig. 3r) and move the observer to laughter, she puts herself at risk of precisely the ridicule she wishes to avert; her wish that her condition should be recognized as truly afflicted, spiritually suffering, may be undermined. She was 'as on uterly depryved of all senc & understanding,' she writes, 'kising ther hands and eting the coles out of the fier with a senclis smyling at whatsoever they sayd or did to me' (169, sig. 3v). Her problem is to persuade the reader that the absurd is not comical; that her distracted behaviour was not representative of her inner truth, should not make her into a Bedlam laughing-stock. So her actions may seem ridiculous; she may be as one deprived of sense; but the sensitive reader is to know the difference between what something looks like, and what it truly is.

Problems of perception and recognition are thus central to her characterization of her own malady, as well as other people's understanding of it. While both in diagnosis and in the curative approaches she recommends, Fitzherbert emphasizes the importance of true perception, the question of how far the truth is available to perception is one that can hardly be resolved, and her explanations are contradictory. On the one hand, she appeals to the reasonable understanding of the onlooker, possessor of 'well-seeing eyes', as the guarantor of truth; and at the same time, since onlookers were led by their reasonable understanding to regard her as insane, she has to discount the common opinion of the world as prejudiced and mistaken. In her recommendations for the cure of disorders of perception, she asserts the senses as reliable, and the external world as accessible to true knowledge. But from another point of view, in relation to those who observe her during her affliction and identify her as insane, she adopts an opposite project. The external world, she must demonstrate, is not reliable at all; it is precisely the source of all error and misinterpretation on the parts of the observers, because they judge by appearances; and appearances inevitably mislead.

Her recommendations for treatment are founded on the assumption of some elements of understanding in the sufferer; they attempt to establish a rational basis for the disorder, on which reasoned argument can operate. Thus if one can only demonstrate reality with sufficient conviction, the logical errors into which the sufferer has been drawn will be dissipated; argument and persuasion will do more than medicine. Fitzherbert herself, she claims, helped 'one who affirmed that she had noe head nor any hands to help her self withall': she 'by Censible experience made her feele and Confesse she had both and by that meanes rendred her more Capeable of what perswasion I would' (154, sig. 10v). The disordered perceptions once restored, the truth will be acknowledged. Moreover – and this for Fitzherbert is perhaps the crucial element of the cure – once the possibility of error in one field of perception has been recognized by the afflicted, this will then lead them to accept that they may be mistaken in other respects too, and are possibly not damned:

> When they fall into Conceite of this nature, the onely way is to give them all possible satisfaccon by their senses for thereby yow shalbe better able to lett them know howmuch they may be deceaved in their opinion, that they are out of the favour of God and soe none of his ... the which being done all these things vanish like smoake together, the which plainely declares what the ground of them all was. (154, sig. 11r)

Thus the disordered senses are the route to their own restoration, by contrast with true melancholy, where their disorder, being physiological in origin, can only be cured physiologically. If error is confined to the mind, and the mind is not organically afflicted, then only reason need be persuaded for all error to be cleared up at once.

What Fitzherbert recommends, in effect, is more or less a technique described by Foucault as the need 'to continue the delirious discourse', that is, to go along with the grammar of madness until it reaches the point of collapse under its own internal contradictions:

> Before us appears the great theme of a crisis that confronts the madman with his own meaning, reason with unreason, man's lucid ruse with the blindness of the lunatic – a crisis which marks the point at which illusion, turned back upon itself, will open to the dazzlement of truth.[21]

But where for Foucault this treatment forms part of the classical apprehension of unreason as a whole phenomenon, for Fitzherbert what differentiates her state from madness is precisely that at the moment of crisis only the not-mad will be able to break open the illusion. The mad, who have no access to reason, will not be able to follow through the logic of the confrontation. The lunatic is blind; others, ultimately, can see, even if they may be looking in the wrong place. On this appeal to sense and reality she elaborates her distinction between madness and spiritual distress. Because those in her case are not truly mad, if they can be brought to acknowledge their own errors of perception progress can be made; whereas if they were mad, then first, they would not recognize their mistakes, and second, if they did it would have no effect, since their bewildered minds would not be susceptible to rational persuasions.

It is on a similar basis that she argues that the afflicted should not be kept from study. The significance of this again lies in the way in which treatment is derived from cause. As Bright explains, the problem with study is physiological; by excessive study the 'spirits' are distracted from the body to the mind, 'and the humours ... setle into a melan-cholie thicknesse, and congele into that cold and drie humour, which rayseth these terrours and discouragements'. And the more attached the sufferer had been to a particular study, the more it is to be avoided, since 'if the affection of liking go withall, both hart, and braine do over prodigally spend their spirits, and with them the subtilest partes of the naturall juyce, and the humours of the bodie' (*Treatise*, pp. 243, 244). Dionys Fitzherbert, on the contrary, asserts the need for those suffering as she did to be encouraged in their 'exercises' (i.e. religious meditations and prayers), because they are not sick in the head, but sick at heart:

> And here are some much to be blamed who by all meanes seeke to keepe them in their Cases as much as may be from reading and their accustomed meditations happily thinking their distempered heads cannot so well beare ytt, but many tymes as I my self was they never feele paine nor any the least jott of evil humor in their heade or any

part of their bodies, but all their Complaints is att their harts the fountaine indeed of all their distempers and trouble. (154, sig. 11r)

Since reason itself is not diseased, she argues, but merely temporarily overpowered, by re-establishing its government the disorder will be brought under control; and how should the forces of unreason be opposed but through study and prayer? 'It is as dangerous I dare avouch yt to theis,' she continues, 'to be perswaded from their exercises in this Case, as for any man to lay aside his weapons in his most extreame needs, nay our best indeavours ought by all meanes to incourage them to yt as their onely way to return them to them selves againe' (154, sig. 11r). Here she is in agreement with Burton, who recommends a judicious balance of physic and counsel, 'hearing, reading of Scriptures, good Divines, good advice and conference', although he warns against too much meditation (*Anatomy*, III, p. 468). Access to knowledge, nonetheless, she advises should be carefully controlled – only the right sort of study will help, and sufferers are all too adept at finding discouraging passages in the Bible to confirm rather than amend their despair.

But despite her determination that what happened to her should be read as an intellectual problem, whose solution is located in the intellect, the attempt to give such an account produces confusion and contradiction. Her always erratic syntax starts to break down entirely under the strain of her efforts to identify the difference between appearance and essence, those who look mad and those who are truly so:

True it is that oftentymes they will both doe and speake soe ridiculously, that even the most stayed mynde cannot almost abstaine from laughing att them, although in this, their misery is impossible to be uttred, which I know not whether to impute ytt, more to the malice of the divell in joining and mixing theis things soe together to make them thereby the more undescernable in the eye of the world, or to their deluded Judgments, but they likely soone find it out, and yt dejects them into wonderfull Contempt of them selves to see as they thinke that they are the very sinck of all wretchednes. (154, sig. 10v)

Here, sufferers and observers alike have become entangled in deluded judgments; to distinguish between distraction and misinformation is as difficult as it is to know a truly staid mind. The indistinguishability of the distracted and those being tried by God may be a consequence of Satan's direct malice. The blurring of the boundaries between observers and observed, however, is a consequence of Fitzherbert's own uncertainties.

Writing insanity

Dionys Fitzherbert's appeal to reason and the senses as highest authority and guarantors of truth is of course (to put it mildly) paradoxical, given her own problems with delusion, in which reasoned argument was absolutely unable to prevail. If the senses must be established as reliable, and the external world as fully available to knowledge, it is because the internal world is deeply problematic. Her fragile subjectivity is shored up by an insistence that the truth is in fact accessible to perception, even though much of her account of her own experience runs counter to this insistence; her sanity, it seems, depends on external guarantees (the world as knowable) against threats both internal and external. The instability of her position on this problem is apparent, and becomes particularly conspicuous in her discussion of ways of bringing the deluded out of their delusions: is she the diagnostician or the sufferer? Whose version of reality is to be credited, and how is it to be enforced?

Thus she is continually drawn into a transition from agent to patient in which the boundaries between persons (as so often in her narrative) start to disintegrate. The shifting pronouns in this passage illustrate the problem; she is discussing the use of guile (Foucault's 'lucid ruse') in dealing with the sufferer:

> also my self and many others as I have heard of, have been in danger to be famisht if such meanes had not been wrought; by a wyle although we then thought it to be well done, abstayning from meate, for when by noe meanes they could make me take any, they would put it to my mouth and soe lett yt fall to the ground then perswade me they thought I would not for all the world offend God soe as to spill his Greatness in that manner ... & other meanes they used in this kind and it is very needefull, but great Care must be had that noe extreame terror be used; When they fall into Conceite of this nature, the onely way is to give them all possible satisfaccon by their senses for thereby yow shall be better able to lett them know (154, sig. 10v–11r)

'I' describes both herself as the recovered and competent diagnostician who can sympathetically treat the disorders of others, and herself in the past as the sufferer, the one to whom things are done. 'You', in a general sense the Christian reader, is here specifically the Christian reader attempting the cure of such lost souls. But 'they', the groups from which she excludes or distinguishes herself, are at once those who had the care of her in her illness, who treated her, and also those suffering in the way that she did; and in contrast to them she becomes 'we', who will deceive these people for their own good, even though,

in a disorientating contradiction, in the deceit she goes on to describe
('a wyle although we then thought it to be well done') she is the one
deceived.

This problematic positioning, in which she is at once subject and
object of her own treatment, as she is of her own narrative, is among
the most compelling qualities of her text. For what is unique about
Dionys Fitzherbert's narrative of madness – or rather, her narrative
contestation of that identity – is the fact that it is indeed her own, that
she rather than anyone else tells the story; and the voices of the insane
emerge very seldom from the history of which they are the objects.
She writes with a solipsistic intensity, from inside a lost place – and
yet also after having emerged from it. The necessary paradox of the
autobiographical mode, in which the narrator is both subject and object
of the narrative (and thereby destabilizes the distinction between the
two), is in the case of madness crystallized into an irreconcilable
separation: the speaking subject, the narrator, here thinks in a mode
absolutely different from the subject spoken. The contrast is more than
that of the classical conversion narrative; it is as if one were to tell the
story of a past lived in a forgotten language. Inevitably, it is a story
which she can only tell by virtue of having escaped the condition, a
narrative of rescue whose outcome is known in the bare fact of its
being recorded; she does not speak from inside insanity, speaks indeed
to deny it and to recast her experiences into a more acceptable framework. But even as she denies it she is caught by it, seems almost to
speak again from within it. To recount is to reanimate; in a sense, she
seems to relive the experience in the act of recall.

For Fitzherbert, who mentions a long-standing affection for the
written word, the act of writing seems to have been almost a process
of catharsis, a 'talking' – writing – cure performed on herself. Her first
move after her recovery was to leave her family home; her next, she
declares, was to write; to recreate and renarrate the experience, to
produce an account which would make sense of it to herself and to
others. There is in her narrative a sense of urgency, a desire to put
down everything, to make sure that nothing is missed or misunderstood.
The possibility of forgetfulness on her part or misunderstanding on
the reader's, which often gives anxiety to religious writers of the
mid-century, is particularly acute in a writing which attempts to give
a reasoned account of something that took place in the absence of a
guiding reason; to bring to consciousness the unknown and the unthinkable. In describing the course of her affliction she is writing across
a chasm, as she acknowledges herself; the problems of memory and
reconstruction which any autobiographer must address become acute
when attempting to describe such episodes. 'I can not yet remember
whate was done untell they had me out of my bed & suffred me to

walke about the chamber', she confesses, writing of the most desperate phase of her disorder; again, 'whether I did resist them ... & that was the caus they bound my hands I do not well remember ... I was as I remember for the most part spechles many dayes after if not alltogether' (169, sig. 3v).

Problems of memory and of control over the meanings of the text are thus multiplied for Fitzherbert by the presumption of insanity. The blank spaces in the memory cannot signify simple forgetfulness; each failure of knowledge threatens to undermine her project by reminding the reader of a possible failure of sanity. For her text is to demonstrate through its lucidity – its ability to reason, to follow a coherent path and offer a convincing explanation of events – the sanity she insists on. The narrating subject must here be seen to be firmly in control of her own meanings and intentions, rather than resorting to a rhetoric of spiritual abandonment and helplessness to resolve the problem of a faulty memory, as later writers do. Moreover, to write as a channel for divine power, or to write in a spirit of ecstasy or abandonment, would surely be inappropriate to her own therapeutic project. The text is after all reappropriating and giving significance to an experience of being out of control, an experience acknowledged as being often one of pain and distress. The madness of divine inspiration, perhaps, even in its most minor forms, seemed of little help in dealing with what she was anxious above all should not signify madness.

And yet in all this, and however she may try to block off all exits and ensure a single and constant meaning for her disorder, the meaning given by a rational and devout woman, she is left with a problem. It is in fact necessary that she accept elements of that rejected other version of herself, the woman out of her wits, distracted; for not only was she behaving in general with great oddity, but more importantly, she was blaspheming, crying out in hatred or disbelief against God. As she explains to Mr Hall, when she spoke such wild words about the Bible and about Christ ('thos bookes weer made but to deceve such foles as I was ... take me said I and naile me up so as that booke saith hee was and see when I shall die thinging in very ded I could never die'), it could not have been her true self speaking: 'I apele to them all that have knowen me if I were like to geve such a reson if I had bene in my right sences' (169, sig. 23r–v, 23v). And her reiterated assertion that she did not understand 'the sencabels things that be' testifies to the same need to distance herself from the self that spoke then (169, sig. 23r). Unlike Job, she did not hold her tongue in patience; and the only way she can excuse that failure is to explain that she was not herself at the time, she knew not what she said. She not only behaves 'like' a madwoman, in terms of outward appearance; like a madwoman, she has been deprived of control over or knowledge of herself. The question of responsibility thus cannot be altogether suppressed. Either she has committed the sin against the Holy Ghost, wilfully calling out against God; or (being in a state of delusion) she did not know what she said, as Dr Chetwynd proposes. Fitzherbert herself attempts an account which is neither of these two unacceptable alternatives. Her will being absent, she has been subjected to a particular and painful test, in which she may indeed at times have been distracted – but not mad; this is the balance she attempts to hold.

It is perhaps significant that notwithstanding her resistance to terms such as 'melancholy' and 'mad', she will describe herself, or at least her symptoms, as 'distracted', which Michael MacDonald identifies as one of the more extreme words for mental disorder at the time – it is one of three words used by the physician Richard Napier to describe the 'patently insane', along with 'mad' and 'lunatic'. Distraction, Macdonald suggests, is distinguished from other forms of advanced and violent insanity in a particular way; the distracted might be violent, 'but their distinctive action was idle talk – raving, seemingly incomprehensible speech'.[22] To accept distraction, then, while refusing madness, would be a way of discounting the content of her speech (at least during the worse periods) without giving way to the notion that her mind was seriously disturbed. The distinction operating (recalling the discussion above of the question of true and false perception) is again in a sense that between inner and outer, with speech being attributed to the surface of the body. Reading by way of Foucault's distinction between passion and delirium – one an extravagance of the body, the other of the mind – one might suggest that in her engagement with her own case she is attempting to move it from passion to delirium, to locate it in the realm of language rather than the body.

Her words, then, must be set at a distance; unreason is located in language. The extent to which any possible spiritual validity in the language of madness itself has been written out of her text is one of its most striking features, by comparison with the writings of the mid-century prophets; women such as Anna Trapnel, for instance, in whose narratives the pleasure of prophecy in its uncontrolled and unreasoning aspects is powerfully evoked: 'The life of vision here is excellent, and precious, and glorious … Vision! the body crumbles before it, and becomes weak'.[23] What Dionys Fitzherbert describes is delusion and misery. For Fitzherbert it remained impossible to find anything but catastrophe in her 'idle speech'; if her soul was indeed breaking its chains, as one tradition in Christianity might have read it, it had quickly to be locked up again. But there remain suggestions that another context could have found another and more ecstatic meaning to put on her affliction – prophecy, perhaps, or mystic trance.

At the outset of her malady, she spent a night convinced that she was about to die, and calling 'Come Lord Jesus, come quickly'; but in the morning, when he had failed to appear, she writes, 'I fell into strang & fantasticall Imaginations such I think as are not mete to be repeted for I confes they were both wiked and prosumtious' (169, sig. 3v). The strange and fantastical imaginations cannot be represented; and yet neither can they be completely excluded. Humility must be written into her elucidation of her affliction, as a quintessentially religious quality; hence her stress on the self-abasement of the religiously afflicted, by comparison with the grandiosity of the mad. But humility, containment and rationality are disrupted by hints of other symptoms appearing behind the scenes. If she is capable of unspecified 'prosumtious' imaginings, what else is she capable of? What might be the rewards of self-abandonment? It is tempting to speculate that forty years later, a more receptive audience than the aristocratic Anglicans surrounding her at the time might have hailed her as a new prophet; to conclude, even, that this case demonstrates above all the sense in which insanity is socially constructed, that one generation's mystic is another's hysteric. This may indeed be one meaning of Fitzherbert's history; but not the only one.

Mysticism and irrationality have been central to the debate on femininity initiated by French theorists (notably Cixous and Irigaray, and to a lesser extent Kristeva) who have seen the self-abandonment of the mystic as the site of *jouissance*, and potentially the disintegration of the boundaries between self and other. 'She is transformed into Him in her love,' writes Irigaray, 'this is the secret of their exchange. In her and / or outside her, as in her *jouissance*, she loses all sense of corporeal boundary'.[24] Kristeva, also dealing with the body's boundaries, declares, 'The mystic's familiarity with abjection is a fount of infinite jouissance'.[25] But for Dionys Fitzherbert, the problems of abjection and the body's boundaries, live issues for her though they are, appear to have little connection with *jouissance*. Mystical ecstasy and the pleasures of delirium (perhaps as the excess of femininity?) must be excluded to keep her narrative and along with it herself in the world of rational debate; the dangers of madness are too serious to be indulged, and reasoned argument is her shield against them. Veering between the categories of madness, distraction, melancholy, and affliction, between conduct and inner truth, apparent and essential significance, she attempts to find a balance in which – against the self-evident categories of the knowable world – she can assert her own sanity.

Thus the story she tells is one less of mystical ecstasy than of great psychic difficulty and suffering. If in triumphalist mode this might be read as a narrative of defiance, of a refusal to be bound or limited by the definitions of those who in one way or another had power over her (her father and brothers, clergy, doctors), it should not be overlooked that defiance is not without its cost, and the results for her were not altogether happy. The problematic connections between femininity, mysticism and madness have a long history; this case may remind us of the perils of attempting uncritically to celebrate those connections. Actually to experience mystical disintegration may have little to do, in the end, with *jouissance*.

Notes

1. Timothy Bright, *A Treatise of Melancholie* (1586), (Amsterdam: English Experience Reprints no. 212, 1969), p. 3.
2. Richard Burton, *The Anatomy of Melancholy*, 3 vols (1621), (Oxford: Oxford University Press, 1926–7). For accounts of madness and melancholy in the early modern period, see Lawrence Babb, *The Elizabethan Malady: A Study of Melancholia in English Literature from 1580 to 1640* (East Lansing: Michigan State College Press, 1951); Michael MacDonald, *Mystical Bedlam: Madness, Anxiety and Healing in Seventeenth-Century England* (Cambridge: Cambridge University Press, 1985); Michael Macdonald (ed.), *Witchcraft and Hysteria in Elizabethan London: Edward Jorden and the Mary Glover Case* (London: Routledge, 1991), Introduction. Roy Porter, *Mind-Forg'd Manacles: A History of Madness in England from the Restoration to the Regency* (London: Athlone Press, 1987) looks at the long eighteenth century.
3. Ms. Bodley 154, sig. 10r. This is the second of two copies of Dionys Fitzherbert's manuscript in the Bodleian Library, Oxford: Fitzherbert's original, numbered Ms. E. Mus. 169, and a fair copy in another hand, Ms. Bod. 154. The two are not quite identical. The most significant difference for the purposes of this essay is the inclusion in the fair copy of a lengthy preface headed 'To the Christian Reader', which contains most of Fitzherbert's medical discusion. Quotations are taken from the original except in the case of this preface (and a copy of a letter); they are henceforward cited in the text as 169 and 154.
4. Michel Foucault, *Madness and Civilization: A History of Insanity in the Age of Reason*, trans. Richard Howard (Harmondsworth: Penguin, 1987). Roy Porter's *A Social History of Madness: Stories of the Insane* (London: Weidenfeld & Nicholson, 1987) discusses various autobiographical accounts of insanity from the seventeenth to the twentieth centuries.
5. Bright, *Treatise*, discusses the cure of melancholy in the last five chapters; see in particular pp. 257–261, for recommendations on diet and conduct. Burton, *Anatomy*, passim: the reference to 'hemrods and passions' is from the 'Synopsis of the First Partition', p. 146.
6. See Ian Maclean, *The Renaissance Notion of Woman: A Study in the Fortunes of Scholasticism and Medical Science in European Intellectual Life* (Cambridge: Cambridge University Press, 1980); Natalie Zemon Davis, 'Women on top', in her *Society and Culture in Early Modern France* (Stanford: Stanford University Press, 1977).
7. Maclean, *Renaissance Notion of Woman*, p. 41. Hysteria and melancholy are

of course separate maladies, differing in both causes and symptoms; but in relation to women's mental disorders, the theoretical distinction does not always seem to have been very clearly drawn, nor preserved in practice. If the organic aetiology of the disorders differed, all nonetheless hinted at feminine sexuality (in particular its excess) as the root cause. See Carol Thomas Neely, '"Documents in madness": reading madness and gender in Shakespeare's tragedies and early modern culture', *Shakespeare Quarterly* 42, 3 (1991), pp. 315–38, for further discussion of this point. Foucault in his discussion of hysteria cites an early seventeenth-century text by Jacques Ferrand, entitled *Maladie d'amour ou mélancholie érotique*; lovesickness, melancholy and hysteria, it seems, have a tendency to merge into one another.

8. Juliana Schiesari, *The Gendering of Melancholia: Feminism, Psychoanalysis and the Symbolics of Loss in the Renaissance* (Ithaca NY: Cornell University Press, 1992), p. 15.

9. Not a great deal has been written on women and melancholy or madness in this period, although there is more on later centuries. See MacDonald, *Mystical Bedlam*, for some discussion of the subject; also his Introduction in *Witchcraft and Hysteria*. Schiesari's *The Gendering of Melancholia* is a detailed psychoanalytic account of mourning and melancholia, focusing on writers of the Italian Renaissance. See also Elaine Showalter, 'Representing Ophelia: women, madness and the responsibilities of feminist criticism', in Patricia Parker and Geoffrey Hartman (eds), *Shakespeare and the Question of Theory* (London: Methuen, 1985); Neely, '"Documents in madness"'.

10. The process is similar to the 'hysterization of women's bodies' identified by Foucault: the female body is represented as 'thoroughly saturated with sexuality', and thereby pathological. For Foucault this is a mechanism of power / knowledge which emerges as one of four 'strategic unities' in the eighteenth century; but he suggests that there had been an earlier period of development. See *The History of Sexuality*, I. *The Will to Know*, trans. Robert Hurley (Harmondsworth: Penguin, 1981), p. 104.

11. The section on women's melancholy occupies five pages – pp. 476–81 – which is indicative of the small claim women have on this enthralling affliction.

12. Most of the works cited in n. 2 above give some discussion of religion and madness. See in addition Michael Macdonald, 'Religion, social change and psychological healing in England 1600–1800', in W. Sheils (ed.), *The Church and Healing* (Oxford: Basil Blackwell, 1982); Susan Snyder, 'The left hand of god: despair in medieval and Renaissance tradition', *Studies in the Renaissance* 12 (1965), pp. 18–59. For more general background discussion see John Stachniewski, *The Persecutory Imagination: English Puritanism and the Literature of Religious Despair* (Oxford: Clarendon Press, 1991), chapters 1 and 2; Keith Thomas, *Religion and the Decline of Magic* (New York: Scribners, 1971), chapter 5; Macdonald, *Witchcraft and Hysteria*, Introduction.

13. William Perkins, *The Whole Treatise of the Cases of Conscience* (1606), Book I, p. 194.

14. The link with unreasoning beasts is also made, in relation to the poor: 'the common people are as a flock of sheep, a rude illiterate rout ... a mere beast'; *Anatomy*, III, p. 388.

15. This assumption is based primarily on a letter to the Church of England on behalf of ancient virgins, written at some later date, in which she complains about the neglect suffered by those who have decided to dedicate themselves to God rather than to marriage, and how little appreciated such a sacrifice is by either church or family. It may also be significant that she claims to have left home initially because she rejected a candidate for marriage put forward by her father; and that her temptations during her crisis included the wish to convert to Catholicism and lock herself up in the strictest order possible.

16. Quotations are from the copy of Dr Chetwynd' s letter in Ms. Bod. 154.

17. The excess of heat is not of course strictly consistent with the humoral account of melancholy, but even physicians were not always very precise; excess heat seems in some cases to be taken as a cause of melancholic enthusiasm; see John P. Sena, 'Melancholic madness and the Puritans', *Harvard Theological Review* 66, 3 (1973). Melancholy adust – burnt melancholy – was also governed by an excess of heat.

18. The autobiographer Hannah Allen, similarly identified as suffering from mental anguish some fifty years later, uses a strikingly similar phrase to make the opposite point: 'if the Body be out of frame and true', she declares, 'the Soul cannot well be at ease'; *Satan his Methods and Malice Baffled* (1683), 'To the Reader'.

19. Perkins also insists on the uselessness of physic: 'distresse of Conscience, cannot be cured by any thing in the world but one, and that is the blood of Christ'; *Treatise of Conscience*, Book I, p. 195.

20. *Mind-Forg'd Manacles*, p. 35.

21. *Madness and Civilization*, p. 189.

22. *Mystical Bedlam*, p. 123.

23. Anna Trapnel, *The Cry of a Stone* (1654), p. 74.

24. Luce Irigaray, 'La mystérique', in her *Speculum of the Other Woman*, trans. Gillian C. Gill (New York: Columbia University Press, 1985), p. 201.

25. Julia Kristeva, *Powers of Horror: An Essay on Abjection*, trans. Leon Roudiez (New York: Columbia University Press, 1982), p. 127.

The Torture of Limena: Sex and Violence in Lady Mary Wroth's *Urania*

Helen Hackett

My interest in the *Urania* began from a sense that Renaissance culture tended to construct romance as a feminine genre, both in terms of its imagined readership, and in more metaphorical senses, as being a low genre, unintellectual, associated with leisure and with the private sphere. Yet until Wroth no woman seems to have presumed to write a romance; even the notable case of Margaret Tyler's translation of *The Mirror of Knighthood* in 1578 was precisely that, a translation, rather than a work of authorial creation. I was therefore interested in what happened when a woman dared to assume the role of author in a genre categorized as feminine, yet in which her models of authorship were all male.[1]

I also became increasingly interested in the *Urania* as a *roman à clef*, in the ways that it self-consciously plays with the boundaries between fact and fiction. As we know, the 1621 *Urania* was read by a number of courtiers as a scandal novel, and Edward Denny in particular took violent exception to an episode which he thought was a fictionalization of recent sensational events in his family.[2] The *Urania* seems also to fictionalize events in Wroth's own life: her main heroine, Pamphilia, is not only a princess but also a writer, and her constant love for the inconstant Amphilanthus resembles Wroth's own long-running affair with her married cousin, William Herbert. The romance is therefore much concerned with questions of self-representation.

This essay continues these lines of inquiry, but does so through a focus on Wroth's representation of violence against the female body in one specific episode of her fiction. This is the story of Limena in Book 1 of the published *Urania*.[3] To summarize briefly: Limena is married to Philargus but is loved by, and in love with, Perissus. When Philargus discovers this secret love, he accuses Limena of dishonouring him and threatens her. Limena does not deny that she loves Perissus, but does deny that she is guilty of any sexual crime. As she repeatedly protests her innocence, Philargus inflicts various violent punishments upon her. This is one of the many stories in the published *Urania* in which extramarital love is idealized as a pure, true love, and the unloved husband is the villain of the piece; other examples include the story which Denny objected to, which he thought depicted his daughter's suspected adultery and satirized his fury against her.

The story of Limena is also one of the many intertwined plots of the *Urania* which surface in the narrative, recede from view, and then reappear again later. The first instalment of this story is related by Perissus, the lover, to the character Urania. Perissus, having been expelled from Philargus's household, believes Limena is dead. He relates what happened to Limena after his expulsion as she told it to a servant who told it to him. Philargus threatened Limena with death; she deflected it as follows:

> 'Said he: "Prepare then quickly, this shall be your last." "My Lord," said she, "behold before your eyes the most distressed of women, who if you will thus murder is here ready." Then, untying a dainty, embroidered waistcoat, "See here," said she, "the breast" – and a most heavenly breast it was! – "which you so dearly loved, or made me think so, calling it purest warm snow. Yet never was the colour purer than my love to you, but now 'tis ready to receive that stroke shall bring my heart blood, cherished by you once, to dye it, in revenge of this my wrong revenge. Nay, such revenge will my death have, as though by you I die, I pity your ensuing overthrow."
>
> 'Whether these words or that sight (which not to be seen without adoring) wrought most, I know not, but both together so well prevaile[d] as he stood in a strange kind of fashion, which she, who now was to act her part for life or death, took advantage of.' (Wroth, ed. Salzman, pp. 17–18)

Philargus gives her a two-day reprieve in which to confess.

The story is taken up again some pages on, first of all narrated by the authorial voice, who describes how a third knight, Parselius, encountered a beautiful lady being persecuted by an armed man.

> The Morean prince stayed to behold and, beholding, did admire the exquisiteness of that sad beauty, but more than that did the cruelty of the armed man seem wonderful for, leading her to a pillar which stood on the sand (a fit place that the sea might still wash away the memory of such inhumanity), he tied her to it by the hair, which was of great length and sun-like brightness. Then pulled he off a mantle which she wore, leaving her from the girdle upwards all naked, her soft, dainty white hands he fastened behind her with a cord about both wrists, in manner of a cross, as testimony of her cruellest martyrdom.

When she was thus miserably bound to his unmerciful liking, with whips he was about to torment her. But Parselius with this sight was quickly put out of his admiration. (Wroth, ed. Salzman, pp. 101–2)

Parselius rides in to attack the armed man, while another knight suddenly appears and frees the lady. They turn out to be Philargus (the husband), Perissus (the lover), and Limena. Philargus dies repentant and urges Perissus and Limena to marry.

Limena herself fills in the intervening events, which are mainly Philargus's tortures of her:

'When I had put off all my apparel but one little petticoat, he opened my breast and gave me many wounds, the marks you may here yet discern' – (letting the mantle fall again a little lower, to show the cruel remembrance of his cruelty) which although they were whole, yet made they new hurts in the loving heart of Perissus, suffering more pain for them than he had done for all those himself had received in his former adventures. Therefore softly putting the mantle up again, and gently covering them, lest they might chance to smart, besought her to go on, longing to have an end of that tragical history and to come again to their meeting, which was the only balm could be applied unto his bleeding heart. (Wroth, ed. Salzman, pp. 105–6)

Limena goes on to describe, at some length and in some detail, how she was threatened with burning, dragged through bushes to tear her skin, gagged, whipped and pinched with irons daily, had salt water rubbed into the wounds, and finally was threatened with drowning, until her rescue.

At first this story seemed to me to be problematic in a text by a woman, because of the way it displays naked parts of a female body which has been subjected to sadistic tortures. Much of the renewed interest in Renaissance women writers like Wroth is of course motivated by feminism: readers like me are delighted to rediscover forgotten women writers from the past, and we inevitably tend to look to them in a spirit of sisterhood, in the hope of finding sentiments which are recognizable as a kind of protofeminism. What, then, to make of this apparently sadistic and pornographic use of the female body in a text by a woman?

Part of the problem is that we have become accustomed to thinking of such displays of the female body in terms of the 'male gaze'. Originally, Laura Mulvey discussed sadistic and fetishistic 'scopophilia' in film as a system in which the female body becomes a token of exchange between the male filmmaker, male characters within the film, and the viewer of either sex, who is put in a masculine position.[4] Subsequently,

Nancy Vickers in her discussions of Petrarch and of the *Rape of Lucrece*, and Patricia Parker in *Literary Fat Ladies*, showed how usefully this idea of the gaze can be applied to Renaissance texts by men.[5] They read the female body in such texts as a token of exchange between male characters and between the male writer and male readers. They see these exchanges as part of the construction of masculine subjectivity, so that texts which are apparently descriptive of women may, in a sense, not be about women at all.

In the Limena episode, the way in which attention is fetishistically drawn to parts of Limena's body does seem similar to the kind of material which is often interpreted in terms of the male gaze. Perissus, when describing Limena's exposure of her breast, has that appreciative interjection, 'and a most heavenly breast it was!' Philargus is amazed and disabled by this display of the breast, a stupefaction and dis-empowerment very like that described by Vickers in her essay 'Diana described': according to her model of interpretation, the female body is perceived by the masculine subject as threatening, an emblem of castration, and provokes first a state of disempowerment and then defensive sadistic violence. There also seems to be an eroticization in the presentation of Limena – not just her amazing breast, but also her sun-bright hair. Very striking is the phrase 'letting her mantle fall again a little lower', to show her wounds – it is easy to read this as a kind of coquettishness whereby an apparently accidental partial display of the body tantalizes and provokes the viewer to imagine more.

So can we assume that, as the first published woman author of a romance, a genre whose conventions have been established by male authors, Wroth inevitably adopts a masculine authorial position? E. Ann Kaplan, in her essay 'Is the gaze male?' suggests that whenever the gaze is deployed, it is inevitably and inherently an instrument of mascu-line power, and the deployer of the gaze, whatever their biological sex, becomes masculinized.

> Perhaps we can ... say that in locating herself in fantasy in the erotic, the woman places herself as either passive recipient of male desire, or, at one remove, positions herself as *watching* a woman who is passive recipient of male desires and sexual actions ... The gaze is not necessarily male (literally) but to own and activate the gaze, given our language and the structure of the unconscious, is to be in the male position.[6]

Here, this would mean assuming that inherently masculine positions in a homosocial exchange were adopted not only by Wroth as author, but also by the character Urania who is the audience for Perissus's description of Limena's breast; and by the female reader implied in the romance's full title, *The Countess of Montgomery's Urania*, which dedicated it to Wroth's friend Susan Vere. The idea of homosocial exchange between masculine agents seems to be stretched rather far here; and the idea that a female author working in a genre established by male authors inevitably writes 'as a man' really does not seem adequate as a way of interpreting what is going on in this case.

A different way of reading the Limena episode is suggested by Mary Ellen Lamb's reading of the *Arcadia*, in her book *Gender and Authorship in the Sidney Circle*.[7] The *Arcadia* was a romance written by a man, but women were prominent in both its original coterie readership and its later wider following. Lamb argues that this generic femininity is connected with its celebration of a distinctively feminine heroism. This is especially evident in the captivity episode of Book 3 of the 'New' *Arcadia*, where Philoclea and Pamela withstand a succession of tortures and death threats in a way which integrates previous models of romantic heroines who die for love, Christian martyrs and Stoic heroes. It is a heroism which consists in passive resistance rather than action, which is enacted in the closed private spaces of Cecropia's castle, and which is grounded in constancy in love, that is, in an inner emotional integrity. In all these respects, it is a form of heroism which is enabled within conventions of feminine virtue; it is not an appropriation of masculine public and martial valour which might be seen as disturbingly Amazonian and unnatural. Indeed, this feminine heroism is increasingly shown to be superior to the futile and bloody martial valour exercised by the battling knights outside the castle walls.[8]

One might easily apply Lamb's reading to the Limena episode, to argue that what look like eroticizations of the suffering female body can be read as examples of feminine heroism. It is clear that Wroth was strongly influenced by the *Arcadia* in many respects, including her treatment of violence. For example, in another episode from Book 1 of the published *Urania*, a lady called Meriana is subjected to a mock-execution in a way which strongly recalls the mock-executions of Pamela and Philoclea in Book 3 of the 'New' *Arcadia*. Meriana's husband takes her up onto the roof of his castle and apparently executes her in the sight of her lover, who sees her head on top of a pillar, with her golden hair hanging down, but it emerges later that this was a hollow pillar and the live Meriana was actually concealed inside it, with her head sticking out of the top (Wroth, ed. Salzman, pp. 189–92). This especially recalls the mock-execution of Philoclea, who is made to stick her head up through the bottom of a gold basin full of blood, so that it appears to Pamela and Zelmane to have been severed.[9]

However, Lamb acknowledges that the tortures of the princesses in the *Arcadia* seem likely also to have provided spectacles of erotic pleasure for male readers. She comments, for instance, that the scene where the two princesses' 'beautiful' bodies were beaten with rods by spiteful old women (*Arcadia*, pp. 551–4) 'surely contained considerable erotic appeal for at least some readers'.[10] She encounters some difficulty in reconciling these models of a feminine reading which sees the princesses as models of heroism, and a masculine reading which enjoys them as erotic objects. She compares the captivity episode with the death of Parthenia, in which Parthenia's dying body, marked by violence, is blazoned in a way which creates an aesthetic and erotic spectacle as well as an example of feminine heroism:

> her neck, a neck indeed of alabaster, displaying the wound, which with most dainty blood laboured to drown his own beauties, so as here was a river of purest red, there an island of perfectest white, each giving lustre to the other. (*Arcadia*, p. 528)

Lamb comments that the dying Parthenia and the suffering princesses:

> may have elicited a sexual as well as, or even instead of, a compassionate response ... The valorization of the female body as the site of heroic virtue becomes, then, a mask covering sadistic voyeurism based on pleasure in women's pain.[11]

This leaves us in some confusion: is the representation of feminine heroism just an excuse for the enjoyment of sadistic voyeurism by the male author and male readers, and if so where does this leave the female reader? Is she just a dupe, or does she have to be a resistant reader, reading against the grain to find positive models of feminine heroism where none were intended? More problematically still, where does this leave the female writer who describes similar spectacles?

It is perhaps not necessary to set up a rigid opposition, as Lamb tends to do, between female readers who find pleasure in noble examples of feminine heroism, and male readers who take an ignoble or indeed deplorable pleasure in sadistic spectacles of women's suffering. We must acknowledge, I think, that there is a range of possible responses to these scenes, which might encompass a pleasurably masochistic identification by female readers with the female victim, and also an identification by female readers with the persecutor, the exerciser of strength and power. Recent work on the idea of the gaze has been helpful in pushing beyond a simplistic model whereby the gaze is always male, heterosexual, sadistic and bad: a good example of this is Valerie Traub's essay, 'Desire and the differences it makes', where as part of her discussion of different critical approaches to Shakespeare she writes:

When viewing a love scene on a movie screen, you experience pleasure by watching an interplay of power and erotic desire. Your eye is drawn to particular body zones, and you are aroused not only by body type and position, but also by the 'scene', the pace of interaction, the affective content. But whether you are aroused by watching a woman's body or a man's, two women together or two men, a woman with a man, or any other combination imaginable, the mere fact of your excitement does not explain what is happening on the dual levels of identification and erotic desire. That is, is your arousal dependent upon a process of identification with or desire for an eroticized object? To state it simplistically, do you *want* or do you *want to be* one of the images on the screen? Which one? Can you tell? Does your identification and / or desire shift during the interaction? And are your desire and identification dependent upon the *gender* or any one of many other constituents of the image: power, class, status, age, relative aggressiveness, vulnerability, energic level, clothing, skin color / texture, hair type / length, genital size / shape ...? [12]

Traub's discussion is useful in foregrounding the fact that a female writer or reader might take both sadistic and masochistic pleasure in the torture of Limena. In any case, the kind of self-justification involved in Lamb's idea of feminine heroism might be described as masochism under another name.

Traub also points out that the viewer's or reader's pleasure in a fictional scene can be a complex flux of identification and desire; and such fluidity is evident in the Limena episode in its interplay between objectification of the woman and an invitation to sympathize and identify with her. This interplay is developed through the alternation between third-person narrations of events by Perissus and by the authorial narrator, and the attribution of direct speech to Limena. The variation of voices entails a variation between views of Limena from the outside, and her voicing of her experience from the inside. Moreover, within this dialogue, the very issue at stake is precisely the relation between inside and outside in constituting personhood. The relation between body and voice, body and selfhood, seems to be crucial both in this isolated episode, and in the *Urania* as a whole, and in the whole question of how we read Renaissance women writers.

The Arcadian princesses, like Limena, put up a stoical endurance to torture, and make repeated assertions that they are willing to die rather than change their affections or dishonour themselves. Running through this is an implicit split between self and body: Pamela, for instance, after her beating, tells Cecropia: 'Thou mayest well wreck this silly body, but *me* thou canst never overthrow' (my emphasis;

Arcadia, p. 553). This separation between body and self, outside and inside, is clearly important in Limena's story. In the eyes of Philargus, her husband, her outside and inside are one: the knowledge that she is in love with Perissus becomes for him an assumption that she has allowed Perissus access to her body, and thereby sullied her own honour, and her husband's honour. He says: 'But if you will speak, confess the truth, O me, the truth: that you have shamed yourself in my dishonour. Say you have wronged me, giving your honour and mine to the loose and wanton pleasure of Perissus' (Wroth, ed. Salzman, p. 16). It is a feature of adultery that although it is thought of as something enacted by and on the body, the signs of it are in fact usually not evident on the body. Even a pregnant female body reveals the fact that a woman has had sex, but does not reveal who with. For verification of a sexual crime, the body must be supplemented by confession, naming, verbalization.[13] Here Philargus seeks verification through confession, demanding that Limena produce her presumed inner shame in spoken utterance, convert it into outer knowledge. Within this, he assumes that her body, her honour and his honour are all identical – her body has been spotted, albeit invisibly, and therefore her honour and his honour are likewise spotted. As she repeatedly refuses to confess, he reacts with an increasingly violent desire to mark her spottedness upon her body.

Limena, however, consistently separates her body and her mind, body and soul, outside and inside. She tells Philargus:

> 'This wretched and unfortunate body is, I confess, in your hands, to dispose of to death if you will, but yet it is not unblessed with such a mind as will suffer it to end with any such stain as so wicked a plot and miserable consent might purchase ... I will with more willingness die than execute your mind, and more happily shall I end, saving him innocent from ill, delivering my soul pure and unspotted of the crime you tax me of, or a thought of such dishonour to myself.'
> (Wroth, ed. Salzman, p. 17)

Here, Limena asserts the separation of her body and soul, her transcendence of her body in her conviction of her inner innocence. However, she goes on to link her honour with her body in asserting the purity and unspottedness of both. When she exposes her breast, she reminds Philargus that he used to call it 'purest warm snow', and asserts: 'never was the colour purer than my love to you'. This is strikingly similar to the exposure of the breast in the source in Boccaccio for the wager story in *Cymbeline*. Genevra, the wife wrongly accused of adultery, tears open her male disguise to show her breasts, and this is taken as proof not only that she is a woman, but also that her assertions that she is Genevra, and that she is innocent, are all true.[14] It is a striking example of the exposure of the breast as an assertion not only of gender, but also of identity and of virtue. In both stories, the strategic exposure of the breast not by a lover or a husband but by the woman herself serves as an emblem of feminine purity: a self-willed and purposeful disclosure of the female body to an exclusive audience serves as a guarantor of inner virtue, a sign of purity, integrity and selfhood.

As the story proceeds, though, it is the marking of Limena's body which becomes increasingly significant; and this marking becomes increasingly reminiscent of the iconography of Christian martyrdom. We are told that Philargus had fastened her hands 'behind her with a cord about both wrists, in manner of a cross, as testimony of her cruellest martyrdom' (Wroth, ed. Salzman, p. 102).[15] Finally, Limena herself makes another strategic display of her own body to a select audience, Perissus and Parselius. This time, her body is not a sign of pure whiteness, but is marked by wounds. Within the iconography of martyrdom, however, this outer markedness itself becomes a token of inner purity. Philargus sought to mark her shame upon her body, but the effect is the opposite: the marks denote her stoical endurance of suffering. There is another analogy here in the figure of Portia, in both Shakespeare's *Julius Caesar* and his source in Plutarch. Portia secretly wounds herself in the thigh, then after a speech protesting of her heroic fortitude and ability to share in Brutus's political anxieties and keep them secret, she shows the wound as proof of this fortitude.[16] In both her case and Limena's, the controlled disclosure of a hidden wound to a select audience is used as a proof of virtue. The body acts as a surface or text on which the signs of virtue are written. It acts as a screen between the character's inside and outside, and as such is the medium of representation of honour, a quality which is itself intermediate between what we might call the private self and the public world of society.

In thinking about the relation betwen body and selfhood as it is represented in the Limena episode, I have been struck by correspondences to several recent analytical discussions of torture.[17] Elaine Scarry, in *The Body in Pain*, remarks on the difficulty of representing pain in words: pain has to be verified through marks on the body, or through the display of the torture weapon, or in some other material form.[18] At the same time, though, Scarry argues that what these material forms represent is not really pain, but the exercise of power. The torturer, by subjecting the victim to pain, seeks to emphasize the latent split between body and selfhood; to confine the victim to a consciousness entirely occupied by the body; and to deprive the victim of language, to reduce the voice to an inarticulate scream, denying the extension of selfhood beyond the body which is enabled by

language.[19] Limena's ultimate victory over Philargus is perhaps most
marked by the fact that the episode ends with her voice, with her telling
her own story.

For Page duBois, in her book *Torture and Truth*, the history of
torture stretching back to ancient Greece is crucially based on 'a
mystical vision of the secret nature of truth, its residence elsewhere'.[20] For the torturer, truth is a hidden and elusive thing located
in the dark recesses of the body of the other; the purpose of torture
is to tear truth out from that body. This corresponds to Philargus's
obsessive and fanatical attempts to force a confession from Limena. He
defines his own identity in terms of a nebulous concept of honour which
he locates within his wife's body. When he perceives this honour as
having been sullied, he attempts to tear out of her not only information,
but also the stain, the inner corruption, which he regards her as having
contracted.

Elizabeth Hanson's article 'Torture and truth in Renaissance England' is concerned with the torture of Catholics under the Elizabethan
regime. Hanson shows how the opposed goals of torturer and tortured,
of eliciting confession and resisting confession, give rise to two different
evaluations of truth:

'Truth', which both perpetrators and victims make the issue of
torture, is not so much a specific content as a sign for the validity
of the competing epistemologies of the torture chamber: 'Truth is
that which is susceptible to discovery' versus 'Truth is that which is
felt in resisting discovery'.[21]

This conforms to Limena's definition of her own truth as lying in
reticence and resistance; she says: 'My Lord ... threatenings are but
means to strengthen free and pure hearts against the threateners, and
this hath your words wrought in me, in whom it were a foolish baseness
for fear of your sword or breath to confess what you demand' (Wroth,
ed. Salzman, p. 16).

Hanson goes on to discuss differing Elizabethan and Jacobean
theories and practices of torture, and decides that the Renaissance body
under torture was radically ambiguous, perceived as at once distinct
from truth and selfhood and the abode of truth and selfhood.[22] In
Catholic martyrologies, the marking of pain on the body is evidence
of a truth which is distinct from the body, an inner faith and knowledge
which is not revealed. Hence the emphasis in martyrologies on the
marking and tearing of the body and the instruments of torture: these
can all be read as material proofs of the inner truth of the sufferer.
They may also of course offer sado-masochistic pleasures to the reader
in a way analogous to the Limena episode. But they serve another

function still in that they are evidence of an *external* noncorporeal truth, that is, the external force of the Elizabethan regime, of whose cruelty the marks of truth are a proof.

Similarly, the marks on Limena's body are evidence not only of her virtue, but also of her torturer's cruelty. Scarry, duBois and Hanson all in their different ways write of the marking of the body in torture as a material inscription of the power relations between torturer and tortured. Limena's persecutor is not an oppressive public regime like that of ancient Athens, of Elizabethan England, or of twentieth-century dictatorships, but her husband. As I mentioned before, this episode is one of many in the *Urania* in which extramarital love is seen as heroic and the unloved husband is cast as the villain of the piece. To some extent this may reflect Wroth's own experience: her family arranged her marriage to Sir Robert Wroth, and there is evidence that it was not a happy one. As I said before, she appears to have been in love with her cousin William Herbert; it was an affection which quite probably went back to their childhood, and which seems after her husband's death to have become a full-blown and long-running affair, producing two children (Wroth, *Poems*, pp. 24–6). Limena's love for Perissus is validated by the facts that it predated her marriage, and that her marriage was arranged by her father and entered into out of duty.

Many of the narratives of the *Urania* demonstrate an interest in romantic love outside marriage, from the main narrative frame of the love between the constant Pamphilia and the inconstant Amphilanthus, to inset stories like those of Lindamira and Bellamira. The names of these two characters might mean 'of fair looks': 'bella' means 'beautiful', 'linda' is Spanish for 'lovely, pretty', and 'mirar' is the Spanish verb for 'to look'.[23] However, their names also confirm the impression given by their life-stories that they are fictionalized versions of Wroth herself: 'Mira' is an anagram of 'Mari' or 'Mary', and 'Linda' sounds not unlike 'Lady', so 'Lindamira' could be 'Lady Mary', 'Bellamira' 'the fair Mary'. 'Limena' too contains the initials 'L. M.' for 'Lady Mary', and this character may also be one of these semi-autobiographical projections. She can certainly be understood as an example of the martyrdom of women in marriage: her physical torture and pain can be read as an allegory of the mental and emotional pain suffered by women trapped within loveless unions. Philargus's intention in his torture of his wife is to extract the truth he wants to hear, and to punish her. The effects of his torture, though, are to legitimize his wife's escape from him, and to leave an indicting physical witness on her body of his cruelty to her. We can return to Scarry's idea of an emphasis on the weapons and marks of torture as a way of giving material form to inarticulable pain. In Limena's case, a narrative of torture is not so much about the representation of physical pain as about finding a means of representing the mental and emotional pain of marriage without love. Her wounds are images of physical pain, and that physical pain itself is a metaphor for metaphysical suffering.

And yet not only metaphysical suffering either: Limena's torments may represent the horror of repeated submission by a wife to sexual intercourse with a husband she does not love. Her wounds may stand for the combined emotional, psychological and physical scarring of marital rape; or, at least, of repeated stoical endurance of a sexual act which revolts her. At an early stage in the narrative, the description of her feelings on her marriage conveys this combination of duty and disgust:

> She, seeing it was her father's will, esteeming obedience beyond all passions how worthily soever suffered, most dutifully though un-willingly said she would obey, her tongue faintly delivering what her heart so much detested, loathing almost itself for consenting in show to that which was most contrary to itself. (Wroth, ed. Salzman, p. 8)

I want to stress the idea of the body as text in the Limena episode, and to link it to the fact that the episode closes with Limena telling her own story. This sets up important correspondences between the body, selfhood and narrative. The *Urania* is a complex network of stories in which the characters relate to one another the adventures they have encountered. Within this, there is a distinct sense of the pleasure of converting experience into narrative, of conferring aesthetic form upon it in the process of giving it utterance. Many of the stories within the *Urania* are presented either as true-life experiences, or as fictions whose pleasure lies in their emotional truth. For instance, at one point the Queens of Naples and Sicily walk in woods, 'telling stories of themselves, and others, mixed many times with pretty fine fictions, both being excellently witty' (Wroth, 1621, Book 3, p. 415). Narrative in the *Urania* is like honour and like the body in that it is a medium which lies between public and private, because it involves the representation of personal experience to an audience.

Narrative seems to have a particular function for women in the *Urania* in that it can offer consolation for emotional suffering. Inter-estingly, in Book 2 of the published *Urania*, the heroine Pamphilia, saddened by her secret and unfulfilled love for Amphilanthus, seeks the company of none other than:

> the sweete *Limena*, who accompanied her, into her sad fine walkes[;] being there alone, (save with her second selfe,) surely said [Pamphilia], you that so perfectly and so happily haue loved, cannot in this delightfull place, but remember those sweete (yet for a while curst)

passages in love, which you haue overgone: speake then of love, and speake to me, who love that sweete discourse, (next to my love) above all other things, if that you cannot say more of your selfe, then your deare trust hath grac'd me withall, tell of some others, which as truly shall be silently inclosed in my breast, as that of yours; let me but understand the choice varieties of Love, and the mistakings, the changes, the crosses; if none of these you know, yet tell me some such fiction. (Wroth, 1621, Book 2, p. 188)

It seems to be implied here that if Limena wants to conceal her own private experiences, she could partially reveal them in disguised fictional form. Mary Wroth herself could be said to be doing this in the extent to which the Urania is a roman à clef. As I have said, Pamphilia's experiences of unhappy love resemble aspects of Wroth's own life; and Pamphilia herself tells the story of Lindamira, which is another fictionalized version of Wroth's own life.[24]

Narrative can therefore operate as a more or less veiled means of uttering one's own emotional experiences, and as a solace for those experiences. Much recent criticism of contemporary romantic fiction has explored the idea of it as 'compensatory literature', salving a sense of lack in life, and this seems to be paralleled in the Urania.[25] At one point, Melasinda, Amphilanthus and Pamphilia 'past the best part of the night in pleasing discourse of the flowring time of their first lovings, euery one, nott nice, butt truly telling their infinitely suffering passions, butt the prize fell to Pamphilias share by their owne confessions' (Wroth, Newberry MS, Book 2, f. 57v). The implication here seems to be that because Pamphilia has suffered most, she is the best story teller. Experience is constitutive of selfhood, and productive of good narrative. Within this there is a refined sense of how narrative hovers on boundaries between fiction and fact, and between private and public: it is a means of making the private public, bringing the inside to the outside.

The link between narrative and the body is made clear in one of the contemporary reactions to the publication of the Urania. John Chamberlain, assuming the Urania to be a roman à clef, said that Mary Wroth 'takes great libertie or rather licence to traduce whom she please, and thincks she daunces in a net' (Wroth, Poems, p. 36). This seems to be an idea a little like that of the Emperor's new clothes: George Gascoigne's Adventures of Master F. J. (1573) includes a mention of 'the fond devices of such as have enchained themselves in the golden fetters of fantasy, and having bewrayed themselves to the whole world do yet conjecture that they walk unseen in a net'.[26] The implication, then, is that Mary Wroth, thinking herself secure behind a veil of fiction, has displayed too much of the private lives of herself and her acquaintances, and in doing so has improperly exposed herself. Narrative which makes the private public is here represented as an improper exposure of the private parts of the female body. Moreover in Lord Denny's verses, accusing Wroth of being a 'Hermophradite [sic] in show, in deed a monster / As by thy words and work all men may conster' (Wroth, *Poems*, p. 32), the strong implication is that what Wroth has metaphorically exposed through her act of authorship is not merely the female body, but a sexually monstrous and unnatural body.

In the case of Limena, narrative and the body operate together in the process of uttering her emotional suffering. Her narrative and her body are alike screens between her inner state and her outer self-representation; they can both be seen as texts in which her virtue is inscribed. Her account of her ordeal ends:

> 'Thus, my lords, have you heard the afflicted life of poor Limena, in whom these tortures wrought no otherwise than to strengthen her love and faith to withstand them. For could any other thought have entered into my heart, that would have been a greater affliction to my soul than the cursed strokes were to my body, subject only to his unnaturalness, but now by your royal hand redeemed from misery to enjoy the only blessing my heart can or ever could aspire to wish. And here have you now your faithful love Limena.' (Wroth, ed. Salzman, pp. 106–7)

Here Limena reverts to the opposition between body and self which she had asserted at the outset, so that the marks on her body become proofs of the unspottedness of her virtue. She closes her story by referring to herself in the third person: the process of verification of her constancy and virtue has involved the conversion of the experience of suffering into narrative, the construction and display of the figure of the suffering Limena, and this, 'your faithful love Limena', she now formally presents to Perissus. She even gives her own story, her 'tragical history' as it has already been called (Wroth, ed. Salzman, p. 106), a title, 'the afflicted life of poor Limena', closing and containing it as a narrative which is now ended and can be admired as an artefact.

It is fascinating to speculate as to the possible significance of Limena's name, which of course means threshold or boundary, as in the adjective 'liminal'. Wroth certainly thought of her characters' names in allegorical terms: the authorial narrator of the *Urania* points out that the name of the inconstant anti-hero, Amphilanthus, means 'the lover of two'. It might not be far-fetched, then, to suggest that Limena's name is equally significant. At first Philargus's accusations and threats throw Limena into a liminal state:

She, sweetest soul, brought into this danger (like one being between a flaming fire and a swallowing gulf, must venture into one, or standing still, perish by one) stood awhile not amazed, for her spirit scorned so low a passion, but judicially considering with herself what might be good in so much ill. (Wroth, ed. Salzman, p. 17)

The simile used here is later realized when Limena finds herself caught between a danger of being burned alive and a danger of being cast into the sea by Philargus. The very fact that Limena is taken to the seashore moves the action to a liminal setting: the edge of the land, the margin of the social world, is a fit place for extreme actions and extreme sufferings which place Limena on the brink of death, but result in Philargus passing over the brink of death. The shore, as so often in literature, is a place of testing, bare of all other concerns. Limena's name might therefore represent the extremity of the events in which she participates. Or, it can be connected to her, and Wroth's, liminal or socially marginal position as women who dare to assert the virtue of love outside marriage. Or, Limena can be seen as liminal in a literary historical sense: although it is probably fanciful to suggest that Mary Wroth was conscious of this herself, Limena can be read as a liminal figure between the objectification of the female body in fiction and the construction of a female voice and female selfhood.

The *Urania* seems to me to be an extremely interesting text for any history of the modern idea of the self in literature, clearly containing as it does a concept of interior selfhood, and of experience as formative of the self. In part, of course, this follows the precedent of the *Arcadia*, where, as we have seen, heroines distinguish between inner and outer self to assert: 'Thou mayest well wreck this silly body, but *me* thou canst never overthrow'. In the *Urania* itself, much stress is laid on the virtue of self-government in Wroth's heroines: this too depends on the idea of an interior self which must not be allowed to show in public but which is nevertheless where emotional truth resides. Wroth's heroines could say with Hamlet, 'I have that within which passes show' (*Hamlet*, I. ii. 85). An idea of shared female experience, so important in modern feminist writing, also seems to be present in some form in the *Urania*: think of Pamphilia's request to Limena, quoted above, to tell her of the 'passages in love, which you haue overgone'.

I therefore feel confident that discussion of female selfhood in the *Urania* is not necessarily an anachronistic kind of feminist reading. What concerns me more, however, is a consciousness that in finding such concepts as a female voice and female selfhood in the Limena episode, I am in danger of smoothing over some of the problems from which I started. I am being drawn back towards a reading of Wroth which would make her acceptable in certain conventionally respectable feminist terms. I hope, though, that I have gone some way to suggest that we do not need to settle for diametrically opposed readings of the text as 'good' in expressing a female voice and female selfhood, or as 'bad' in celebrating masculine sadism and feminine masochism. Instead, it might be possible to develop a reading in an area where these categories intersect, where there is interplay between them – again, a 'liminal', or 'Limenal', space.

Notes

1. See Helen Hackett, '"Yet tell me some such fiction": Lady Mary Wroth's *Urania* and the "femininity" of romance', in Clare Brant and Diane Purkiss (eds), *Women, Texts and Histories 1575–1760* (London and New York: Routledge, 1992), pp. 39–68.

2. See *The Poems of Lady Mary Wroth*, ed. Josephine A. Roberts (Baton Rouge and London: Louisiana State University Press, 1983), pp. 31–6.

3. The first part of the *Urania*, consisting of four books, was published as *The Countesse of Mountgomeries Urania* (London, 1621), hereafter referred to parenthetically as Wroth, 1621. There is also an unpublished manuscript sequel in two books, now in the Newberry Library, Chicago (Case MS. f. Y1565. W95), hereafter referred to parenthetically as Wroth, Newberry MS. Book 1 of *Urania*, 1621 is available in Paul Salzman (ed.), *An Anthology of Seventeenth-Century Prose Fiction* (Oxford and New York: Oxford University Press, 1991), pp. 1–209, hereafter referred to parenthetically as Wroth, ed. Salzman.

4. Laura Mulvey, 'Visual pleasure and narrative cinema', *Screen* 16, 3 (1975), pp. 6–18.

5. Nancy J. Vickers, 'Diana described: scattered woman and scattered rhyme', in Elizabeth Abel (ed.), *Writing and Sexual Difference* (Brighton: Harvester, 1982), pp. 265–79; Nancy J. Vickers, '"The blazon of sweet beauty's best": Shakespeare's *Lucrece*', in Patricia Parker and Geoffrey Hartman (eds), *Shakespeare and the Question of Theory* (New York and London: Methuen, 1985), pp. 95–115; Patricia Parker, *Literary Fat Ladies: Rhetoric, Gender, Property* (London: Methuen, 1987), pp. 65–6, 126–54.

6. In Ann Snitow, Christine Stansell and Sharon Thompson (eds), *Desire: The Politics of Sexuality* (London: Virago, 1984), pp. 328, 331.

7. Madison: University of Wisconsin Press, 1990.

8. Lamb, *Gender and Authorship*, chapter 2.

9. Sir Philip Sidney, *The Countess of Pembroke's Arcadia [The 'New' Arcadia]*, ed. Maurice Evans (Harmondsworth: Penguin, 1977), pp. 563, 568–9.

10. Lamb, *Gender and Authorship*, p. 104.

11. *Gender and Authorship*, p. 109.

12. In Valerie Traub, *Desire and Anxiety: Circulations of Sexuality in Shake-spearean Drama* (London and New York: Routledge, 1992), pp. 100–1.

13. See Susan J. Wiseman, '*'Tis Pity She's a Whore*: representing the incestuous body', in Lucy Gent and Nigel Llewellyn (eds), *Renaissance Bodies: The*

THE TORTURE OF LIMENA

Human Figure in English Culture c. 1540–1660 (London: Reaktion, 1990), pp. 180–97.

14. Genevra, who has been in exile in male disguise as Sicurano, reveals her identity and her innocence in the presence of the Soldan who has employed her, her husband Bernardo who believes she was killed at his command, and her false accuser Ambrogiuolo. 'Afterward, desiring such garments as better fitted for her, and shewing her breasts, she made it apparant before the Soldane and his assistants, that shee was the very woman indeede.' The Soldan is 'amazed in his minde', but then 'found it to be reall and infallible'; Giovanni Boccaccio, *The Decameron*, trans. Anon. (1620), 2nd Day, 9th Novell, in Geoffrey Bullough (ed.), *Narrative and Dramatic Sources of Shakespeare*, 8 vols (London: Routledge, 1975), VIII, pp. 61–2.

15. As Philargus prepares to inflict blows on her body, Parselius intervenes, but in trying to separate them he himself marks Limena's body:

> Parselius came and struck down the blow with his sword, though not so directly but that it a little razed her on the left side, which she perceiving, looking on it, and seeing how the blood did trickle in some (though few) drops, 'Many more than these,' said she, 'have I inwardly shed for thee, my dear Perissus.' But that last name she spoke softlier than the rest, either that the strange knight should not hear her or that she could not afford that dear name to any but her own ears. (Wroth, ed. Salzman, p. 102)

This recalls the two grazing blows which Britomart suffers in Book III of *The Faerie Queene*, first at the hands of Gardante, then at the hands of Busirane (III. i. 65, III. xii. 33). In both these incidents she sheds a few drops of blood; and the second wound, by Busirane, is a smaller replication of the wound to the heart which he has inflicted on Amoret. Britomart describes the love for Artegall which she has conceived after seeing him in the magic mirror as a wound which has penetrated to her bowels and her entrails (III. ii. 39); so that these grazing wounds can be interpreted either as marks of her entry to a mature state of desire, or of the fact that Artegall is the only combatant who can administer a conquering blow to her, both physically and emotionally, as he does in Book IV. In the case of Limena, her outer wound is made both to resemble the inner state of her heart, which is wounded by love, and to contrast with it, since her inner wounds are infinitely worse than anything that can be inflicted on her body. At the same time, the fact that she speaks the name of Perissus softly in order to keep it to herself enacts in words the interiority and privacy of her passion.

16. In Plutarch, Portia 'took a little razor such as barbers occupy to pare men's nails, and, causing her maids and women to go out of her chamber, gave herself a great gash withal in her thigh, that she was straight all of a gore-blood'. She makes a speech to Brutus about her ability to 'constantly bear a secret mischance or grief with thee', then 'With those words she showed him her wound on her thigh and told him what she had done to prove herself.' ('Passages from North's Plutarch', in William Shakespeare,

Julius Caesar, ed. Arthur Humphreys [Oxford: Oxford University Press, 1984], pp. 236–7). In Shakespeare, Portia says:

> Tell me your counsels, I will not disclose 'em.
> I have made strong proof of my constancy,
> Giving myself a voluntary wound
> Here, in the thigh. (II. i. 299–302)

In both texts, Portia asserts herself able to rise above the disability of her sex, and Brutus praises her as noble.

17. I am grateful to Adrian Poole, whose paper 'The flayings of Marsyas: pain, punishment and tragedy', given at the staff / graduate seminar, English Department, University College London in the autumn term 1992 helped me to think further about torture.

18. New York and Oxford: Oxford University Press, 1985, pp. 13–15.

19. Scarry, *The Body in Pain*, pp. 48–9.

20. New York and London: Routledge, 1992, p. 140.

21. *Representations* 34 (Spring 1991), pp. 53–84 (p. 56).

22. 'Torture and truth', esp. pp. 65–6.

23. I am grateful to Kate Chedgzoy for this information.

24. This is not unlike Viola in *Twelfth Night*, in both the 'willow cabin' speech and the lines which follow 'My father had a daughter loved a man', I. v. 272–80, II. iv. 108–22). Viola speaks her desire in a disguised version of her own voice, and in doing so speaks of a fictionalized version of herself. For both Viola and Wroth, this is simultaneously a safe way of speaking of personal feeling, and very dangerous, hovering precipitously on the boundary between public and private, self-concealment and self-exposure.

25. See, for instance, Tania Modleski, *Loving with a Vengeance: Mass-produced Fantasies for Women* (repr. New York and London: Routledge, 1990 [1982]); Janice Radway, *Reading the Romance: Women, Patriarchy and Popular Literature* (Chapel Hill and London: University of North Carolina Press, 1984), esp. pp. 86–118, 209–22.

26. Paul Salzman (ed.), *An Anthology of Elizabethan Prose Fiction* (Oxford: Oxford University Press, 1987), p. 3.

The Iconography of the Blush: Marian Literature of the 1630s

Danielle Clarke

The visibility of Henrietta Maria's devotion to the Virgin Mary caused some alarm to Puritan critics of the court in the 1630s as one of the central tenets of Reformation doctrine was seemingly undermined before their very eyes: at court, in the Queen's chapel, by the Queen herself.[1] Not only was the Queen seen to be introducing a heretical object of worship into England, she was also perceived to be adapting profane methods to the act of devotion, as the cult of the Virgin Mary took on a worldly, secular cast which had close visual and verbal affinities with Henrietta Maria's court entertainments.[2] In addition, the Queen's devotion to the Virgin Mary exemplified a widespread fear about female agency, and about Henrietta Maria's power to influence religious and political policy. In the unsettled political and religious climate of the 1630s in England, the figure of the Virgin Mary is extraordinarily volatile, as one strand of the Catholic / Puritan debate focuses on her as a particular site of doctrinal and political tension.[3] The Marian texts linked to Henrietta Maria employ a courtly discourse and embrace modes of signification which in Protestant eyes apparently destabilize their self-professed notions of purity and devotion, as they incorporate aspects of the continental counter-Reformation, such as neo-Platonism, *préciosité*, and devout humanism of the type encouraged by St Francis de Sales and his followers.[4] Critics of the court quite frequently point to the gap between the notions of devotion and chastity encouraged by these texts and actual court practices as evidence of the Catholic party's attempts to insinuate Catholicism into the church hierarchy by hypocritical means.

The Queen's circle at court and its Mariolatry thus become a site where various anxieties are brought together and identified: iconophobia, xenophobia and the fear of the effeminization of the state by Catholicism (seen as a feminocentric faith) and by Charles's uxoriousness. Puritan observers focus upon four closely linked areas: the extent of Catholic influence at court and over the King;[5] the power of

Henrietta Maria over the King;[6] fears about Catholic plots fomented by Jesuits and Spaniards (Prynne, *Popish Royall Favourite*, pp. 52–5); and concern that the church hierarchy is turning towards Rome.[7] It is my contention here that the figure of the Virgin Mary, as represented in the texts connected with Henrietta Maria in the 1630s, becomes a site of political and representational struggle, and that the books of Marian devotion come to exemplify all that Puritans fear about the French, Catholic queen.

That the number of texts devoted to the worship of the Virgin Mary increased during the 1630s is hardly in question.[8] The activities of the continental Catholics and the presses operating in St Omer and Douai ensured a steady, if not altogether reliable, stream of Catholic books coming into England.[9] Naturally, some of these were books on how to say the rosary, or recite the Litany, or lives of the Blessed Virgin, which drew on established doctrines and traditions. But there was a new form of Marian devotion coming into England, heavily influenced by developments in French Franciscan thought. The brand of devotion fostered by de Sales, based upon neo-Platonic ideas of the relationship between beauty, the senses and the soul, was particularly influential.[10] The ideas of devout humanism built upon existing traditions and transformed them, so that part of the proselytizing mission was concerned with reclaiming what was profane for the glory of God. Furthermore, de Sales's work had a particular appeal to women, and placed some degree of emphasis upon the worship and the example of the Virgin Mary.[11] The texts associated with Henrietta Maria and her court in the 1630s bear traces of these influences, and tend to appropriate other literary forms in order to promote devotion to the Virgin Mary – the emblem book and poetry, to take but two examples. Yet it is precisely these links with forms more usually associated with the celebration of secular love and beauty that contribute to the perception that Virgin-worship is profane and idolatrous, as their methods are misunderstood by Puritan readers.

The status of the Marian books of devotion in England was additionally complicated by the widespread misunderstanding of Laud's reforms of church ceremonial, which meant that devotional languages and practices were open to interrogation. The Archbishop of Canterbury's ideas about the necessity of reverence and the 'beauty of holiness' were manifested as a concern with the positioning of altars, the question of bowing, and an attempt to restore English churches to their pre-Reformation glory.[12] These, together with the Laudian stress upon the primacy of the sacrament and a concern with the value of vestments and chalices meant that his brand of Protestantism (which had roots which reached back as far as Hooker) was widely characterized as crypto-Catholicism. As early as 1627 Laud and Neile were seen as close to the Catholic position. The Venetian ambassador reported in May 1627 that they had been added to the Council of State: 'one of them being about to publish a book of the seven sacraments, whereby the Anglican Church would draw somewhat nearer to the Catholic'.[13] In the same year, John Cosin's *A Collection of Private Devotions* had provoked an outcry from Puritans who saw in it a return to outlawed practices, such as praying for the souls of the dead and using saints as intercessor.[14] Henry Burton, for example, asserted that 'the whole booke is popish, & weares the Jesuites badge in the front of it' (Burton, *Jesuites Looking Glasse*, p. 117). These examples demonstrate the facility with which one strain of discourse is conflated with another, and that these complex doctrinal battles were fought out upon the field of representation itself. I shall argue that Puritan critics, such as Burton and William Prynne, deliberately exploit the multiplicity of the languages used to describe the Virgin, in order to characterize crypto-Catholic and Catholic texts as woman-centred, immoral and iniquitous, in opposition to the Marian writers' own rationalization of their stylistic methods.

One of the most important, and most contentious texts associated with the Marian 'cult' was Anthony Stafford's *The Femall Glory: Or, the Life and Death of our Blessed Lady* (1635). As (nominally) a non-Catholic Marian text Stafford's text seems to have brought together these conflicts most powerfully, perhaps because *The Femall Glory* cannot be clearly placed as either Protestant or Catholic, and seems to derive its authority from Arminian (or at least anti-Calvinist) reforms. Debates over the form of worship become relevant, as Stafford's text asserts a Laudian concentration upon the importance of external forms of devotion, which for the Puritan detractors are indistinguishable from popery. Worship of the Virgin Mary was officially banned in England, as George Herbert reminds us: 'But now (alas!) I dare not; for our King, / Whom we do all jointly adore and praise, / Bids no such thing'.[15] Stafford plays upon the dearth of material as a selling point for his text: 'I am the first (to my knowledge) who hath written in our vulgar tongue on this our blessed Virgin' (sig. cv). Stafford's text reads almost as a practical application of Laud's ideas regarding the importance of ceremony and the value of the sensual in promoting devotion. In 'A Just Apology', Stafford asserts the importance of images:

> For whatsoever invigitates the eye, leaves a stronger impression in the Soule, then that which onely pierceth the Eare; which Truth, hee shall easily discover, who shall first heare a History only reade, & after see it acted on the Theatre.[16]

This passage constitutes a reversal of his position as stated in *The Femall Glory*, where he writes that 'I abhorre to write of things Divine in the stile of the stage' (p. 158). Stafford is careful here only to use the history translated to the stage as a comparison, yet it is a comparison with implications which undermine his stand against using the language of the stage to describe 'things Divine'. His stress upon the eye recalls Laud's reformation of church ceremony, but muddles one strand of discourse with another in a way that Prynne and Burton found unacceptable. One of the objections to Stafford's book was to the inclusion of certain engravings, part of Stafford's attempt to 'invigitate the eye'. Prynne writes: 'There is a picture of her fabulous Assumption into *Heaven*, cut in brasse, after the *Popish* forme, with men and women devoutly kneeling and praying to her'.[17] Prynne chooses his words carefully, using 'fabulous' in its strict etymological sense, as 'fable', 'untruth'. He continues this idea, maligning and undermining Stafford's earlier claim that his book is a 'history':

> hee spends many pages to prove '*the verity* [of *S. Mary's* Assumption, as an] '*undoubted truth.*' Whereas indeed, it is a meere *Popish* ridiculous false Legend. And to prove this, he makes her to be borne without Sinne. (Prynne, *Canterburies Doome*, reprinted in Stafford, *The Femall Glory*, 1869, p. xvi)

The attack deviates from doctrine, and becomes far more concerned with language and method; Stafford uses up 'many pages' to put forward a 'ridiculous false Legend'. Henry Burton, similarly, attacks Stafford's book on both doctrinal and stylistic grounds, vilifying *The Femall Glory* 'wherein he mightily deifies the Virgin *Mary*' and 'seemes to hold the Virgin Mary to have beene without sinne' (Burton, *Jesuites Looking Glasse*, pp. 123–4). Burton objects to the representational value of Stafford's depiction of the Virgin Mary (whom he presents to his female readers as 'a Mirrour of Femall perfection' [sig. b3r]), '*not as a meere woman, but as a type and Idea of an accomplist piety*' (p. 124). Burton further accuses Stafford of self-contradiction, and of elevating the Virgin Mary to the status of a goddess who challenges the supremacy of Christ himself: 'Loe therefore what a Metamorphosis of our Religion is here. Here is a new goddesse brought in amongst us' (p. 126).

What aroused the Puritan critics more than anything else was the fact that Stafford's book was backed as embracing Protestant orthodoxy by Laud's chaplains, Peter Heylyn and Christopher Dow, resulting in the perception that a Catholic book was being defended by the church hierarchy, compounding fears about the Catholic threat.[18] Dow's and Heylyn's defences answer a number of accusations from Henry Burton, of which Stafford's book is only one, but the Puritan anxiety about *The Femall Glory* indicates the degree to which issues of representation and interpretation are at stake in the perception of the state as increasingly effeminized and threatened by the foreign power of Catholicism. Dow claims not to have seen Stafford's book, and takes up a stance of power-lessness: 'what if a Romanist ... indeavour to pinne such a sense upon our *Articles*, as may make them almost *Romish*. Who can hinder such mens tongues and pens?' (*Innovations*, p. 44). If the Bishop of Chichester has authorised it, Dow argues, then 'Mr. *Burton* will never bee able to finde the least point of Popery in it' (*Innovations*, p. 54). Heylyn similarly writes that Stafford's book contains nothing 'contrarie unto any point of doctrine established and received in the Church of *England*' (*Brief and Moderate Answer*, p. 123). This is all a matter of where devotion becomes idolatry and the difficulty of distinguishing *latria* from *dulia*.[19] Stafford's 'A Just Apology' demonstrates the slipperiness of these distinctions, and the way in which the available languages of devotion can be misread, as he tries to ally *The Femall Glory* with Protestant orthodoxy: 'the meere quoting of diverse places in it, which directly make against the profane Idolatrizing of this *Superlative Saint*, will justifie me in all eyes, but in those of Envy, and her brood' ('A Just Apology', p. lxxxii). Stafford insists upon the usefulness of images, pictures and the veneration of the saints, and via a close examination of the passages which Burton attacked, attempts to head off criticism by powerfully asserting that his text is not '*Popishly* affected' ('A Just Apology', p. lxxxviii).

Stafford confronts an age-old problem in relation to the repre-sentation of the Virgin Mary: that of finding an appropriate language which does not invite the wrong kind of devotion. Henry Hawkins's descriptions of the Virgin Mary in *Partheneia Sacra* (1633), perhaps the text which most clearly exemplifies the Queen's influence and interest, indicate some of the problems of finding a decorous language with which to describe her:

> Seeke not Vermilion or Ceruse in the face, bracelets of Oriental-pearles on her wrist, Rubie-carknets on the neck, rich pendants in the eares, and a delicious fan of most exquisit feathers in her hand, nor al that magasin of Feminin riches, or richest ornaments of Beautie, enough to belye beauties rather, and destroy them quite, then to afford them, where they are not found; they being nothing els then a precious Scene of fopperies, which they only seeke with a curious wastfulnes, who wil needs be wholy mad with the greatest sumptuousnes and cost.[20]

His description of what the reader should *not* look for concentrates upon jewels, ornaments, colours, and physical attributes, which Hawkins calls 'counterfet and Sophisicat'. Yet the rest of Hawkins's text revels in an imagistic density, ornamental symbolism, and the adornments of the Virgin Mary. Hawkins's Virgin becomes the ornaments which describe her, so that the distinction between signifier and signified is repeatedly collapsed and turned inside out. Like other Marian writers, Hawkins works within a hermeneutic which assumes that the physical and bodily is a mirror in which the spiritual and the heavenly can be perceived. The stress upon sensuality is incorporated into the form of the text itself, as the reader is asked to contemplate the emblems, and to move through the various stages of explication.[21] Whilst Hawkins attempts to alter the relationship between body and ornament, he cannot shrug off the language of sensuality and excess, nor can he escape from the conventions used to describe the beauties of mortal women. He aims to shrink the distance between observer and observed:

> Nor would I wish you perfunctoriously to view her only, and passe her over with a slender glance of the eye, but to enter into her *Garden*, which she is herself, and survey it wel. Where, to the end you may not erre, mistake, or goe astray, in wayes so new, and strange, and (for ought I know) as yet untraced and trod of anie, take heer, I pray, for Guide, my proper *Genius*, wel acquainted with al passages of them. (*Partheneia Sacra*, sig. Aiir)

This approach has a curiously erotic subtext, entering the garden, which *is* the virgin, fixing it with one's gaze, together with the possibility that one may 'erre, mistake, or goe astray'.[22] The Virgin is translated into an image which is spatial, geographic, and the reader is figured as an adventurer, colonizing new land. Hawkins uses his 'ornaments' in a double sense, initially treating the symbols as separate from that which they denote. As the narrative of each 'devise' progresses, however, the distinction he has set up begins to collapse, the Virgin as virgin and as body disappears:

> Then had she the flowers of al Vertues and Graces within *her*, to wit, the diversities of al vertues, the *lillies* of *chastity*, the blush and *modestie* of the *rose*, the *hope* of the *Violet*, the *charitie* and divine Love of the *Heliotropon*, and the like. Her soule was a *Garden* of al flowers, and no lesse then a Paradise. (*Partheneia Sacra*, p. 76)

Under the guise of finding the essential, the reader is led away from the Virgin to the contemplation of the symbols that represent her. She is always seen as the outside, a way of leading the reader to the inside. She is a vessel, a mediator, the means to an end – Hawkins asserts that she is not the pearl, but the shell, the mother of 'that precious *Pearl*, *Christ Jesus*' (*Partheneia Sacra*, p. 192). The Virgin Mary mediates the Word, as well as mediating the words of Hawkins, Stafford and other Marian writers, and (supposedly) transforming them from their immoral contexts into signs of chastity and modesty. The process of moving past the Virgin's attributes to the Virgin herself is frequently seen as a sensual one, presented here by Hawkins: 'The Rose growes on a speckled thorn, swelling into sharp or pointed buttons somwhat green, which rives [sic] by little and little, and opens at last, then unbuttons and discloses its treasure' (Partheneia Sacra, p. 20). The parallel of undressing is one which would not escape readers familiar with contemporary poetry, such as the work of Herrick, Waller or Crashaw. The idea of the treasure contained within the rose, supposedly the Virgin, the signified, is also associated with the conquest of feminine virtue, as Patricia Parker has said in Literary Fat Ladies.[23] Hawkins explicitly posits the Virgin as a treasury and as a cabinet:

> The ROSE is the Imperial Queene of Flowers, which al doe homage to, as to their Princesse, she being the glorie and delight of that Monasterie. She is herself a Treasurie of al Sweets, a Cabinet of Musks, which She commends to none to keepe, but holds them folded in her leaves. (Partheneia Sacra, p. 17)

The idea of a cabinet or a chamber is effectively turned inside out, as the 'treasure' contained in the treasury is precisely the Virgin's purity and freedom from sin: the treasure is in fact the chamber, the Virgin's womb:

> And to conclude, as the Bed-chambers of Kings are adorned with Lillies, that they may rest more deliciously among them: so the Virgin, not the Chamber only of a KING, but of GOD also, was dressed-up and beset al with Lillies round-about. (Partheneia Sacra, p. 34)

This factor serves to explain (partially) the confusion and slipperiness at work in the use of an ambiguous iconography to represent the Virgin. Hawkins, in particular, uses a narrative strategy that presupposes the inside / outside division, when, by his own admission, the importance of the Virgin is dependent upon the collapse of outside and inside: her essential role is to be the enveloping vessel bearing the Word into the world.

The circumlocutions necessary to portray the essential qualities of the Virgin constantly pull away into a concentration upon surface, revelling in the power of invention to the point that Marian authors often become embroiled in the sensuality of language, and in the eroticism of the Virgin's femininity. Their language crosses the boundary with other discourses, and uses the vocabulary of woman-worship and suppressed sexuality. The Virgin's garden, according to Hawkins is: 'the Pallace of Flora's pomps, where is the ward-robe of her richest mantles, powdred with starres of flowers, and al embroadred with flowrie stones' (*Partheneia Sacra*, p. 6). In attempting to 'fix' the reading of his text, Stafford complains that Erasmus:

> compares GOD to a Woer; the *Angell* to a Sollicitour; and *Mary*, to the Beloved; and proceeds further than either Divine Will, or humane Modesty permit. He treates of this venerable, this stupendious en-counter betweene the Divinity and Humanity, in the same amorous phrase with which the Poets describe the wanton meeting of *Dido* and *Æneas* in the Cave. I will not rip up the particulars in which he is faulty this way; lest I runne into the same errour which in him I reprehend, and imprint a blush of the cheekes of my bashfull *Readers*. (*The Femall Glory*, p. 72)

Stafford is here asserting the propriety of his own language, but his concern is with misleading or leading astray his 'bashfull' readers. It is at this point that the collapse of the distinction between different kinds of discourse is asserted as a problem – and the problem is seen to be most pressing in relation to Stafford's women readers. His preface also attempts to prescribe their reading of the text, and confine it to the search for virtue via the imitation of the Virgin, rather than using her as a mirror in which they can improve their beauty (sig. b3r–b4r). It is they, he seems to imply, who are likely to be led astray by the 'amorous phrase'.

In many texts about the Virgin Mary – Anthony Stafford's *The Femall Glory* (1635), Henry Hawkins's *Partheneia Sacra* (1633), *Maria Trium-phans* (1635), we find a high concentration of the use of the word 'blush' as an important attribute of the Virgin Mary. The idea of the blush is one which is also frequently utilized in love poetry, encomia and rom-ance.[24] The *OED* entry for the word 'blush' reveals a confusing array of conflicting meanings. The earliest meanings of 'blush' denote an idea of shining forth, a gleam, a glance. This is compounded by the expan-sion of the word to denote the movement of colour into the face – due to *either* shame *or* modesty. Most of the examples cited in the *OED* refer to women – a significant fact, as in the representations of the Virgin Mary we find that the pressure of expressing divine virtue and the prece-dent of her silence in the Bible leads the writers of the 1630s to resort to images culled from contemporary poetry and romance to make the Virgin eloquent – she 'speaks' with her body, which is a site upon which such writers can inscribe her essential qualities without compromising them. This appropriation of a secular language is seen as problematic by Puritan critics, like Henry Burton, who accuse both Laudians and Catholics of 'Goddesse-worship' and of a prurient sexual interest in the Virgin, who for them is not a legitimate object of Christian worship.

The idea of the blush as a sign of perfection or modesty is not confined to religious texts. Brabantio, when railing at Desdemona's falling in love with Othello, says:

> A maiden never bold of spirit
> So still and quiet, that her motion
> Blush'd at her self: and she, in spite of nature
> Of years, of country, credit, everything
> To fall in love with what she fear'd to look on?
>   (*Othello*, I. iii. 94–8)

Desdemona's blush is central to her lost identity, to her confinement within the private sphere; any movement provokes shame and confirms her modesty. This is contrasted with her boldness in defying her father, her confrontation of her sexual being in seeking out Othello. Here the blush is a sign of male-defined virtue, a blazon subject to male interpretation.[25]

Whilst the meaning of the blush is always more than double, some poetic texts incorporate this dual aspect into the meaning of the blush itself. It becomes a part of wooing, a sign simultaneously of innocence and knowledge. It is the woman's proof that she is innocent and that she has been unfairly taken advantage of, at the same time as it is read by her male wooer as a sign of her compliance with his designs. Thus the duality central to the blush can signify either way – it can attest to a woman's guilt or to her virtue.[26] Which way depends upon the interpretation of this bodily 'language' which is woman's response to imposed silence. These meanings surely complicate the presentation of the Virgin, as they demand that the reader exercises some discretion in her or his selection of meanings for the word 'blush'.

The blush could be seen to be an attempt to resolve the problem of the Virgin's body, on display and to be worshipped for its beauty, and that of speech. Yet the blush is also an assertion of the bodily, frequently used to signify a stage in the process of sexual conquest, adored by male wooers for its beauty and eroticism, and used by them as a key to the 'true' feelings of the wooed. The blush is indeed a text, written on the face of women, but however hard the Marian authors try to direct and confine the reading, it slips away from their grasp and takes refuge in the autonomy of paradox and indeterminacy, wrenching the texts away from their supposed purity and chastity. The problematics of the use of imagery more usually found in secular contexts are explicitly addressed in *The Paradise of Delights* in a series of meditations upon the *Ave Maria*:

> Neither was her virginal comelynes such as usually doth stir up
> wanton lustes, or inflame bad desires; but altogeather so far contrary,

that who so should behold the beautifull blush of her modest and
virginall countenance, could not chose, but be inflamed with most
chast desires and fervent love towardes this vertuous Queene.[27]

Here we have precisely the transposition of discourses that Burton
and Prynne objected to so strongly, pinpointed by the echoes in the
language used for erotic desire and heavenly desire respectively.

Hawkins exploits the duality of the blush in his explication of the
emblem of the rose. The blush is an involuntary outward sign of an
inward perturbation, yet the relationship between signifier and signified
is unstable and open to interpretation. Hawkins makes an explicit
comparison between the Virgin Mary (the heavenly ideal of chastity)
and Lucretia (the earthly ideal of chastity), differentiating them in terms
of the blush:

> *Lucretia the Chast* chose rather to wallow in her bloud, then to survive
> her shame, wherin she blushed indeed, but yet without cause; ...
> [when blushing] ... The hart is put into a fright; the obsequious
> bloud comes-in anon, and asks: What ayle you, Sir? Goe, get you
> up, and mount to the turret of the cheeks ... the bloud obeyes, and
> makes the blush, that rayseth such alarmes, in tender Virgins most
> especially. What feares the Virgin, when she blushes so? The wrack
> of her honour; you wil say How so? Is Honour in the Bodie, or the
> Mind? If in the Mind, the Mind is a Citadel impregnable, not subject
> to violence, not to be betrayed, but by itself. (*Partheneia Sacra*, p. 19)

The blush is represented as something which mediates between the
inner and the outer, it is a visible manifestation of inner purity, a
response to a perceived threat. Hawkins emphasizes that the Virgin
Mary has no need to blush at the approach of Gabriel ('blush not ...
thy hold is sure enough'), yet goes on to represent her as doing exactly
that:

> this of al other Vertues, never is safe and secure enough ... Now
> lookes she pale like a verie clowt; and now through modestie, the
> colour mounts into her cheeks, and there sets-up his ruddie standard,
> as if the Fort were his; til feare againe prevayling, plucks it downe.
> And these were the vicissitudes our Sacred VIRGIN had, when her
> glorious Paranimph discovered his Embassage to her in her secret
> closet, presenting her a shadow only, seeming opposite to her chast
> Vow. (*Partheneia Sacra*, pp. 19–20)

Hawkins reorientates the sexual elements of the woman's blush so that
it becomes an expression of Mary's extreme modesty and excessive care

for her chastity, carefully writing its meanings away from the secular contexts that undoubtedly inform his description. The rewriting of secular imagery is part of the project of Hawkins's text in using the visual and sensual as a means of meditating upon the heavenly virtues of the Virgin.

The blush is only one aspect of the appropriation of secular discourses in the Marian texts of the 1630s – *Partheneia Sacra* uses the traditional figure of the *hortus conclusus* as a structure within which the various emblems which represent the Virgin Mary are placed, but translates it into visual and physical form, a means for meditation. Yet it is this appropriation of form that leads to the identification of the Marian cult with the excessive and destabilizing influence of Henrietta Maria. For example, courtly imagery is often used in the 1630s texts, influenced by the Platonist cult, and by French devout humanism, fostered by Henrietta Maria in her support for and sponsorship of the Capuchin order. It was this passage in *The Femall Glory* that prompted Burton's attack:

> At length the Worlds greedy expectation was satisfied; and this Cynthia, this chast Starre was delivered of a *Plannet* farre greater, and brighter then her selfe; of whose all gladding shine, the first man participated, and the last shal. (*The Femall Glory*, pp. 12–13)

Despite the theological orthodoxy of this passage in attributing a higher status to Christ than to Mary, and reducing her role to that of delivering the Messiah, it was the attribution of the name of 'Cynthia' to the Virgin that Burton objected to most vehemently.[28] Its language recalled all too clearly courtly spectacle – Joseph Rutter's *The Shepheards Holy-Day*, or the masques of Davenant, which used Platonist ideas and images to represent the immanent virtues of the King and Queen.[29] Hawkins employs these images to a greater degree than Stafford, due partly to his continental connections. He uses pagan goddesses to illuminate aspects of the Virgin: 'This *Starre* is the blessed *Virgin*, that may wel be tearmed *Venus*, because she enflames mens harts with *Divine love*; and therefore is sayd to be *the Mother of faire dilection*' (*Partheneia Sacra*, p. 119). Venus is used elsewhere to convey physical and sexual love, and adds an element of eroticism to the description which is compounded by vocabulary such as 'enflames' and 'dilection'. Such transference of discourse is also apparent in the use of star symbolism, and it is here that the link between the Marian texts and those of the court becomes most clear. The issue is that such texts are open to misinterpretation, and a 'wrong' reading amounts to idolatry. Hawkins writes:

> They are the silver Oes, al powdred heer and there, or spangles sprinckled over the purple Mantle or night-gowne of the heavens:

the seed of pearle, sowne in the spacious fields of the Heavens, to bring forth light. Have you seen a statelie Mask in Court, al set round, and taken up with a world of beautiful Ladies, to behold the sports and revels there? Imagin the *Starres* then, as sitting in the Firmament, to behold some spectacle on Earth, with no other light then their owne beauties. (*Partheneia Sacra*, pp. 114–15)

The comparison with the masque exemplifies exactly the critiques the Puritans were making of Laud's reforms, and in consequence points out the immorality and licentiousness (as they saw it) of court spectacle. Not only is there a problem of decorum involved in the parallel with the masque, especially when read against the critical discourses of, for example, Prynne's *Histriomastix* (1633), but the colouring which is lent by it to the Virgin removes her from the sphere of the sacred, pure and divine. Mary, as the signified of the star, is pictured watching a masque at court, an accessory to what the Puritans saw as unchaste love and lust masquerading as purity and morality. Alexis de Salo's *An Admirable Method to Love Serve and Honour the Virgin Mary* (1639) reads, as Sensabaugh has said, 'like a book of courtly compliment',[30] as it places stress upon the role of the Virgin Mary as mediatrix.

A Marian text which makes clear the divisions between Catholics and Puritans over the representation and doctrinal status of the Virgin Mary, as well as associating Henrietta Maria closely with the renewed interest in the cult, is the anonymous *Maria Triumphans* of 1635.[31] This text is specifically directed against the Puritan attack upon devotion to the Virgin Mary, whose accusation is that of idolatry, based upon the methods and language of worship. The text adopts a dialogue form, consisting of a 'discussion' between Mariadulus and Mariamastix. Mariamastix, the Puritan, is represented as extreme, bombastic, breathless and full of unfounded prejudice. Mariadulus, by contrast, is seen to be reasonable, reasoned and sympathetic. The author's portrait of the Puritan conforms to a common, but very specific stereotype, although it is notable that both parties employ the same kinds of critique and languages of criticism to attack one another. The debate in *Maria Triumphans* becomes more textual and personal than doctrinal or rational. The argument is concerned with whose words 'mean' more, whose language can claim to signify. It is not so much a debate as a statement of two opposing positions, with a stylistic bias towards the Catholic point of view. Mariamastix allies the Catholics' beliefs with fiction, calling their belief in the Immaculate Conception a 'Phantasy' (*Maria Triumphans*, p. 48). In turn, Mariadulus accuses the Puritan of fabricating evidence: over the issue of calling the Virgin a 'Goddesse', he says 'I do not thinke, you can alledge any one approved Catholike Authour, so stiling the *B. Virgin*' (*Maria Triumphans*, p. 81). Mariadulus

goes on to accuse the Puritans of reading too literally: 'as
so speaking were verily persuaded, that the *B. Virgin* (as
scending the Nature of a Creature) were a true *Goddesse* indeed.
Triumphans, p. 82). This is an accusation frequently levelled at the
Puritans by the Catholics in the 1630s, as the Catholics assert that their
vision of the Virgin Mary is more theologically and philosophically
complex, as befits her paradoxical and mysterious status. Words become
twisted and altered to suit individual purposes. Mariadulus argues that
'you shall fynd ... the Word *Goddesse* to be ascribed by any Catholike,
to the *Blessed Virgin* only in a secondary, and *Analogicall* Construction'
(*Maria Triumphans*, p. 84). He stresses that the Catholics place emphasis
upon the intention behind what is said rather than upon the words
themselves, whilst the Puritans are characterized as verbal wranglers,
caught up in the beguiling aspects of language. Mariadulus defends the
Catholic form of worship by making a secular comparison:

> Thus (for example) the Honour exhibited to any great favorite of a
> Prince, may be justly said to be given to the Prince himselfe; since
> the true Cause of the exhibition of the Honour, is the Grace and
> Favour, which the Prince beareth to such a Worthy Personage.
> (*Maria Triumphans*, pp. 187–8)

Yet this defence is precisely what the Puritans object to – the lack
of distinction between the sacred and the secular, and the displacement
of the proper object of worship by Mary. As Mariamastix says,
'you make to your selfe a *She Saviour*, I meane, a Woman' (*Maria
Triumphans*, p. 91).

The Preface to *Maria Triumphans*, which is dedicated to Henrietta
Maria, makes explicit the identification of Virgin and Queen, such that
Henrietta Maria is posited as Mary's representative upon earth:

> In your Patronage wherof, She, whome it chiefely concernes, will a
> new become your Patronesse: And thus will *Mary* intercede for *Mary*;
> the *Queene of Heaven, for a great Queene* upon earth ... you are the
> daughter of a *King*, sister to a *King*, Spouse to a *King*; and (notwith-
> standing Your weake-strong Sex) do persever with more then manly
> Resolution in Practise of Piety, & in inviolably professing the Ancient
> Apostolicall Fayth. (*Maria Triumphans*, pp. 4–6)

The identification of Henrietta Maria with the Virgin paradoxically
recalled Elizabeth I's appropriation of Marian iconography in her own
representation, thus providing a native model for the association between the Virgin Mary and political intervention.[32] Similarities in poems
of praise addressed to the Queen and to the Virgin Mary served to

compound this construction of Henrietta Maria as the earthly mediatrix
and mother-figure for English Catholics, intervening on their behalf
with King and clergy, and playing a role in negotiations between
England and Rome.[33] Francis Lenton, the author of *Great Britains
Beauties, Or, The Female Glory* (1638) – a text which gestures at Stafford's
Marian one in its title – reveals the extent to which the languages of
love and religion were interchangeable, and, in Puritans' eyes, indistinguishable. As Veevers points out, Lenton's verses deliberately
seem to 'echo the language and imagery of Marian devotion'.[34] The
Queen's name is anagrammatized as 'I AM A TRU STAR' (Maria Stuart),
an obvious reference to Mary as *stella maris*. Lenton elevates her to a
level comparable with that of the Virgin: the Queen's motto is '*A Royall,
Sacred, bright*, tru *fixed* Star / In whose compare, all other Comets are'
(*Great Britains Beauties*, sig. Bv). As the star, she is a powerful influence
for good, who ultimately, like the Virgin, derives her power from her
male superior:

> A morning *Star*, whose Rose at blush and smile,
> Shewes the dayes solace, and the nights exile;
> A radient *Star* whose lustre, more Divine,
> By *Charles* (our Sun) doth gloriously shine ...
> ... *A Star* whose influence, and sacred light,
> Doth beautifie the day, and blesse the night
> (Great Britains Beauties, sig. Bv)

The connection with Henrietta Maria was exploited both to support
and to criticize the Queen. Writers seeking her patronage usually call
attention to her power over the position of English Catholics via her
influence with Charles I. Richard Broughton, for example, describes
her constancy in faith, her help to her Catholic subjects, and then refers
to Britain as the 'Dowrie of Marie', arguing that three Maries have
favoured Catholics: Henrietta Maria herself, Queen Mary, and Mary
Queen of Scots.[35] By the same token, the correspondence between
Henrietta Maria and the Virgin Mary, worked through the transposition
of descriptive languages from one sphere to another, can be used against
her. William Prynne, notably, used the idea of the Virgin as mediatrix
to compound his vision of the popish conspiracy, which for him had
been mediated primarily through the Queen:

> And which was *instar omnium*, they had *Queen Mary* herselfe in the
> Kings own bed and bosome for their most powerfull Mediatrix, of
> whom they might really affirme in reference to his Majesty, what
> some of their popish Doctors have most blasphemously written of
> the Virgin *Mary* in relation to *God and Christ, That all things are*

subiect to the command of Mary, even God himselfe: That she is the Empresse and Queen of Heaven. (*Popish Royall Favourite*, p. 56)

Prynne thus draws together several threads, whereby Catholicism is reduced to the worship of the Virgin Mary, and the Queen's devotion to the Virgin posits her as the prime agent of Catholic subversion of the English state and religion, effected by means of female wiles. Prynne writes that the Queen is

> left free, by all meanes and acts that may be, to withdraw the King from the Protestant Religion to her owne, and his children too: Wee have great cause to feare (if *Adams*, *Solomons*, or *Ahals* seducements by their wives be duly pondered). (*Popish Royall Favourite*, p. 59)

It is the implications of the intertextual networks of meaning that the Virgin's descriptions associate themselves with which prompt Puritan criticism, as much as straightforward doctrinal disagreement. Such languages of devotion serve to place Marian devotion, and by implication Catholicism, at the centre of power, and cannot remain confined to the sphere and specific purposes for which they were originally employed. The wider implications of sensual and courtly language render the discourses of these Marian texts political in much the same way that Kevin Sharpe has claimed that the language of love and compliment at court is politically charged.[36] If the language of love is 'political', so too is the language of religious love, particularly when religious texts persistently appropriate other 'languages' of love, and intersect with discourses which properly belong to other arenas.

Notes

1. For a useful account of Henrietta Maria's Mariolatry, see Erica Veevers, *Images of Love and Religion: Queen Henrietta Maria and Court Entertainments* (Cambridge: Cambridge University Press, 1989), pp. 92–109. On 17 April 1616, the ambassador Salvetti reported that the Queen and her ladies 'sang the hours of the Virgin, and lived together like Nuns', *Historic Manuscripts Commission, Tenth Report*, Appendix I (Skrine MSS), p. 57.
2. Veevers, *Images of Love and Religion*, ch. 5.
3. For the background to the position of English Catholics in the 1630s, see Gordon Albion, *Charles I and the Court of Rome: A Study in Seventeenth-Century Diplomacy* (London: Burns, Oates & Washbourne, 1935); Martin Havran, *The Catholics in Caroline England* (London: Oxford University Press, 1962); John Bossy, *The English Catholic Community 1570–1850* (London: Darton, Longman & Todd, 1975); Caroline Hibbard, *Charles I and the Popish Plot* (Chapel Hill: University of North Carolina Press, 1983),

and Peter Lake, 'Anti-popery: the structure of a prejudice' in Richard Cust and Ann Hughes (eds), *Conflict in Early Stuart England: Studies in Religion and Politics 1603–1642* (Harlow: Longman, 1989), pp. 72–106.

4. On Catholic devotion in England, see Helen C. White, *English Devotional Literature [Prose] 1600–1640* (Madison: University of Wisconsin Press, 1931), chs. 4 and 5; Louis L. Martz, *The Poetry of Meditation: A Study in English Religious Literature of the Seventeenth Century* (New Haven: Yale University Press, 1954, repr. 1962); and Anthony Raspa, *The Emotive Image: Jesuit Poetics in the English Renaissance* (Fort Worth: Texas Christian University Press, 1983).

5. George Con, the Papal envoy to the English court in the 1630s, became a great favourite at court, and much was made of Charles's interest in him. See Hibbard, *Charles I*, ch. 3.

6. See William Prynne, *The Popish Royall Favourite* (London, 1643), passim, for the association of popish plotting with the Queen's influence over Charles.

7. For the view that a return to ceremonialism masked a plot to reconcile England and Rome, see Henry Burton, *For God, and the King. The Summe of Two Sermons* (London, 1636) and *The Jesuites Looking Glasse* (1636), in Prynne, pp. 65ff. See also Hibbard, *Popish Royall Favourite*, ch. 3.

8. The main texts of Marian devotion are Louis Richeome, *The Pilgrime of Loreto. Performing his Vow Made to the Glorious Virgin Mary Mother of God*, trans E. W. (1629); John Brereley, *Virginalia, or Spirituall Sonnets* (1632); Henry Hawkins, *Partheneia Sacra* (1633); N. N., *Maria Triumphans* (1633); *The Devotion of Bondage* (1634); Anthony Stafford, *The Femall Glory* (1635); *The Arch-Confraternity of the Holy Rosary* (1636); *The Mistical Crowne of the most Glorious virgin Mary*, trans. R. H. (1638); and Alexis de Salo, *An Admirable Method to Love, Serve and Honour the B. Virgin Mary* (1639).

9. There is as yet no comprehensive study of the circulation of Catholic books in Charles's reign, but most scholars assert that these books were relatively freely available. See Caroline M. Hibbard, 'Early Stuart Catholicism: revisions and re-revisions', *Journal of Modern History* 52 (1980), pp. 1–34 (p. 12).

10. On de Sales in England, see White, *English Devotional Literature*, pp. 111–15, and A. F. Allison, 'Crashaw and St François de Sales', *Review of English Studies*, o.s. 24 (1948), pp. 295–302.

11. See Elizabeth Rapley, *The Dévotes: Women and Church in Seventeenth-Century France* (Montreal: McGill-Queen's University Press, 1990).

12. On Laud and Arminianism, see J. Sears McGee, 'William Laud and the outward face of religion' in Richard L. DeMolen (ed.), *Leaders of the Reformation* (London: Associated University Presses, 1984), pp. 318–44; Nicholas Tyacke, *Anti-Calvinists: The Rise of English Arminianism c. 1590–1640* (Oxford: Clarendon Press, 1987), ch. 8; Kevin Sharpe, 'Archbishop Laud and the University of Oxford', in his *Politics and Ideas in Early Stuart England* (London: Pinter Publishers, 1989), pp. 123–46; Peter Lake, 'The Laudians and the argument from authority', in Bonnelyn Young Kunze and Dwight D. Brautigam (eds), *Court, Country and Culture: Essays on Early Modern British History in Honor of Perez Zagorin* (Rochester NY:

University of Rochester Press, 1992), pp. 149–75; and the essays by Tyacke, Fincham, Lake and White in Kenneth Fincham (ed.), *The Early Stuart Church, 1603–1642* (Basingstoke: Macmillan, 1993).

13. *Calendar of State Papers: Venetian, 1626–28*, p. 218.

14. For opposition to this book see William Prynne, *A Briefe Survay and censure of Mr Cozens his Cousening Devotions* (London, 1628).

15. George Herbert, 'To All Angels and Saints', ll. 16–18, in *The Complete Poems*, ed. John Tobin (Harmondsworth: Penguin, 1991).

16. Anthony Stafford, *The Femall Glory*, ed. O. Shipley (London, 1869), p. lxxxvii. This is the only text which reprints 'A Just Apology'.

17. William Prynne, *Canterburies Doom*, in Stafford, *The Femall Glory* (1869), p. xvi.

18. See Peter Heylyn, *A Briefe and Moderate Answer to the … Challenges of Henry Burton* (London, 1637) and Christopher Dow, *Innovations Uniustly charged upon the Present Church and State* (London, 1637).

19. That is, where images are being valued as a means to an end (*dulia*) versus being adored as ends in themselves (*latria*).

20. Henry Hawkins, *Partheneia Sacra. Or the Mysterious and Delicious Garden of the Sacred Parthenes* (Rouen, 1633), sig. A4r-v.

21. On the text as an emblem book, see Rosemary Freeman, *English Emblem Books* (London: Chatto & Windus, 1948), ch. 7 and Appendix 3, pp. 243–8, and Michael Bath, *Speaking Pictures: English Emblem Books and Renaissance Culture* (Harlow: Longman, 1994), ch. 9.

22. See Patricia Parker, *Inescapable Romance: Studies in the Poetics of a Mode* (Princeton: Princeton University Press, 1979), pp. 16–31 on the sexual implications of 'erring' and 'error'.

23. Patricia Parker, *Literary Fat Ladies: Rhetoric, Gender, Property* (London: Methuen, 1987), ch. 7.

24. For discussions of the blush, see David Lee Miller, *The Poem's Two Bodies: The Poetics of the 1590 Faerie Queene* (Princeton: Princeton University Press, 1988), pp. 172–5, and Gerald Hammond, *Fleeting Things: English Poets and Poems, 1616–1660* (Cambridge, MA: Harvard University Press, 1990).

25. See Nancy Vickers, '"The blazon of sweet beauty's best": Shakespeare's *Lucrece*', in Patricia Parker and Geoffrey Hartman (eds), *Shakespeare and the Question of Theory* (London: Methuen, 1985), pp. 95–115.

26. For other examples, see Ben Jonson, 'Epistle to Katherine, Lady Aubigny', ll. 110–17, in *Ben Jonson*, ed. C. H. Herford and Evelyn Simpson (Oxford: Clarendon Press, 1947), vol. VIII; John Donne, 'On His Mistress', ll. 27–30, and 'Sapho to Philaenis', ll. 57–60, in *John Donne: The Complete English Poems*, ed. C. A. Patrides (London: Everyman, 1985), and *Much Ado About Nothing*, IV. i. 40–1 and IV. i. 159.

27. I. Sweetnam, *The Paradise of Delights. Or the B. Virgins Garden of Loreto* (1620), pp. 85–6.

28. See Burton's marginal comment, *For God, and the King*, p. 125: 'Lo here the new great Goddesse, Diana, whom the whole Pontifician world worshippeth'.

29. On the perceived connections between courtly spectacle and Catholicism, see Veevers, *Images of Love and Religion*, chs. 5 and 6, and G. F. Sensabaugh,

'Platonic love and the Puritan rebellion', *Studies in Philology* 37 (1940), pp. 457–81. On the Jesuits' use of drama see Suzanne Gossett, 'Drama in the English College, Rome, 1591–1660', *English Literary Renaissance* 3 (1973), pp. 60–93, and William H. McCabe, *An Introduction to Jesuit Theater* (St Louis: Institute of Jesuit Sources, 1983).

30. 'Platonic love', p. 477.
31. 'N. N.', *Maria Triumphans; being a discourse wherin the B. Virgin Mary is defended* (St Omer, 1635). On the authorship of this text, see Erica Veevers, 'The authorship of *Maria Triumphans*', *Notes & Queries* 34 (1987), pp. 313–14.
32. See Robin Headlam Wells, *Spenser's Faerie Queene and the Cult of Elizabeth* (London: Croom Helm, 1983), pp. 14–21; John N. King, *Tudor Royal Iconography: Literature and Art in an Age of Religious Crisis* (Princeton: Princeton University Press, 1989) and 'Queen Elizabeth I: representations of the Virgin Queen', *Renaissance Quarterly* 43 (1990), pp. 30–74. Carole Levin, 'Power, politics, and sexuality: images of Elizabeth I' in Jean R. Brink, Allison P. Condert and Maryanne C. Horowitz (eds), *The Politics of Gender in Early Modern Europe* (Sixteenth Century Essays and Studies, XII; Kirksville: Missouri, 1989), pp. 95–110.
33. See Hibbard, *Charles I*, chs. 2 and 3. For a poem which uses Marian imagery in praising Henrietta Maria, see Ben Jonson's poem, 'An Epigram to the Queen', 'Herford and Simpson', VIII. It opens, 'Haile Mary, full of grace, it once was said'. Crashaw also transposes discourses of love and religion in his poems. See Veevers, *Images of Love and Religion*, pp. 104–6.
34. *Images of Love and Religion*, p. 146.
35. Richard Broughton, *The Judgement of the Apostles* (Douai, 1632), sigs. *7r–v.
36. See Kevin Sharpe, *Criticism and Compliment: The Politics of Literature in the England of Charles I* (Cambridge: Cambridge University Press, 1987).

Playing the 'Masculine Part': Finding a Difference within Behn's Poetry

Bronwen Price

In the preface to *The Lucky Chance* the speaker makes an important and revealing request that bears upon the problem of voice and speaking positions in Behn's writing:

> All I ask, is the Priviledge for my Masculine Part the Poet in me, (if any such you will allow me) to tread in those successful Paths my Predecessors have so long thriv'd in, to take those Measures that both the Ancient and Modern Writers have set me.[1]

What is interesting about this preface is the way it draws our attention to the interface between text and context, between the speaking subject and the conditions of speech which inform what may be spoken, where, by whom and how.

At first glance it seems that clear demarcations between gender positions are drawn up. To enter into the public domain and speak as a poet means privileging a 'masculine part', while covering up and keeping private the feminine. For the speaker 'to take those Measures' of masculine privilege appears to do nothing more than reaffirm conventional gender divisions of the seventeenth century, which associated masculinity with speech and what was properly feminine with silence. Behn's literary cross-dressing merely enables her to speak like a man. It involves joining forces with 'my Brothers of the Pen' (*Works*, ed. Summers, III, p. 187), becoming one of the boys by following the 'Paths' set out by her literary forefathers.

However, in the process of affirming the 'Masculine Part ... in me', the speaker acknowledges that it is not hers to possess through the marginal comment '(if any such you will allow me)'. Her acquisition of such a role is subject to audience recognition and permission. It depends on the audience's willingness to go along with a masquerade which permits her to have a masculine part.

The admission of the performance and audience element involved in privileging a masculine part signals a point of disruption in the text, displacing the binarism between masculine and feminine which on the surface seems to be affirmed. The privileged masculine part is revealed to be not a substance, but an effect of reading, a reading which is born out of the subordination of a feminine other.[2] The preface, however, exposes the suppressed term upon which the identity of the favoured part depends by siting this other in the speaker. At the moment in which the speaker asks for her masculine part to be privileged, we are given a different view which discloses what is at stake in complying with such a request. We are required to read the speaker's words with this difference in mind.

In this essay I will examine whether and to what extent this ambivalence within speaking positions, between one voice and another, is registered within Behn's lyric poetry. The majority of Behn's poems are concerned with love and sexual desire, and frequently play out the familiar tropes of Ovidian, Petrarchan and Platonic love. Conventionally in such poetry the woman is sited as the textualized object-body of a male voice and gaze. She rarely takes the part of speaking subject.[3] In what sense, then, does Behn's use of such poetic forms mean privileging a masculine part? In what ways do her poems negotiate positions from which to speak? Do they expose a difference of view; other ways of reading love and desire?

I

Many of Behn's poems employ an ostensibly female voice. One such example is 'The Willing Mistress' in which the usually silent pastoral nymph is, it seems, given licence to respond both verbally and sexually to her lover's advances. Significantly, though, the poem also appears in another version, 'I led my Silvia to a Grove', in which the speaker is male and which takes the form of a seduction lyric.[4] Both poems present a narrative which begins with the lovers' entry into the enclosed realm of the grove and recounts the events leading up to consummation:

SONG
The Willing Mistress

Amyntas led me to a Grove,
  Where all the Trees did shade us;
The Sun it self, though it had Strove,
  It could not have betray'd us:
The place secur'd from humane Eyes,

No other fear allows,
But when the Winds that gently rise,
     Doe Kiss the yielding Boughs.

Down there we satt upon the Moss,
     And did begin to play
A Thousand Amorous Tricks, to pass
     The heat of all the day.
A many Kisses he did give:
     And I return'd the same
Which made me willing to receive
     That which I dare not name.

His Charming Eyes no Aid requir'd
     To tell their softning Tale;
On her that was already fir'd,
     'Twas Easy to prevaile.
He did but Kiss and Clasp me round,
     Whilst those his thoughts Exprest:
And lay'd me gently on the Ground;
     Ah who can guess the rest?

                         (*Works*, ed. Summers, VI, p. 163)

The uneasy relation between speech and silence is indicated by the depiction of the pastoral setting. While the grove is presented as a retreat, protected from the constraints imposed by the public domain, it is nonetheless constructed with direct reference to the codes of social decorum through which such concealment is deemed to be necessary. The grove's seclusion is underpinned by 'fear' of exposure and betrayal (ll. 4, 6). Even within this private place, sex is not mentioned overtly, but is implied within a coded polite language, loaded with a sense of the illicit as 'That which I dare not name' (l. 16). The licence and intimacy that the grove seems to provide are thus subject to a social frame which determines boundaries for the conduct and discourse of sexual desire. The nymph's words are censored by codes of propriety and decorum even as she appears to be given a voice.

However, this regulation of the terms in which sexual desire is spoken is not specific to the female voice, as it also applies to the male speaker of the original version of the poem.[5] What is more significant is the sexual politics underlying these terms. Here, too, there is a marked similarity between the two poems. While 'The Willing Mistress' seems to give voice to female sexuality and desire, these are defined only in reference to the male lover who leads and controls the proceedings. It is Amyntas who is granted agency throughout, while the nymph is located as the obedient, passive recipient of his actions, merely returning and receiving what he gives (ll. 14, 15). Although the poem presents a first-person narrative, the female 'I' is defined as the object of the proprietorial 'charming eyes' of the male lover.[6] She plays the conventional female part, in which, although speaking, she is spoken for, as it is he who is perceived as being author and possessor of her sexuality.

In the final stanza the first-person subject is indeed severed from itself, alluded to as 'her': it is now fully absorbed into a male narrative (l. 18), where entry into the grove signals entry into and enjoyment of an open, available and receptive female body.[7] Moreover, while the grove is presented as being 'secur'd from humane Eyes' (l. 5), the poem invites the reader to view illicitly these private parts and enter into a male voyeuristic fantasy, in which we are required to fill in the gaps of the nymph's half-spoken utterances.

The nymph's lips are thus opened only to be closed. Her reading of Amyntas's 'Tale' indicates her seduction by it. It is the masculine part which is privileged, for her voice is penetrated by the underlying narrative which informs both versions of the poem and sets the terms in which her sexuality may be expressed. The poem's final question seems to point us to an irresistible reply, which observes the compliant responses of the receptive nymph. Yes, we can guess the rest, for the question directs us towards a familiar story of male sexual fantasy which we are asked voyeuristically to follow.[8]

Or are we? While it seems that the narrative leads towards an inevitable conclusion, the final question remains unanswered. The story is incomplete and thus opens up the possibility of another reply, a different ending.

II

'The Disappointment' takes us a stage beyond the sexual encounter of 'The Willing Mistress' signalling one possible different ending from that which we may assume follows 'the rest' of the latter poem. Like 'The Willing Mistress', 'The Disappointment' takes the form of a narrative, but this time the speaker is a third party, voyeuristically looking on at the sexual exchange between 'the Amorous *Lysander*' and 'fair *Cloris*':

The Disappointment

I

One day the Amorous Lysander,
By an impatient Passion sway'd,

Surpriz'd fair Cloris, that lov'd Maid,
Who could defend her self no longer.
All things did with his Love conspire;
That gilded Planet of the Day,
In his gay Chariot drawn by Fire,
Was now descending to the Sea,
And left no Light to guide the World,
But what from *Cloris* Brighter Eyes was hurld.

II

In a lone Thicket made for Love,
Silent as yielding Maids Consent,
She with a Charming Languishment,
Permits his Force, yet gently strove;
Her Hands his Bosom softly meet,
But not to put him back design'd,
Rather to draw 'em on inclin'd:
Whilst he lay trembling at her Feet,
Resistance 'tis in vain to show;
She wants the pow'r to say – *Ah! What d'ye do?*

III

Her Bright Eyes sweet, and yet severe,
Where Love and Shame confus'dly strive,
Fresh Vigor to *Lysander* give;
And breathing faintly in his Ear,
She cry'd – *Cease, Cease – your vain Desire,*
Or I'll call out – What would you do?
My Dearer Honour ev'n to You
I cannot, must not give – Retire,
Or take this Life, whose chiefest part
I gave you with the Conquest of my Heart.

IV

But he as much unus'd to Fear,
As he was capable of Love,
The blessed minutes to improve,
Kisses her Mouth, her Neck, her Hair;
Each Touch her new Desire Alarms,
His burning trembling Hand he prest
Upon her swelling Snowy Brest,
While she lay panting in his Arms.
All her Unguarded Beauties lie
The Spoils and Trophies of the Enemy.

V

And now without Respect or Fear,
He seeks the Object of his Vows,
(His Love no Modesty allows)
By swift degrees advancing – where
His daring Hand that Altar seiz'd,
Where Gods of Love do sacrifice.
That Awful Throne, that Paradice
Where Rage is calm'd, and Anger pleas'd,
That Fountain where Delight still flows,
And gives the Universal World Repose.

VI

Her Balmy Lips incountring his,
Their Bodies, as their Souls, are joyn'd;
Where both in Transports Unconfin'd
Extend themselves upon the Moss.
Cloris half dead and breathless lay;
Her soft Eyes cast a Humid Light,
Such as divides the Day and Night;
Or falling Stars, whose Fires decay:
And now no signs of Life she shows,
But what in short-breath'd Sighs returns & goes.

VII

He saw how at her Length she lay,
He saw her rising Bosom bare;
Her loose thin Robes, through which appear
A Shape design'd for Love and Play;
Abandon'd by her Pride and Shame,
She does her softest Joys dispence,
Off'ring her Virgin-Innocence
A Victim to Loves Sacred Flame;
While the o'er-Ravish'd Shepherd lies
Unable to perform the Sacrifice.

VIII

Ready to taste a thousand Joys,
The too transported hapless Swain
Found the vast Pleasure turn'd to Pain;
Pleasure which too much Love destroys:
The willing Garments by he laid,
And Heaven all open'd to his view,
Mad to possess, himself he threw

On the Defenceless Lovely Maid.
But Oh what envying God[s conspire]
To snatch his Power, yet leave him the Desire!

IX

Nature's Support, (without whose Aid
She can no Humane Being give)
It self now wants the Art to live;
Faintness its slack'ned Nerves invade:
In vain th'inraged Youth essay'd
To call its fleeting Vigor back,
No motion 'twill from Motion take;
Excess of Love his Love betray'd:
In vain he Toils, in vain Commands;
The Insensible fell weeping in his Hand.

X

In this so Amorous Cruel Strife,
Where Love and Fate were too severe,
The poor *Lysander* in despair
Renounc'd his Reason with his Life:
Now all the brisk and active Fire
That should the Nobler Part inflame,
Serv'd to increase his Rage and Shame,
And left no Spark for New Desire:
Not all her Naked Charms cou'd move
Or calm that Rage that had debauch'd his Love.

XI

Cloris returning from the Trance
Which Love and soft Desire had bred,
Her timerous Hand she gently laid
(Or guided by Design or Chance)
Upon that Fabulous *Priapas*,
That Potent God, as Poets feign;
But never did young *Shepherdess*,
Gath'ring of Fern upon the Plain,
More nimbly draw her Fingers back,
Finding beneath the verdant Leaves a snake:

XII

Than *Cloris* her fair Hand withdrew,
Finding that God of her Desires
Disarm'd of all his Awful Fires,

And Cold as Flow'rs bath'd in the Morning-Dew.
Who can the *Nymph*'s Confusion guess?
The Blood forsook the hinder Place,
And strew'd with Blushes all her Face,
Which both Disdain and Shame exprest:
And from Lysander's Arms she fled,
Leaving him fainting on the Gloomy Bed.

XIII
Like Lightning through the Grove she hies,
Or *Daphne* from the *Delphick God*,
No Print upon the grassey Road
She leaves, t'instruct pursuing Eyes.
The Wind that wanton'd in her Hair,
And with her Ruffled Garments plaid,
Discover'd in the Flying Maid
All that the Gods e'er made, [o]f Fair.
So Venus, when her Love was slain,
With Fear and Haste flew o'er the Fatal Plain.

XIV
The *Nymph*'s Resentments none but I
Can well Imagine or Condole:
But none can guess *Lysander*'s Soul,
But those who sway'd his Destiny.
His silent Griefs swell up to Storms,
And not one God his Fury spares;
He curs'd his Birth, his Fate, his Stars;
But more the *Shepherdess*'s Charms,
Whose soft bewitching Influence
Had Damn'd him to the Hell of Impotence.

(Works, ed. Todd, I, pp. 65–9)

On the surface the poem seems to present the pastoral figures in conventional subject positions, drawing on standard conceits of seventeenth-century sexual love poetry. Cloris is depicted as a site of military conquest, the virginal territory into which Lysander drives, to become the sacrificial 'Victim' of his 'Vigor', the booty of his plunder where she is forced to surrender herself as 'The Spoils and Trophies of the Enemy' (ll. 68, 23, 40). She is merely the vehicle through which Lysander's virility may be displayed and affirmed. He demonstrates that he is 'unus'd to Fear', for Cloris's apparent attempt to repulse him 'Fresh Vigor to Lysander give[s]', so that ultimately 'Resistance 'tis in vain to show' and she 'could defend her self no longer' (ll. 31, 23, 19, 4).

As in 'The Willing Mistress' the nymph's sexuality, it seems, is created and defined through the rule of the masculine part. Her apparent lack of resources to withstand Lysander's authority over and authorship of her sexual identity is manifested in her voicelessness, which is presented as signifying the submission of a 'yielding Maids consent' (l. 12). Even when Cloris does speak she is barely audible and her words have no effect (ll. 24–30). Her assertion of 'I' is intruded upon and broken up by Lysander's more forceful utterance of his desire and recalls her previous submission to him which demands a negation of 'I' (ll. 29–30).

However, the poem plays with these familiar tropes and lets slip the conventional roles of the lovers, which are unsettled by the troublesome desires that underlie them. The poem's bathetic humour is furnished by an ambivalence of meaning which disturbs the terms of the pastoral fiction. Cloris's request for Lysander to '*take this Life*' rather than to relinquish '*My Dearest Honour*' (ll. 29, 27), seems simultaneously to express a desire for sexual death, as she acknowledges that he has already conquered and possesses the '*chiefest part*' of her life, '*my Heart*' (ll. 29–30). This call for death prefigures the nymph's 'half dead and breathless' state in which 'no signs of Life she shows' after her 'transports Unconfin'd' (ll. 55, 59, 53). Indeed, from the outset she has displayed 'a Charming Languishment' (l. 13), suggesting her already aroused state beneath the mask of feminine modesty. Similarly, 'her swelling Snowy Brest' (l. 37) provides an ambiguous image of purity and sexual excitement.

Cloris's entry into the sexual exchange may therefore denote not so much submission to Lysander's vigorous desires as an articulation of her sexuality. While acting the part of coy nymph, she appears also to be an active participant in the encounter, bent on arousing and exciting Lysander (ll. 13–17). She invites Lysander to view her as a sexual object, 'A Shape design'd for Love and Play' (l. 64) which he must overcome and through which he may affirm his prowess, as these, it seems, are the only terms available in which her sexuality may be expressed. The nymph thus appears to follow the rules of the traditional sexual game within which she simultaneously plays another, opening her lips at the same time as she appears to close them. Ultimately, though, Cloris cannot accommodate this incongruity, 'Her Balmy Lips' at last encountering Lysander's (l. 51). This slippage between one role and another is suggested by the marginal light cast by her eyes after orgasm (ll. 56–7). Her initially apparently guarded body breaks out of its confinement to resemble the licence of the male lover's figure when they both 'Extend themselves upon the Moss' (l. 54).

Lysander is represented in a similarly ambivalent way. The conventional Petrarchan pose of deference towards the 'lov'd Maid' (l. 3) is dismantled by the excesses of his desire. When lying 'trembling at' Cloris's 'Feet' (l. 18), Lysander displays not so much reverence for her, as sexual excitement. Although it is initially Cloris's eyes whose 'Light' is 'Brighter' than 'That gilded Planet of the Day' (ll. 6–10) which envelop Lysander's vision, he swiftly passes through each part of her body (ll. 34–8) to reach the central 'Object of his Vows', which is sacrilegiously 'seiz'd' even as it is exalted (stanza V). This bold icono-clastic gesture marks the displacement of the increasingly Petrarchan stance by the apparently more forceful Ovidian one of intrepid male sexual potency and conquest, when Lysander's 'daring Hand' reaches for the sacred desired object 'without Respect or Fear' (ll. 45, 41).

However, the pose of virile captor has already been unsettled by the ambivalence of Cloris's performance, for the fiction of the nymph's passivity and submission questions the extent of Lysander's power and control. This 'misplacement' of roles signals displacement when, at the crucial moment in the fray, Lysander finds himself 'Unable to perform the Sacrifice' (l. 70). The penis deviates from its 'proper' place, appear-ing as a separate 'self' (l. 83), a rebellious subject, possessing a life, and so death, of its own, as it first seems to lead the proceedings and then refuses to stand to the attention of its owner.[9] Power is quite literally out of Lysander's hands (ll. 89–90). The poem inverts the Ovidian conceit in which the deftness and efficiency of the phallic sword under-lies sexual conquest. Here, this manly weapon becomes the object of attack when 'Faintness its slack'ned Nerves invade' (l. 84).[10] The swain is indeed 'betray'd' (l. 88) by his penis as the masculine part turns against the whole. The climactic aggrandisement of the phallus – 'the Nobler Part', *Nature's Support*' (ll. 96, 81), animating what passively lies waiting to be created – works up to a big come-down, as it is shown to be unfit for its task and is thus transformed from a source of pleasure to pain, from strength to weakness, from potency to humiliation, as 'Heaven' is turned into '*Hell*' (ll. 76, 140).

'The Disappointment' thus seems to offer another tale from that implied by 'the rest' of 'The Willing Mistress'. Its voyeurism plays with the masculine part only to refuse to oblige it. 'That Fabulous *Priapas*' is disclosed to be something which 'Poets feign' (ll. 105–6). The hyper-bolic fiction of 'That Potent God' emerges in a debased text where it is shown as being 'Disarm'd of all his Awful Fires' (ll. 106, 113). Having uncovered a different reading of male sexuality, the nymph flees dishevelled from the grove, disrupting the boundaries of pastoral mythology.

However, in spite of its apparent disintegration, the rule of the phallus still resides veiled within the text. Sex is defined with reference to phallic performance or non-performance and is identified as satis-factory only in terms of penetration and male orgasm. While it appears that the nymph achieves orgasm, the separation between the lovers' parts is presented as a deficiency. When Cloris discovers the protagonist member to be limp and inert, she identifies it as a 'snake' (l. 110), a dangerous poison in the Edenic grove. Ultimately, though, it seems that the masculine part reaffirms itself when the nymph's 'bewitching Influence' is blamed for Lysander's fall so that she is made the guilty party (ll. 139–40). It is Lysander's reading of events which is apparently given the last word in the story, as he transfers his sense of shame and lack onto her. As with 'The Willing Mistress', female sexuality is apparently given voice only to be closed within an alternative patriarchal myth.

However, the narrative we have been offered does not so readily follow a direction which leads to the swain's version of events. As the nymph flees from the place of seduction, so the voyeur speaker enters the text in the first person for the first time to provide another reading of the story, one which identifies itself not with Lysander, but with Cloris (l. 131). What is significant here is not simply, as Todd suggests, that the poem apparently concludes by 'sympathising with the woman' (*Works*, ed. Todd, p. 393), but that 'The Disappointment' points to the existence of another narrative which infects the swain's, for the voice of the speaker opens up the seeming closure of the swain's story to give an ironic difference of view.[11]

III

'To *Lysander*, on some Verses he writ, and asking more for his Heart then 'twas worth' takes us out of the private elysium of Behn's pastoral fiction and into the urban domain of the marketplace. The speaker and her lover conduct a private transaction, in which the speaker responds to the bargaining conditions set out in Lysander's verses. Here, the female reply is not compliant with or receptive to her inscription within the masculine narrative, but instead revises the terms into which she has been written:

> *To* Lysander, *on some Verses he writ,*
> *and asking more for his Heart then 'twas worth*

> I
> Take back that Heart, you with such Caution give,
>   Take the fond valu'd Trifle back;
> I hate Love-Merchants that a Trade wou'd drive;
>   And meanly cunning Bargains make.

II

I care not how the busy Market goes,
   And scorn to Chaffer for a price:
Love does one Staple Rate on all impose,
   Nor leaves it to the Traders Choice.

III

A Heart requires a Heart Unfeign'd and True,
   Though Subt'ly you advance the Price,
And ask a Rate that Simple Love ne'er knew:
   And the free Trade Monopolize.

IV

An Humble *Slave* the Buyer must become,
   She must not bate a Look or Glance,
You will have all, or you'll have none;
   See how Loves Market you inhaunce.

V

Is't not enough, I gave you Heart for Heart,
   But I must add my Lips and Eies;
I must no friendly Smile or Kiss impart;
   But you must Dun me with Advice.

VI

And every Hour still more unjust you grow,
   Those Freedoms you my life deny,
You to *Adraste* are oblig'd to show,
   And give her all my Rifled Joy.

VII

Without Controul she gazes on that Face,
   And all the happy Envyed Night,
In the pleas'd Circle of your fond imbrace:
   She takes away the Lovers Right.

VIII

From me she Ravishes those silent hours,
   That are by Sacred Love my due;
Whilst *I* in vain accuse the angry Powers,
   That make me hopeless Love pursue.

IX

Adrastes Ears with that dear Voice are blest,
   That Charms my Soul at every Sound,

And with those *Love-Inchanting* Touches prest:
  Which *I* ne'er felt without a Wound.

        X
She has thee all: whilst *I* with silent Greif,
  The Fragments of thy Softness feel,
Yet dare not blame the happy licenc'd Thief:
  That does my Dear-bought Pleasures steal.

        XI
Whilst like a Glimering Taper still *I* burn,
  And waste my self in my own flame,
Adraste takes the welcome rich Return:
  And leaves me all the hopeless Pain.

        XII
Be just, my lovely *Swain*, and do not take
  Freedoms you'll not to me allow;
Or give Amynta so much Freedom back:
  That she may Rove as well as you.

        XIII
Let us then love upon the honest Square,
  Since Interest neither have design'd,
For the sly Gamester, who ne'er plays me fair,
  Must Trick for Trick expect to find.

                    (*Works*, ed. Todd, I, pp. 92–3)

In the opening stanzas the speaker undoes the bargaining terms within which Lysander's verses transact. This economy, the speaker shows, inscribes her as currency with which he may 'drive' and 'Monopolize' a 'Trade' (ll. 3, 12), 'Chaffer' and 'advance the Price' by imposing on her his own 'Rate' (ll. 6, 10–11). Within such a transaction she would be excluded from negotiations, and merely operate as a speculative mirror of male power, 'An Humble Slave', subject to his 'Subt'ly' and 'meanly' driven 'cunning Bargains' (ll. 13, 10, 4), as that which he 'will have', whether it be 'all' or 'none' (l. 15). While the speaker would thus be transfixed as the private property of Lysander's estate, Lysander would be enabled to circulate his revenue and have shares in more than one investment, so as to accumulate a number of seductions / properties. For him the market is open. He possesses an unrestricted exchequer, the carte-blanche.[12]

However, the speaker refuses 'to go to market'[13] and to be the site / sight of Lysander's speculation, but answers back, opening up new terms which dislodge the privilege of the masculine part. She proposes a different exchange mechanism from his in which love is aligned with honesty and egality, 'one Staple Rate' (l. 7). She demands a fair deal – equal quantities of give and take, where she is afforded as much freedom as Lysander, so that they are 'Heart for Heart' (l. 17).

This apparent attempt to establish a sense of proportion, though, points to disproportion, for in requesting 'Freedoms you my life deny' (l. 22), the speaker ironically invests Lysander with the power to set the terms in which such civil liberties are granted. Inevitably, then, he must receive more than his fair share, for the speaker's humanist sense of justice and equality fits neatly within the same economy as Lysander's capitalist self-interest. The speaker's appeals for her 'Lovers Right' and property entitlements of 'my due', 'my Dear-bought Pleasures' (ll. 28, 30, 40), merely locate her as Lysander's small change which can only beg to be his major source of interest.

This sense of '(dis)proportion' [14] is highlighted by the shift in the poem's initial position with the introduction of a third party, Adraste, the other woman who apparently commands Lysander's attention at stanza VI. The effect of Lysander's business dealings is to produce a black economy, onto which blame may be transferred, as woman is set against woman. It is Adraste who is presented as illicitly appropriating the speaker's pleasure as the 'happy licenc'd Thief' of 'all my Rifled Joy' (ll. 39, 24). It is this silent 'she' who 'Ravishes' what is 'my due' and 'takes the welcome rich Return: / And leaves me all the hopeless Pain' (ll. 29–30, 43–4).

While the first-person subject attempts to assert her claims against this 'she', however, both parties are identified in reference to the masculine part, Lysander, to whom each is an object of exchange. Their struggle to compete in the market-place is underpinned by the primacy of this pervasive phallic signifier which holds them apart and sets a price on them as the indispensable key term of all commerce. The women, it seems, possess nothing of worth within themselves, but adopt significance and value only with regard to the authorizations of the male consumer.[15] Having initially dismantled the frame of Lysander's transactions, the voice of the poem now seems to inscribe itself within the terms of his economy. No longer is the poem one of rejection, but rather Lysander becomes 'that dear Voice' which 'Charms my Soul at every Sound' (ll. 33–4). It is Lysander's language which penetrates negotiations and whose withdrawal of interest apparently results in the speaker's self-negation (stanza XI). Without consumer demand, she consumes herself (ll. 41–2).

The end of the poem, however, presents a further shift of conditions which seems to destabilize the central part of the text. The speaker's statement of her name (l. 47) signals a redefinition of her position which inaugurates a renegotiation of the terms of exchange. No longer is she a self-consuming object of Lysander's denial, but demands as much freedom as him, 'That she may Rove as well as you' (l. 48). The transference from 'I' to 'she' signifies a dislocation of subject position which raises the possibility of the speaker's placing herself outside Lysander's speculations.

However, this new point of departure involves merely returning full circle to the place where the poem began, when the speaker requests that she and Lysander 'love upon the honest Square' (l. 49). This circling round of the argument, though, throws off balance the proportions of this square, signalling the (dis)proportionate interests which inform the entire poem, where in each case the masculine part is privileged and the woman cheated. This mismatching of positions is suggested by the uncomfortable juxtaposition between the call for fair play and the speaker's threat to answer Lysander 'Trick for Trick' in the final lines. This slippage from fair dealing to double dealing indeed implies the underlying condition of transactions, in which the woman's 'Freedom' entails merely playing the man at his own game rather than offering a different course of action.

The revisions the poem offers to Lysander's verse therefore remain a problem, indicating the precarious position of the female speaking subject. Her attempt to shift and manoeuvre the frame of Lysander's dealings signals the tricksiness of the masculine part, its ability to penetrate each position the female voice attempts to occupy. In all of its turns the speaking subject becomes entangled in Lysander's text, responding only to the terms it has already laid out, pulling in different rhetorical directions only to hold in place the central signifier of the phallus.

If 'To *Lysander*' challenges the privilege of the masculine part only to reinstall it, the reply 'To *Alexis*, On his saying, I lov'd a Man that talk'd much' would appear to go even less far. The speaker seems submissively to accept the position into which the male voice has placed her, apparently repeating and reaffirming her inscription within his text:

To Alexis, *On his saying, I lov'd a Man that talk'd much*

> *Alexis*, since you'l have it so
>   I grant I am impertinent.
> And till this moment did not know
>   Thro all my life what 'twas I ment;
> Your kind opinion was th'unflattering Glass,
> In which my mind found how deform'd it was.
>
> In your clear sense which knows no art,
>   I saw the error of my Soul;

And all the feebless of my heart,
  With one reflection you controul,
Kind as a God, and gently you chastise,
By what you hate, you teach me to be wise.

Impertinence, my sexes shame,
  (Which has so long my life persu'd,)
You with such modesty reclaim
  As all the Woman has subdu'd.
To so divine a power what must I owe,
That renders me so like the perfect – you?

That conversable thing I hate
  Already with a just disdain,
Who Prid[e]s himself upon his prate
  And is of word, (that Nonsense,) vain;
When in your few appears such excellence,
They have reproacht, and charm'd me into sense.

For ever may I listning sit,
  Tho but each hour a word be born:
I wou'd attend the coming wit,
  And bless what can so well inform:
Let the dull World henceforth to words be damn'd,
I'm into nobler sense than talking sham'd.
                    (*Works*, ed. Todd, I, pp. 273–4)

Whereas 'To *Lysander*' attempts to negotiate new terms with the male lover, this poem presents itself as a mark of the debt the female speaker owes to Alexis. He has disclosed to her the error of loving 'a Man that talk'd much'. The excesses of her lover, however, become a sign of her own deficiencies. 'That conversable thing' (l. 19) mirrors her own 'Impertinence' (ll. 2, 13): his improprieties are transferred to her.

Alexis, meanwhile, is located as the source of meaning and truth. Hanging on his every word, the poem's very articulation is validated by his 'opinion' (l. 5), the speaker apparently surrendering herself to the penetration of Alexis's stronger, firmer judgment. It is his 'clear sense' (l. 7) which forms the parameters and conditions for understanding, and he who grants the speaker wisdom (l. 12), before which she 'did not know / Thro all my life what 'twas I ment' (ll. 3–4). Alexis conducts her out of this dark state of ignorance and confusion and leads her towards a state of self-revelation. Indeed, in order to achieve self-understanding the speaker has to open herself up to the examination and scrutiny of Alexis's superior insight. To know herself is to be known.

If the speaker's acquisition of 'knowledge' is a mark of submission, it is also apparently one of salvation. The speaker's discourse becomes devotional when Alexis is afforded Christ-like qualities, as 'the perfect', possessing 'so divine a power' and offering moral truth (ll. 18, 17), guiding the speaker from her lost and blind condition to one where she 'found' and 'saw the error of my Soul; / And all the feebless of my heart' (ll. 6, 8–9). Through his 'clear sense' (l. 7) the speaker sees the light. His word, it seems, is gospel, revealing 'my sexes shame' (l. 13). Conversion to Alexis's 'nobler sense' (l. 30), however, provides redemption, through which she takes up her place in his language of silent attentive listener (stanza 5).

The speaker's self-recognition is thus inaugurated by her apparent acceptance of Alexis as her author, and her inscription within the boundaries of his knowledge, where her former 'Impertinence' is now regarded as lying outside the realm of proper meaning (stanza 1). In seeing herself as 'I am' (l. 2), she submits to the 'controul' of his 'reflection' (l. 10), experiencing herself as his negative image, where he is 'th'unflattering Glass, / In which my mind found how deform'd it was (ll. 5–6). She is the supplement through which Alexis's identity is affirmed. The site / sight of her nonsensical conduct provides a mirror for Alexis's 'clear sense'.[16] Indeed, it is Alexis's 'clear sense' which provides, it seems, a sense of proportion, the moderation of his words ironically reflecting the 'modesty' (l. 15) which should belong to, but which has been exceeded by, the speaker.

It is, however, this disruption of a sense of proportion which points to another reading of the poem. Lodged within the speaker's seeming deference to Alexis is a difference of view. While apparently learning to be silent (stanza 5), so she speaks. Although she seems to mouth his words, the speaker's mimicry of Alexis's 'kind opinion' eludes the frame of his 'clear sense', appearing excessive and parodic. His part lacks substance. The dash and question mark which follow the speaker's contemplation of her new self-image (l. 18) signal a blind spot in the text. Does her newly formed likeness to 'the perfect' reflect Alexis, or is she opening this up to question? This ambivalence is underlined by the ambiguity of the poem's final word: is the speaker shamed into silence or is this a sham? The poem seems here to let slip an other, loudly silent, ironic third voice which creates a gap in the text's explicit meaning. It produces double vision, an excess sense, which unsettles the masculine part.

Ironically, then, where 'To *Lysander*'s challenge to the male speaker apparently points to the woman's containment within his terms, the seeming compliance of the female voice in 'To *Alexis*' signals another way of talking. Mimicry of the male voice indicates the displacement of the masculine part, the seeming recognition of its proportions drawing attention to the speaker's disproportionate mode of expression. Her repetition of Alexis's words paradoxically does not provide a straight answer, but unsettles meaning to suggest a way of disentangling her voice from the masculine part. The speaker's acquiescence bends towards transgression, her propriety towards excess, silence towards speech, to let slip 'impertinent' meanings, even as they seem to be censored.

IV

'To the fair *Clarinda*, who made Love to me, imagin'd more than Woman' offers a different tale from that of the above poems. Here, the masculine part is withdrawn, it seems, as the speaker attempts to voice her love for another 'woman'. However, such a task seems to arouse a new set of questions about speaking other than those we have encountered so far in Behn's poetry. In what terms can the speaker express her love? What indeed does it mean to be a woman? What is female sexuality?

To the fair Clarinda, *who made Love to me,*
imagin'd more than Woman

Fair lovely Maid, or if that Title be
Too weak, too Feminine for Nobler thee,
Permit a Name that more Approaches Truth:
And let me call thee, Lovely Charming Youth.
This last will justifie my soft complaint,
While that may serve to lessen my contraint;
And without Blushes I the Youth persue,
When so much beauteous Woman is in view,
Against thy Charms we struggle but in vain
With thy deluding Form thou giv'st us pain,
While the bright Nymph betrays us to the Swain.
In pity to our Sex sure thou wer't sent,
That we might Love, and yet be Innocent:
For sure no Crime with thee we can commit;
Or if we shou'd – thy Form excuses it.
For who, that gathers fairest Flowers believes
A Snake lies hid beneath the Fragrant Leaves.

Thou beauteous Wonder of a different kind,
Soft *Cloris* with the dear Alexis join'd;
When e'r the Manly part of thee, wou'd plead

Thou tempts us with the Image of the Maid,
While we the noblest Passions do extend
The Love to *Hermes*, *Aphrodite* the Friend.

(*Works*, ed. Todd, I, p. 288)

The title itself raises a number of questions, for what is meant by 'imagin'd more than Woman'? Does it mean that the speaker cannot conceive of being 'made Love to' by a woman without imagining that she is more than a woman? What, then, constitutes 'Woman'? Is 'she', for example, the 'nothing' which we find in so much seventeenth-century sexual love poetry? In which case, what does 'more than' comprise – something of man? For Clarinda to be 'more than Woman', though, 'she' must be 'imagin'd' to be so. 'She' must be turned into something other than 'her' self. The title, indeed, requires the reader to puzzle over these various possible gender constructions, while at the same time not allowing us to settle on any one, for 'more than' refuses to supply a stable meaning.

The ambivalences provided by the title are taken up in the opening of the poem in which the speaker attempts to find an appropriate mode of address for Clarinda. She begins by identifying this 'more than Woman' in conventional pastoral terms, as 'Fair lovely Maid' (l. 1). However, the closure in which 'that Title' (l. 1) inscribes Clarinda is immediately qualified and unsettled as 'Too weak, too Feminine for Nobler thee' (l. 2). The speaker thus seems both to affirm and trouble the gender categorization invested in this act of naming, where the apparently complimentary address comprises a specific positioning of the 'Feminine' as passive and impotent.

But as the speaker displaces 'that Title', so she renames Clarinda with one which 'more Approaches Truth: / And let me call thee, Lovely Charming Youth' (ll. 3–4). The 'Lovely' is retained, while the conventional 'Feminine' subject-position implied in 'Maid' is lost. Instead, Clarinda is given a masculine part. Yet 'Youth' does not quite qualify her to be a 'man'. But then again, where is the 'Woman' in 'Youth'? The readjusted title thus points to an irony, for the attempt to identify Clarinda accurately by naming 'her' destabilizes the question of gender. The phrase 'more Approaches Truth', indeed, recalls the ambivalence of 'more than Woman', pinpointing the gap between signifier and signified. Ironically, the act of naming suggests the uncertainty and inappropriateness of the terms of classification. The shift of title implies the fiction inscribed within each address and the impossibility of defining and enclosing Clarinda within fixed bounds of sexual identification.

The irony which arises in the problem of naming Clarinda at the same time calls into question the speaker's subject-position. Who is

the first-person subject who addresses Clarinda? At one level the 'I'
who names and identifies seems to mimic the subject-position of a
speculative phallic eye. And yet, this 'I' draws our attention to a
difference of view, for 'it' signals its inability to site/sight Clarinda.
'Its' classifications point always to a deferral of meaning, a double take,
as 'it' finds the nymph in the swain, the swain in the nymph. Both 'in
view' (l. 8) and out of sight, Clarinda presents a 'deluding Form' (l. 10)
to the speaker, one which eludes representation. This incapacity to
penetrate Clarinda pinpoints the ambivalence of the speaker's own
subject-position as 'she' both replicates and displaces the phallic I/eye.
In assuming this dislocated 'I' which sites/sights and yet does not
site/sight, the speaker displaces the conventional siting/sighting of
the part she takes up, the passive, silent, coy female lover who is the
object of male speculation. She unfixes 'her' inscription within the
pastoral fiction of blushing maid (l. 7), shifting 'her' position in accord-
ance with the difference of her 'view' (ll. 5–6).'Her' I/eye indeed
merges into the plural 'we' (ll. 9ff.), which sees double.

The speaker's double-visioned, non-penetrative I/we, however, po-
sition(s) itself/themselves to some extent with regard to the proportions
of a masculine part. 'She' names Clarinda within the terms of a binary
logic, a fiction of sexual opposition, comprising either nymph or swain.
Clarinda performs an appropriate gender role and is given the 'proper
name', '*Cloris*' or '*Alexis*' to provide the speaker with an approved female
sexual identity in each case. The speaker may 'Love' the swain, for it
is implied that women may love only men sexually, and yet apparently
remain 'Innocent' (l. 13) and 'commit' 'no Crime' (l. 14) if Clarinda
plays the part of nymph. The speaker therefore seems to define her
relationship with Clarinda in reference to official codes of sexual
propriety, demarcating conventional gender positions to signify the
boundaries between what is licit and illicit.

And yet there is an irony in the speaker's regard for such proprieties,
for as they are observed, so they are problematized. The proprietorial
bounds of chastity are worried by the articulation of female desire.
Clarinda's and the speaker's love may be perceived as permissible in
that it is visibly 'Innocent'. There is nothing to be seen which opposes
propriety. Sexual arousal does not make itself manifest. There is no
penetration. The speaker's assertion that they can thus 'commit' 'no
Crime', however, is unsettled as she shifts position. An element of uncertainty arises with 'Or if we shou'd – ' (l. 15), which is then readjusted
to confirm their apparent decorum, ' – thy Form excuses it' (l. 15). But
in between the point of doubt and the re-siting/sighting of the relationship lies a gap '–' which arrests and troubles the site/sight of 'thy Form'.

This gap widens in the following lines in which the text questions
further what can and cannot be seen. Could female sexual propriety

and innocence – 'fairest', 'Fragrant' 'Flowers (ll. 16–17) – contain a snake (l. 17)? – a latent transgression, a deviation from what constitutes pure 'woman'? Does the snake signify a masculine part (as it does in 'The Disappointment'), and if so, is it possible that a masculine part could be invisible – there and not there – something and nothing? The rhetorical question opens up such a possibility, while at the same time displaying an ironic incredulity, which blurs and unfixes the siting/ sighting of sexual difference, propriety and transgression. The allusion to the hidden snake calls into play the wholeness of 'thy Form', which manifestly excuses any criminal implication in the relationship, and recalls 'thy deluding Form', which de-forms form, for it is outside the realm of 'proper' meaning. Through the fragrant leaves of the flowers seeps an unidentifiable scent of an other sexuality which is unpenetrable and unsiteable / unsightable.

The rhetorical question is indeed left open, followed by a stanza break. The poem concludes, however, with further attempts to identify Clarinda's sexuality. The speaker seems to reaffirm sexual difference as Clarinda is presented as incorporating 'Manly' and womanly parts (ll. 20–1), which are classified as distinct, while also apparently being linked in the mythical figures of Hermes and Aphrodite. But the absence which precedes this conclusion troubles this neat closed fiction of oppositional equilibrium, for it creates an asymmetrical hole in the poem which de-forms such proportion. Instead, it points to a 'Wonder of a different kind' (l. 18), an identification which can only defer what is signified, so as to displace and make ambivalent the enclosed polar-ized classification of the conclusion.

In Behn's poetry it therefore seems that female sexuality and desire emerge to offer a reply to the conventional tropes of seventeenth-century sexual love poetry. At first glance, the poems appear to restate old fictions, to reaffirm the masculine part against a female speaking subject as the latent central term of reference. And yet, at the same time, many of the poems provide a difference of view, a point of resistance, which looks beyond these visibly limited bounds to cast a blind spot over what is sited. In between the gaps of the surface text lurks an other subterranean voice, which presents an ironic plural view, throwing off balance the clear sense of what is written by providing a silent excess meaning. We are required to take another look at the poems – to have double vision – which points beyond the edge of what is sited to other possibilities.

Notes

1. Aphra Behn, *The Works*, ed. Montague Summers (New York: Phaeton Press, 1915), III, p. 187.

2. As has been noted by Catherine Gallagher in *Nobody's Story: The Vanishing Acts of Women Writers in the Marketplace, 1670–1820* (Oxford: Clarendon Press, 1994), elsewhere in Behn's work the figure of the prostitute is exploited to represent the role of the female writer (pp. 1–48).

3. Alistair Fowler (ed.), *The New Oxford Book of Seventeenth-Century Verse* (Oxford: Oxford University Press, 1992), quite rightly notes that in the Restoration verse the beloved emerges 'from being the mute subject of rhetoric' to become 'an active adversary in debates of love' (p. xli). Indeed, earlier poetry also sometimes allows the woman a voice. Nonetheless, this is still more the exception than the rule. Moreover, the use of a female voice does not guarantee a non-masculinist view.

4. See Aphra Behn, *The Works*, ed. Janet Todd (London: Pickering, 1992), I, p. 6. According to Sara Heller Mendelson in *The Mental World of Stuart Women: Three Studies* (Brighton: Harvester, 1987), 'The Willing Mistress' was transformed from 'I led my Silvia' (p. 139). Todd suggests that the latter version was first printed in *The Covent Garden Drollery* (1672) and *The Dutch Lover* (1673), appearing in the form of 'The Willing Mistress' in 1684 (*Works*, ed. Todd, I, pp. 375, 461).

5. Todd notes that at the end of the original version is added 'As Amorous as these Verses may be thought, they have been reduc'd to bring them within the Rules of Decency, which all Writers ought to observe, or instead of a Diversion they will become a Nuisance' (*Works*, ed. Todd, I, p. 375).

6. In the original version the male lover's eyes are 'greedy' (*Works*, ed. Todd, I, p. 6, l. 17).

7. In both versions of the poem the 'Tale' (l. 18) belongs to the swain, although in the original version it is 'amorous' rather than 'softning' (*Works*, ed. Todd, I, p. 6).

8. Elaine Hobby, *Virtue of Necessity: English Women's Writing 1649–88* (London: Virago, 1988), suggests that Behn's poetry 'repeatedly declares and enlarges upon the joys of sensuality in a world where men take the initiative and women yield gladly', a view which when connected to 'the idea that women are secretly lustful ... is quite consistent with the dominant ideology of the day' (p. 153). Whether Behn 'could only perceive and write about sexual desire in her poetry within this framework' (p. 153), however, is another matter, as I hope to show.

9. Compare with Rochester's 'The Imperfect Enjoyment', *The Poems of John Wilmot, Earl of Rochester*, ed. Keith Walker (Oxford: Blackwell, 1984), pp. 30–2, where the non-performing penis is also treated as an unruly subject of its owner. However, in Rochester's poem the 'Base Recreant's' (l. 61) refusal to attend to love is matched against its virtuoso performance in the case of 'lewdness' (l. 49).

10. As Todd points out, however, Ovid's *Amores* III. vii contains a 'disappointment' poem which was taken as a model for, among others, Rochester's poem on the subject (*Works*, ed. Todd, I, pp. 392–3).

11. Todd also notes that other versions on the same theme, such as Rochester's 'The Imperfect Enjoyment', are 'told rather more from the male point of view' (Behn, ed. 1992, p. 393).

12. My discussion here is indebted to Luce Irigaray, *This Sex Which Is Not One* (1977), trans. Catherine Porter (New York: Cornell University Press, 1985), pp. 170–91.

13. Irigaray, *This Sex Which Is Not One*, p. 196.

14. See Jane Gallop, *Feminism and Psychoanalysis: The Daughter's Seduction* (London: Macmillan, 1982), who explains that 'proportion is etymologically "for the portion", in favour of the part, on the part's side rather than the whole's. The etymology of "proportion" then leads us to "disproportion", one proportion having a disproportionate share' (p. 20).

15. See Irigaray, who suggests that within this specular economy, '[c]ommodities among themselves are ... not equal, nor alike, nor different. They only become so when they are compared by and for man' (*This Sex Which Is Not One*, p. 177).

16. Compare with Irigaray, *This Sex Which Is Not One*, pp. 176–7.

Read Within: Gender, Cultural Difference and Quaker Women's Travel Narratives

Susan Wiseman

This essay has two aims: first, to offer an analysis of vocabulary and systems of meaning operating between text and reader in 'travel' writing by seventeenth-century Quaker women, and secondly, in making a re-evaluation of the language Quakers use to describe travel and conflict, and the ways in which their encounters with slaves and native peoples figure in their writings, to propose a corresponding re-evaluation of the place of cultural difference and slavery in early Quaker travel writing.

The focus will be on Quaker and other nonconformist vocabulary of travel between 1650 and 1690, analysed briefly in four narratives by women travellers: Barbara Blaugdone, Katherine Evans and Sarah Cheevers, Joan Vokins, and Elizabeth Hooton. In taking a brief time-span this analysis contrasts with the habitual placing of such texts within the structures of the twin teleological narratives in which texts by Quaker women are alternately situated – on the one hand the 'believer's' history of the development of Quakerism, and on the other the narrative of the part played by women in abolition. As Susan Mosher Stuard puts it, Quaker women 'were preachers and prophets' and in the eighteenth century 'followed the call to preach abroad, and joined the transforming movement to abolish slavery from human society'.[1] However, to claim such a clear progression, or in Mosher Stuard's formulation, 'story', is to suppress any detailed account of the shifting implications of mid- to late seventeenth-century Quaker travel.

Historical and literary critical writings which discuss seventeenth-century Quakers in colonial America and the West Indies habitually place Quaker men and women into one of several versions of a narrative of emancipation of slaves which is fulfilled at the moment in the nineteenth century when not only the importation of slaves but the institution (if not the fact) of slavery was abolished in British colonies. The version which accepts the Quakers as a driving force in the campaign against slavery, and those who see their part as more equivocal and sporadic (the London Yearly Meeting of Quakers did not come out officially against slavery until 1760 – long after the first protests), are equally bound up in a teleogical narrative, of which those involved in what is seen as 'proto-abolitionism' had no knowledge themselves.[2] This essay aims to re-examine the very early engagement between Quakers, more particularly Quaker women such as Elizabeth Hooton and Joan Vokins, in travel, and especially their encounters with Indians and slaves in America and the West Indies. It will concentrate on a moment in relations between Quakers and the colonies rather than a narrative, and it will attempt to 'read' these encounters in terms of negotiations to do with culture, status, linguistic dominance and – inevitably – Quaker mythology.

While the Quaker encounter with these peoples was different from that of the official government's own terms, it was by no means disinterested and was related in a peculiarly intimate way to the very hierarchy it struggled to combat and control. 'Travel' for missionary purposes, even when undertaken by Quaker women, who tended to regard themselves as to some extent outside, or in struggle against, the norms of their own society, implies all the most obvious conceptions of power relations between the traveller and those visited (though, of course, in the case of the Quakers power was conceived of as spiritual rather than temporal – hence their ability to visit the Sultan). However, the fact that the destinations visited tended to be ruled by the same figures of authority in secular and church government against whom Quakers struggled at home (or by rival sects) means that their accounts of travel in Ireland, America, Malta and the Caribbean tend to expose their ambivalent relations with the holders of power.

Part of the significance of Interregnum and Restoration nonconformist travel was the presentation of a narrative of the meaning of travel to a peer group. Quakers consistently wrote letters home and made reports of their missions. It was from the mid-1650s, when the Quaker project was under pressure from Cromwell, and the Quakers were locked into internecine struggles with sects at home, that they sought the establishment of the word abroad. We can ask not only what was the meaning of travel in relation to those outside the group, but also what was its meaning for those within the group. For example, Phyllis Mack suggests that some Quaker women began travelling after they encountered difficulty with authority in England – either with the usual authorities or with the Quaker leadership.[3] Travelling seems to have been significant as cultural reinforcement of Quaker self-mythologization as a group and in the structuring of narrative and myth for consumption by this interpretive community.

Encounters with authority and the life of Christ: the writings of Barbara Blaugdone and Katherine Evans and Sarah Cheevers

Myth, including Christian myth, provides a pattern for experience and, in the texts of Quakers examined here, the literalization of the Bible and the life of Christ provides a charter for their social order and behaviour through a central identification with the life of Christ, registered in the texts as an endorsement of their activities. The Bible was their map, their guide to foreign cultures, and above all, their phrase book, providing a significant and overdetermined vocabulary with which to respond to all encounters. Moreover, travel and proselytizing began amongst Christians, particularly amongst fellow sectarian Protestants. In consequence, at least in surviving textual evidence, Quakers made a very specific kind of sense of their meetings with strangers.

Quakers wanted to change people's relationship to the Scriptures so that rather than being what Margaret Fell called 'thieves' of God's words, they could be interpreters in the light. This was in part, certainly in the context of the Caribbean and America, an intra-Christian project in which the Quakers very deliberately sought to differentiate themselves from other, at first more materially powerful, Protestant and Puritan communities and mythologies, from the Church of England to other radicals and Ranters. It is a commonplace that although Quakerism shared the ecstatic aspect of many of the Civil War sects the Quakers were at pains to distinguish their 'living' mode of interpreting Scripture.[4] Particularly during the early years Quakerism and Quakers actively contradicted the dominant religious and political system.

The Quaker traveller is a preacher rather than a pilgrim, and the call to travel was a significant aspect of this polemical Quakerism. It was proof that one was a fully initiate Quaker; the narrative of that travel is also the story of one divinely inspired and, rather than being a journey towards revelation, it is the product of inner light. Quaker preaching and travel was bound to disturb social bonds, and Quaker women travelling were not simply in danger of being found unruly, their mission virtually required it. As in the illuminating case of Barbara Blaugdone, accounts of travel are at pains to emphasize that journeys and conflicts are the physical manifestations of the spiritual journey which both determines and transcends them and the spiritual narrative of God's goodness is the one which can be used to interpret all events.[5]

Blaugdone's narrative of the blessings of her calling to Quakerism focuses on her experiences travelling in the West Country and in Ireland, as occasions of the manifestations of God's grace to her. Her narrative provides evidence of the significance of travel as spiritual but also as emphasising and shoring up Quaker differences from those in authority. The opening passages insist on the interlocking of the physical and the spiritual journey:

> whoever shuns the Cross, and goes out of the Power, they lose their way and dishonour God; but whosoever keepeth in the Faith, and abideth in the Power, they are in Safety: I have living experience of it. (A4r)

> I speak my Experience in the Dealings of the Lord with me in my Travels and passing through my Spiritual Journey for the benefit of those that travel rightly after. (A4v)

The literalization of the spiritual journey is familiar from other radical writings of the seventeenth century, but the co-option of any physical landscape to purely spiritual significance distinguishes a particular Quaker mode of recounting stories of travelling and preaching in the second half of the seventeenth century.

Characteristically of such Quaker writings, a series of encounters with the authorities punctuate the spiritual journey. At Great Torrington Blaugdone was told 'I ought to be Whipt for a Vagabond' (p. 14); in Exeter Prison she says she was housed with gypsies and eventually released with them to be driven several miles beyond the city (only to return to visit her friends). Thus, although such externalities appear only as evidence of the poor spiritual state of her prosecutors, as part of a biblicized vocabulary of persecution, the reader's experience of the text is structured in part by Blaugdone's repeated struggles with authority, in this case the temporal powers.

The other major structuring principle the text uses, again found elsewhere in Quaker writing, is identification with the life of Christ. This is emphasized by Blaugdone's lack of physical maps and guides; she sets off towards Bristol – with no map but God's inner light to guide her: 'In my Travels I went several miles upon long Downs, and knew nothing in the way, but as the Lord was with me and did drive me.' In Blaugdone's account of travel biblical precedent forms an evident subtext and a key to the interpretation, for the reader as for Blaugdone. It also serves as a map. There are no descriptions of where she is because it does not matter where she is; unmapped physically, her experience is an index of the spiritual status of the Christians in each part of the country. Her travels in Devon are mapped not by the connection between places but by the spiritual significance of the incidents at each place. When she has to lodge in a stable the narrative, as if inevitably, echoes Christ's birth, and so on. Indeed, although the incidents emphasize that she was addressed by the authorities according to the dominant codes which they had to interpret unaccompanied travelling women's relation to geography – outcast status, vagrancy, gypsydom – her narrative invokes these interpretations in order to reject them.

Landscape is in part erased and replaced by the Bible as a mythic structure, but importantly, for the Quakers the Bible could only work as a spiritual guide when animated by the spirit, and in her encounters with shipwreck and rejection Blaugdone repeatedly situates her story as interwoven with and reliving that of Christ. Thus, within Blaugdone's narration two separate moments of near shipwreck are recounted intertextually with Christ's adventures but without the inset biblical quotations which punctuate most non-Quaker Puritan writing (Mary Rowlandson's captivity narrative, for instance).[6] For any Christian reader it is immediately evident that Blaugdone, a female traveller, is validating her testimony by a partially articulated typologizing of the life of Christ combined with a cross-gender identification with Christ. When God orders her to remain in a shipwrecked boat tossed in a stormy sea, any Christian reader would link it to Christ's lifetime; 'external' events like shipwreck signify only as support to an inner narrative – something the earlier Quaker leader James Nayler took to an extreme when he wrote an account of his spiritual backsliding in his entry into Bristol, leaving out all the external details.[7]

Thus Quaker accounts of travel work rather differently from the appropriation and 'casual and special naming' of the land which Paul Carter characterizes as the explorer's attitude to space and time.[8] Rather they are constituted paradoxically by simultaneous reporting of engagement with authorities who claim for themselves the right to subordinate Quakers and – at the other extreme – the refusal of the significance of the world through identification with the life of Christ.

Where Blaugdone seeks to differentiate herself from secular persecutors by organizing her story around Christ's life, those Quakers who encountered other Christians needed to establish fully their sense of difference and distinction by pitting their version of the Bible against that of their tormentors. Katherine Evans and Sarah Cheevers, who sailed to Malta and encountered the Italian Inquisition, seem to differentiate their own practices and myths from those of the Catholic Church, achieving almost exactly what Lévi-Strauss describes as a clear distinction between myths with a common origin.[9] Cheevers and Evans set off on a dual mission, first to go to Istanbul and convert the Sultan, and secondly to replicate the voyages of St Paul.[10] But their main purpose was to 'convince' those they met by distributing Quaker 'Books and Papers' and preaching at every possible moment. This entailed constant engagement with Christian hierarchies.

They anticipated a meeting with the Sultan, or with a dangerous cultural other – possibly even cannibals. But they landed in Malta only to be taken from the care of the English Consul by the Inquisition. Their planned conversion of the heathens was transformed into a three-year engagement with that closer enemy, and the one regarded as supremely dangerous in Civil War England, the Catholic Church.

Fundamental to this encounter is the use of the Bible as a myth to shore up the binary distinction between Quakers and their questioners. In response to the threat of absorption into Catholicism the women mobilize their version of biblical myth and map it very literally and typologically onto their present situation. They report that they were called by God to stage disruptive counter-rituals during church services:

> we went in obedience to the Lord to one of their Tower-Houses [churches] in time of their Worship, and stood trembling in the midst of them; and I was made to turn my back to the high Altar, and kneel down, and lift up my voice in prayer unto the Lord, and he that was saying Service drew off his Surplice, and kneeled a little beside us till I had done. (p. 73)

Such theatrical repudiations symbolize the women's refusal of acquiescence in rituals and register their use of theatrically appropriate moments to insist on their religion as the 'opposite' of Catholicism. This use of the Bible to distinguish themselves from their Inquisitors is repeated in my next example, but here it is complicated by the problematics of nation and identification. The figures of authority are recast as biblical oppressors. The English Consul who had finally allowed the Inquisition to take possession of them enters the story as Pilate:

> The day that we were had from the English Consul's to the Inquisition, the Consul's wife brought us meat to eat, and as she past by me, I was smote with an arrow to the heart, and I heard a voice saying It is finished, she hath obtained her purpose. I did not taste of her meat, but went aside and wept bitterly. The Consul did affirm to us the night before, that there were no such thing (as to ensnare us) intended; but it was in us as fire, and our souls were heavy unto death: for many days before us we saw in a Vision our going there (to prison) and we said Pilate would do the Jews a pleasure, and wash his hand in innocency. (p. 5)

The narrative interprets their experience as a reworking of the last days of Christ, which in a peculiar typology are echoed by the women's trials in the present. The text quite explicitly maps the experience of the women onto that of Christ at his trial by Pilate and the garden at Gethsemane. The women become Christ, the Consul becomes Pilate, and the narrative of good and evil, self and other, is preserved. Once again, the Bible functions as a way to interpret the crises of social place, nation and religion which occur amongst Christians – here English Protestants, Quakers and the Inquisition.

Evans and Cheevers's account of the encounter emphasizes the efficacy of Quaker vocabulary in establishing difference between Quakers and others. The emphasis on the 'living' Quaker faith and words (itself the subject of mockery to contemporaries) is echoed in Daniel Baker's presentation of the text upon its publication in the early 1660s when he describes the congregations of separatist non-Quakers as 'dead' (B1v).

Tripartite structures: authority, Quakers, slavery, and cultural difference

As I have suggested, the land signifies for Quakers as a metaphor for spiritual experience through the life of Christ – enabling the Egyptian 'wilderness' to be mapped with equal ease onto New England or Devon. Moreover, it becomes clear that Quaker polemic often takes as its implicit object the English Christian and it is in relation to this that the Quakers proselytize. A crucial reason for Quaker emphasis on language and the repetitive aspect of their violent encounters with Protestants and especially Puritans is the way in which their 'living' use of the Bible, and their way of reading the Bible in terms of 'light', is wholly adapted to debate amongst Puritans. This is illuminated by their accounts of travel in the New World, when we find records of encounters with authority and with slaves.

The Quaker preacher Joan Vokins landed in New England only to find herself locked into a dramatic confrontation with a Christian, even English, other – Ranters and ex-Quakers turned Ranters:

And they that had been convinced, and were *turned again with the Dog to his Vomit*, as saith the Scripture, and with the *Sow that was washed, to wallow again in the mire, and had made Shipwreck of Faith and good Conscience*, they were most wicked and preached scripture, and had Truth's Words, and grieved Truth's spirit and burdened *Friends* exceedingly, and honest Friends could hardly be clear, that they had a Testimony, except they spake while they were speaking: But when Gods Power did arise over them, it many times put them to silence, even to admiration and altho *Friends* Exercise was great, especially them that declared, yet the blessed Effect of the Almighty Power was, and is, a Precious Recompence, and a good Reward.[11]

Vokins's account is the most complex we have seen so far of a Quaker preacher's encounter in New England. Once again, the encounter with

a radically opposed other who is to be 'convinced' is bound up with a
process of differentiation between the Quakers, Ranters and what seem
to be ex-Quakers turned Ranters. These Ranters are presented as using
the Quakers' own techniques to disrupt Quaker meetings in the same
way that Quakers disrupted meetings in steeple-houses. The problem
seems to have been, basically, that the Ranters and ex-Quakers were
using the same religious discourses as the Quakers and could mimic
and parody Quaker testimony. Thus Vokins's narrative presents the
New World as replicating the discursive controversies found in England
twenty years earlier, but in a manifestation even more complex than
the confrontation with Puritans whose counter-vocabulary of 'wandering vagabond Quaker' fed into a narrative of sufferings and persecution.

Vokins and others also record encounters with slave populations in
the Caribbean in a way which suggests the complexity, too, of Quaker
relationships to slavery in the mid- to late seventeenth century. Vokins
reported on the separate meetings of black and white people, noting
that 'my soul was often melted therwith, even in the meetings of the
Negro's or Blacks, as well as among friends'.[12]

Where Blaugdone encounters English authorities, Joan Vokins and
the earlier traveller, Elizabeth Hooton, encountered Puritans in the
New World. In the texts of Hooton, like those of Vokins, it is the
close sharing of Quaker and Puritan mythology which sparks off first
attempts to differentiate through banishment, then an escalating circle
of violence, punishment and mutual attempts to destroy the belief
structure of the other. It is at the borders between different mythic
and social practices and groups, as I have suggested both violently and
imperfectly differentiated, that native Americans (in America) and slaves
(in the Caribbean) are brought into play in these texts – often quite
explicitly as an index of the godliness of the Quakers.

In the 1650s the Quaker preacher Elizabeth Hooton was called by
God to strengthen and refresh the Quaker settlements in the distant
West Indies and New England. Like Blaugdone, Hooton renders the
landscape into spiritual terms, and as with Blaugdone and Evans and
Cheevers, and Vokins, the reader is offered very full accounts of her
encounters with other Christians. It is in her encounter with competing
versions of her and others' experiences that we can begin to read a
social, hierarchical and even gendered context into a text which is
(religiously) resistant to expressing such meanings in the official 'manifest content' of the narrative.

As the term 'manifest content' suggests, these texts emphasize biblical
intertexts and potential points of identification with the life of Christ,
but in doing so tend to occlude or erase issues of gender and cultural,
rather than sectarian, difference. Such questions, which to a twentieth-
century reader might be the areas of most interest, tend to be what

could tentatively be called the repressed of the texts, emerging at moments of stress in the narrative or when the biblicized narrative is challenged by other interpretations. Hooton's writings about America and Barbados thus register questions of gender and cultural difference as they relate to the internecine strife between Protestant mythologies. Read against the grain, these texts do yield traces of the material circumstances which the narratives tend to elide by situating them as aspects either of the life of Christ or of engagement with authority. As I shall suggest, it is at the borders of these texts that slavery is an issue and, even where it becomes a major concern, it is bound tightly to issues of the relative status of Quakers and others rather than being the autonomous discourse suggested by the narrative of the history of abolition.

Notably, Elizabeth Hooton's literary remains are manuscript letters rather than the full-blown and post-hoc biblicized narratives of the other (later) figures, and the typological relation of texts to circumstances fosters a material rather than biblical understanding of her writings. Hooton was an early missionary travelling with George Fox to the Caribbean and America. Such women were among the first Quakers to land in America but terror of them spread quickly and when Mary Fisher and Ann Austin came ashore, the first Quaker preachers to arrive in Boston, their bodies were examined for signs that they were witches. Shipmasters often refused to carry them; Boston in the 1650s was renowned in Quaker mythology as that 'metropolis of blood' where Anne Hutchinson and others had been executed for refusing to obey the sentence of banishment for religious dissent. The Quaker approach to this situation, as manifested in Hooton's two visits to New England, was to visit repeatedly the places from which she was banished, re-enacting and repeating a cycle of witness, imprisonment, whipping, banishment, return, which locked Puritans and Quakers into varying attempts both to distinguish themselves and to dominate each other by their superior moral courage. Hooton was imprisoned while the authorities decided whether to hang the Quakers, whip them at the cart's tail or banish them. In the end:

they called another Jury which caused us to be driven out of their Jurisdiction by men & horses armed with swords & staffes & weapons of warre who went along with us near two days journey into the wilderness, & there they left us towards the night among great rivers & many wild beasts yt useth to devoure & yt night we lay in the woods without any vicutalls, but a few biskets yt we brought with us which we soaked in the water, & so did the Lord help & deliver us & one carried another through the waters & we escaped their hands.

And their lawes were broken, & that they intendet against us it may fall upon themselves, & was a deliverance never to be forgotton.[13]

In the early 1660s Charles II did, temporarily, alter the laws about religious dissent in New England (though he later amended them to point out that he was not advocating fair treatment for Quakers). But, importantly, we see that the early Quakers were not involved in attempting to convert Indians but in an internecine struggle with Boston Puritans who persecuted them and whom they, in turn, refused to leave alone. Hooton's repeated banishments and returns, accompanied by escalating violence, seem like the throes of two similar monsters attempting to achieve separation. And rather than explore the wilderness or look to the native population to convince them, Hooton acts as if magnetically drawn back to Boston and its environs with the endless round of whippings.

Hooton repeated the encounter with the officials of Boston throughout New England and on her second visit she was imprisoned and whipped repeatedly – returning as soon as she had been driven out to insist that she be allowed to use the warrant given to her by the King to buy land. She describes her encounters with authority vividly:

> I said sell me a house or let me rent one yt I may entertaine strangers & laide the Kings promise before them concerning libertie we should enjoy beyond ye seas; but they regarded it not, but made an Warrant to whip me for a wandring vagabond Quaker at 3 townes. (p. 41)

Paradoxically, the violence of the authorities and their refusal to allow her to live and proselytize in their town drives Hooton to invoke the authority of Charles II as a counter to theocratic Puritanism; both orders ultimately defined Quakers as outsiders and characterized their travel precisely as it was most dangerous for women to be perceived – as wandering.

Thus, place and landscape concerned preachers like Hooton at two points: when they intersect with other Christian mythologies while attempting to convince them (as when they disrupt church services), and at the point where they are dominated and 'named' by the systems to which they oppose themselves – such as the legal systems which condemned them to whipping in particular places. The native population of New England barely enters these narratives and these early Quaker reports of their engagement with the New Atlantic world contrast in some ways with the proselytizing stance of colonists such as John Eliot, who set up 'praying towns' for converted Indians.[14]

Cultural and religious differences, and slavery, seem to be registered in the text at points of conflict. From 1650 to 1690 slavery seems to be neither a dominant concern nor to have informed the imagery of Quaker representation of their mission. Elizabeth Hooton, like Margaret Fell's son Henry Fell, appeared to be able to live in the Caribbean without transposing the central Quaker figures of light and dark and the liberation of the oppressed nations onto literal situations of oppression and slavery. Indeed, it seems that such a connection in the circumstances either suggests that light and dark were not yet, even in late seventeenth-century English, dominant tropes for cultural difference; or, rather, that though they were a dominant binary they were not (yet) understood through the matrix of 'race' which would so insistently taxonomize difference around skin colour. It might also imply an active disavowal producing a distinction between spiritual vocabulary and literal circumstances.

In a remarkable instance of the insulatory function of myth shoring up a disjunction between visual 'evidence' and Quaker discourse, Elizabeth Hooton wrote a 'Testimony for dear brother Will Simpson' who 'hath ... laid downe his body in Barbadoes where god made him serviceable in his trueth'. Hooton returns to the Civil War and writes of Simpson's protests in England in the 1650s in terms of blackface protest – against the government in England: 'moreoever he was made oftentimes to colour his face Black, & soe black they [i.e. the government] should bee and appeare to people, for all their great profession'.[15] Certainly at the conscious level, the connection between Simpson's blacking up to show 'badness' and the oppressions of slavery is not made.

However, as the dramatic events recorded by Vokins and Hooton suggest, the differentiation between Quakers and other Puritan sects could not be as fully achieved as the Quakers would have liked (as Owen Watkins notes, what strikes us now is the similarity between Quakers and other Puritan sects[16]). It is in the context of the Quakers' attempts to distinguish themselves from fellow Puritans that the native population begins to figure – it precisely is in the context of such differentiations that Hooton speaks of the native Indians. Her account contrasts with those of Fox (who writes of praying with the Indians but also of war with them). Hooton writes of the Indians as helping persecuted Quakers:

7 or 8 mre friends yt came out of England did they thus abuse wth horrible whippings & mangling of our bodyes with whips fining and imprisoning and banishing into ye Wildrenesse yt when ye snowes were very deep & no tread but wt Wolves had made before me & my life neare lost many times in ye cold of ye Winter and ye hazard of the Journeys, & thus have they used us English people, us Vagabond Rogues and wandring Quakrs wch had not a dwelling place wch were true born English people of their own Nation, yet had ye Endians wch were barbarous savage people, wch neither know God nor Christ in any profession have been willing to receive us into

their Wigwams, or houses, when these professors would murther us.
(pp. 45–6)

The struggles between groups of Christians bring the Indians into
textual play; the native population fulfils a specific role in Hooton's
text. Although ironically called 'barbarian' – implying their lack of
religion but also, crucially, of linguistic competence and therefore the
very opportunity to embrace Christian faith – the Indian population
provides a contrast with the ostensibly Christian 'professors' who sent
Hooton and her companions into the 'Wildreness' to follow the footsteps of the wild beasts.[17]

The Bible serves loosely as a guide for this narrative – we think of
Christ in the wilderness, the Good Samaritan and the Pharisees. Thus
the Indian hospitality – offered by people of radical cultural difference
and, for the Quakers, deprivation – serves to point up the callous cruelty
of Bostonians. Shelter in wigwams is contrasted to the lack of mutual
support between 'English people' and Christians and serves to reinforce
Quaker self-positioning. Crucially, the significance of the native population for Hooton is *in terms of* her relationship to the Bostonians who
would 'murther us'. The way in which the native population appears
here is suggestive of the specific part played by Quakers in recognizing
the importance of both native Americans and slaves. They were initially
seen as important in relation to, or as marginal counters in, debates
over religious and political authority. This tripartite structure, in which
native Americans and slaves emerge at marginal, but crucial, points of
dispute between systems of authority, is illustrated well by a collective
letter from Richard Prior and Jane Gore, Barbados, conveying news of
friends in Maryland and Virginia who are 'wel':

> & ye power of ye Ld is entred among ye indians & one of ym was
> moved to goe abrod in ye power to minister & they did hang him,
> & since 4 or 5 of ym is moved to goe forth and we here as if they
> should have hanged ym soe ye Ld is stird up mightily among ym yt
> they thunder and thresh against wickedness.[18]

This elucidates the incorporation of slaves and Indians into a dynamic
and tripartite struggle in Quaker discourse in which the benevolence
of Quakers signifies in contrast to the barbarism of other Europeans,
especially Puritans.

Hooton's writing about native Americans as a source of succour
demonstrates both differences from and similarities to her writing about
the slave populations of Barbados where the struggle for recognition
is against the English governors. Hooton's peers and fellow travellers,
George Fox and William Edmundson, as well as their critics, also wrote

ambivalently on the slave populations of Barbados. George Fox's epistles illustrate the complex of material interests, Quaker polemic and struggle with other authorities that constitute the complex tripartite dynamic of difference in these early writings. Fox is far from consistent. He comments against slavery and argues strongly for the preaching of the gospel to negro slaves and Indians and their 'equal right' to be Christians. For instance, in the usual biblicized language he advocates rescuing the 'Heathen' from a caricature of African religions by telling them that the Christian god rules the 'Stones, which they make idols of.'[19] In 1672 he advocates spiritual care of the household servants and slaves, exhorting 'Friends in Barbadoes' – who presumably included slave owners – to take care at 'all your Family Meetings do not neglect any among your Whites and Negroes, but do your Diligence and Duty to God and them' (p. 327).

The ambivalence and even contradiction inherent in such a 'position' on slavery through such tripartite struggles emerges in the history of Quakers in the Caribbean during this period and marks their discourse around slavery. For example, during their visit to Barbados, Fox and Edmundson proselytized for religious equality, citing the equality of all men but also the danger of slave uprisings – a particularly acute danger for pacifist Quakers. The pacifism advocated by Quakers after the Restoration of Charles II would have important consequences in a society where slaves might outnumber planters – the reason given by the governor of Antigua for turning away visiting Quakers was that the large number of Quaker converts among the militia would endanger the safety of Europeans. So on the one hand Quakers were seen as luring the European population into a dangerous refusal of arms while, paradoxically, inciting the slave population to rebel. In such circumstances, Edmundson denied that making Christians of slaves incited them to rebellion.[20]

In 1675 the slaves in Barbados planned revolt. When they were discovered and prevented, the governor accused Edmundson and Fox of inciting rebellion. Edmundson continued to speak against slavery. However, in a moment which makes explicit the relationship – for Quakers – between Quakers, authorities and slaves, in 1678 Fox spoke before the govenor denouncing uprisings and suggesting for slaves not only obedience but love towards their owners. Their interventions in the plantation economy put Quakers in paradoxical social and economic positions: not only did Quaker planters own slaves, but the Quaker preachers visiting from England also had contradictory needs in relation to the governments of the islands. On the one hand they sought to establish moral superiority to Charles II's Church of England governors, but equally they needed to be let onto the island in the first place if they were to make converts and, as their journals show, they actively sought the opportunity to meet figures in authority.[21] Thus the discourses around slavery vary not according to the position of the slaves, but according to that of the Quakers in relation to other powers.[22]

The slave population and their religious status and education rapidly became a matter in dispute amongst politico-religious sectors of the Caribbean. One of Elizabeth Hooton's interventions in the debate indicates both its complexity and that, as the example of Fox suggested, a tripartite structure of 'Quakers-authorities-slavery' was in operation, not a simple campaign against slavery. Elizabeth Hooton's surviving document from these years is a formal, possibly public, letter admonishing the government of Barbados and addressed to 'the Rulers and Magistrats of this Island that ought to rule for good':

> I have seen many overturnes, and the Lord will overturne still. Therefore have a Care in the fere of the lord that hee may give a blessing unto you ... And soe Consider what is required for in this Island. There is Great need of Justice and Judgement, for if one goe up into the Countrey, there is A great cry of the Poore being Robbed by Riche men's Negroes, Soe they cannot without great Trouble, keep anything from being stolen; And if they doe complaine they cannot get any Satisfaction; now it is the Duty of Every man to take Care and see there family have Suffitient food and any thing else they stand in need of ... that they may be kept from Stealing and doeing any thing that is Evill; Soe that you may make good Lawes and yor People be kept in good order, according to what is made knowne to them by tem that Rule over them. And soe you Come ... to a true Reformation of yor Selves, first reforming yor selves in yor familys, and you will see Clearly how to Rule others, to a Reformation god looks for Among you and all People.[23]

Such a warning is poised paradoxically between advocating some sort of recognition of slaves as subjects and a much clearer sense of slaves as at the base of the social pyramid – part of the 'family' (i.e. household) unit which is the point at which reformation of the social body needs to take place. However, the warning is not in terms of the treatment of slaves. Slaves feature instead as evidence of the pervasive social collapse of plantation society. The robbing of the poor by rich men's slaves seems to indicate the absolute collapse of the proper order of society to such an extent that rich men's slaves actually have much greater real power then poor white Europeans. That this is an index of social disruption which needs to be put right at the level of individual household units – i.e. by better control of slaves by the rich householders – suggests a conception of society firmly rooted in the status quo and accedes to the prevailing structure of authority with regard to slaves. This particular protest is marked, I would argue, not by gender identification with women slaves nor with the figural use of 'slavery' to describe the condition of women, nor with emancipatory rhetoric, but with the tripartite rather than binary structures produced in negotiations between Quaker discourse and myth in relation to other powers with the slave population making a third counter in this discourse.

Quaker women travellers and their readers

Thus, I have argued that these texts might be read in terms of the Quaker biblicization of experience, identifications with the life of Christ and internecine struggles with other sects. Two questions remain; what relationship do such texts have to questions of cultural and gender difference? And why have they been placed at the start of such narratives and what does that mean?

In terms of culture and gender difference I have argued that, rather than offering overt same-sex identifications, Quaker women use the life of Christ as a point of identification, emphasizing gender often primarily at the point of signature or, as in the case of Evans and Cheevers, in terms of closeness in which both figures are unitarily written as experiencing events analogous to the life of Christ. As I have suggested, this identification with Christ – and with other biblical figures – is an aspect of the way Quaker myth uses the Bible literally to interpret experience and to transform narrative encounters with landscape into spiritual experience. The relationship between Quaker women, land and travel is constructed by their reading of the Bible, as Barbara Blaugdone emphasized. But it is also structured around debates within the mid-seventeenth-century Puritan movements to which Quakerism was responding, and for this reason what the New World – both the important colony in Barbados and New England – represents is not initially a native population of pagans to convert, but a repetition of the spiritual territory of the old world in which Quakerism was locked into a struggle to both convince other sects and differentiate itself from them. While such debates led women to challenge Quaker leadership, and in the 1670s the position of women within the organization changed, such issues have – or had for them – no *natural* or self-evident implications for other struggles or conflicts.[24]

In travel communications they do not call attention to the landscape or external circumstances, and their systems of belief are thrown into relief not by encounters with the 'other' of heathens, pagans or believing slaves, but in encounters with members of their own culture who have different belief systems. It is in relation to these primary distinctions that other differences are organized. However, it is also in the records of these moments of encounter with other Christians that the material struggles for status and place – as well as issues of gender and especially cultural difference – emerge from textual 'repression' to shore up the Quaker discourse of moral superiority while simultaneously providing the reader with an opportunity to read the text against the grain: to find the textual residues of struggles over status and differences.

As Homi Bhabha has argued, 'the locality of culture ... is ... more hybrid in the articulation of cultural differences and identifications than can be represented in any hierarchical or binary structuring of social antagonism'.[25] And, in this case, any imposition of a binary relation between Quakers and either native Americans or slaves serves to over-simplify a complex set of discourses around what was, for Quakers, a situation in which such cultural differences initially emerged and sig-nified in relation to their 'local' power struggles, producing a tripartite rather than binary dynamic with, as Bhabha suggests, many possible participants. Bhabha's observation helpfully reformulates European at-tempts to dominate other cultures because he insists on a strategy which returns to the subject and the object of the text variegated localities and divergent motivations.

If the biblicization of circumstances and appearance of difference at the margins of attacks on Quakers by other sects and obsession with English power structures that I have traced were indeed the dominant concerns of Quaker and racial discourse while involved in travel, why have these texts been placed at the start of such narratives of the interrelationship of gender and slavery? One issue, perhaps, is our contemporary emphasis on alterity theory and some of the binarisms it tends to bring with it; it may be that alongside the conception of culturally different subjects as 'others', other, diverse discourses and investments were at play in seventeenth-century understandings of difference. This is one thing the texts examined here seem to suggest.

Moreover, the retrospective seeking out of Quaker women as a point of origin brings with it troubling issues about the implicit use of the category 'woman' in relation to unspoken, but implicit, assumptions about women's ethical positions. In anticipating women as anti-slavery campaigners we assume, I think, that women 'ought' to have seen what was going on because in certain crucial ways they are considered to be ethically different from 'men'.

Paradoxically, where Freud insisted that women were ethically under-developed, some strands of contemporary feminist history, and certainly Quaker history, seem to assume women as ethically advanced; hence the search for *female* early abolitionists.[26] This desire for positive ethical difference in women's 'moral development' appears in the work of Carol Gilligan under the sign of psychological / ethical theory. Gilligan argues that there are 'two ways of speaking about moral problems, two modes of describing the relationship between other and self'.[27] This difference, she argues, 'is characterised not by gender but by theme. Its association with women is an empirical observation'[28] but, as it is empirically proven, that is the same thing as its being a difference by gender rather than theme – and Gilligan proceeds accordingly to reproduce implicit assumptions about the ethical 'difference' of women. Whatever conditions might produce a gendered difference in ethical development – and there are many, which, indeed, Gilligan's work claims to register – they cannot be assumed, implied or projected into the past except at the expense of complex argument. Such assumptions are in themselves problematic, particularly so when applied retrospectively.

Quaker women's texts can, as I hope I have suggested, be read as marked by interests and as producing discourses of cultural difference in relation to other powers; to assume, on the other hand, that women – as *women* – must articulate such causes as polemic involves silently replicating Gilligan's assumptions about the 'different' ethical status of historical women. Rather, cultural and gender differences might be considered as the partially repressed of such texts. Perhaps it is possible to acknowledge our own interest in reading texts against the grain to find areas of culture and gender difference not necessarily present in the texts as polemic but marking the texts at moments of stress, disavowal or competition with other myths and discourses.

Notes

An earlier version of this article was published by *Baetyl* (1994). Thanks to Kate Chedgzoy, Melanie Hansen and Suzanne Trill, who accepted an early version of this paper for their conference, 'Voicing Women' (Liverpool 1992), and to Susan Bruce, Helen Hackett, Elaine Hobby and Jonathan Sawday for comments there. Thanks to Richard Wilson and the Early Modern Seminar at Lancaster University (1993) for inviting me to give the paper and to Professor L. Boose for comments. Thanks to Kate Chedgzoy for reading and commenting on the manuscript.

1. On 'believer's history' see Patricia Crawford, *Women and Religion 1500–1700* (London: Routledge, 1993), p. 125. Texts on women and the abolitionist movement, such as Jean Fagin Yellin, *Women and Sisters: The Antislavery Feminists in American Culture* (New Haven and London: Yale University Press, 1989); and Moira Ferguson, *Subject to Others: British Women Writers and Colonial Slavery, 1670–1834* (London: Routledge, 1992), tend to concentrate on the interrelationship of gender and slavery in the eighteenth century and later; Ferguson, however, does follow the Quaker narrative in grounding her history in the voyages of Quaker women in the second half of the seventeenth century. See Susan Mosher Stuard, 'Women's witnessing: a new departure', in Elizabeth Potts Brown and

Susan Mosher Stuard (eds), *Witnesses For Change: Quaker Women Over Three Centuries* (New Brunswick and London: Rutgers University Press, 1989), pp. 3–25 (p. 3).

2. My argument traces a rather different pattern to that suggested by Moira Ferguson's sense that 'beginning hesitantly in the seventeenth century, women bold enough to write about slavery … managed to inject their dissent with gender-specific concerns', though this clearly was the case in the later period (*Subject to Others*, p. 3). Investigations of the place of gender in anti-slavery include Fagin Yellin, *Women and Sisters*.

3. Phyllis Mack, *Visionary Women: Ecstatic Prophecy in Seventeenth-Century England* (Berkeley: University of California Press, 1992) p. 208.

4. Owen C. Watkins, *The Puritan Experience* (London: Routledge and Kegan Paul, 1972), pp. 160–4.

5. Barbara Blaugdone, *An Account of the Travels, Sufferings and Persecutions of Barbara Blaugdone* (London, 1691); subsequent references in text.

6. *A True History of the Captivity and Restitution of Mary Rowlandson* (London, 1682). See also Nigel Smith, *Perfection Proclaimed* (Oxford: Oxford University Press, 1989), pp. 24–6, on Puritan versus Quaker use of biblical citation.

7. On James Nayler see Watkins, *The Puritan Experience*, pp. 170–1.

8. Paul Carter, *The Road to Botany Bay* (London: Faber & Faber, 1987), p. 4.

9. Claude Lévi-Strauss, 'Relations of symmetry between rituals and myths of neighbouring peoples', in *Structural Anthropology*, trans. Monique Layton (Harmondsworth: Penguin, 1976), II, pp. 239, 246.

10. Katherine Evans and Sarah Cheevers, *A Short Relation of Cruel Sufferings* (London, 1662). See pp. 1–2, 4–5, 7 et seq. Subsequent references in text.

11. Joan Vokins, *Gods Mighty Power Magnified As Manifested in His Faithfull Handmaid Joan Vokins* (1691), pp. 34–5.

12. For a further analysis of the engagement of Vokins with black congregations, see Ferguson, *Subject to Others*, pp. 63–4.

13. Elizabeth Hooton, D Portfolio iii 27, quoted on p. 31 of Emily Manners, *Elizabeth Hooton: First Quaker Woman Preacher* (London, 1914). Subsequent references in text.

14. See James Holstun, *A Rational Millennium* (Oxford: Oxford University Press, 1987), pp. 118–20.

15. Elizabeth Hooton, 'Testimony for dear Brother Will Simpson', Port. 17, 95. For deployment of imagery of light and dark and the oppressed nations see letters of Henry Fell to his mother, 'Letters and Documents of Early Friends', in transcriptions of Swarthmore Mss, vol. 2. On conflict with Ranters, see p. 103 of the latter.

16. Watkins, *The Puritan Experience*, p. 173.

17. On the importance of the link between the idea of the barbarian and linguisitic competence see Anthony Pagden, *The Fall of Natural Man* (Cambridge: Cambridge University Press, 1982), pp. 15, 20.

18. *Early Friends Correspondence & Documents* (transcripts), vol. 4, p. 296.

19. George Fox, *A Collection of Many Select and Christian Epistles. Letters and Testimonies* (London, 1698), p. 325.

20. William Edmundson, *A Journal on the Life, Travels, Sufferings and Labour*

in the Work of the Ministry (Dublin, 1715), pp. 55, 58–62, and on the Indies, pp. 76–95.

21. Ferguson, *Subject to Others*, pp. 52–3; see her footnote 12 to Aptheker and note 17, *Memoirs of the Life of George Fox, The Friends' Library*, vol. I, ed. William Evans and Thomas Evans (Philadelphia: Joseph Rakestraw, 1838), p. 81; for a full analysis of the debate around Quakers and slavery in the late seventeenth and early eighteenth centuries, see Herbert Aptheker, 'The Quakers and negro slavery,' *The Journal of Negro History* 25.2 (1940), pp. 331–62.

22. For an analysis of Quaker discourse on slavery which responds to the moral/political tussle between Quakers and Anglicans see Morgan Godwyn, *The Negroes' and the Indians' Advocate* (London, 1680), A4r–v.

23. Ms D Portfolio iii, 25, quoted by Manners, *Elizabeth Hooton*, p. 71.

24. Patricia Crawford, 'The challenge to patriarchalism: how did the revolution affect women?', in John Morrill (ed.), *Revolution and Restoration: England in the 1650s* (London: Collins and Brown, 1992), pp. 112–28, esp. pp. 122–3.

25. Homi Bhabha, 'DissemiNation: time, narrative, and the margins of the modern nation' in his *Nation and Narration* (London: Routledge, 1991), p. 292.

26. Sigmund Freud, 'Some psychical consequences of the anatomical distinction between the sexes', *Complete Psychological Works* (London: Hogarth Press, 1961), XIX, pp. 257–8.

27. Carol Gilligan, *In a Different Voice* (Cambridge, MA, Harvard University Press, 1982), p. 12.

28. Gilligan, *In a Different Voice*, p. 2.

Contra-dictions: Women as Figures of Exclusion and Resistance in John Bunyan and Agnes Beaumont's Narratives

Tamsin Spargo

The voices of dissent, raised against dominant structures of authority and in opposition to prevalent meanings in the late seventeenth century, were raised neither in unison nor in harmony. Located within a bitter battle of words about the true meaning of the Word, the combative texts of John Bunyan reveal the extent to which the confident assertion of male authority which permeates much nonconformist writing both depends upon, and attempts to legitimate, the exclusion of women.

In this essay I wish to examine one example of how the attempt to construct and defend an authoritative position, both textually and discursively, within a dissenting movement, depends on strategies of exclusion, of not only challenging the truth-claims of rival speakers or writers but of denying the legitimacy of the rival's claim to a position from which to speak or write. In the example I have chosen the ultimate threat to the fragile stability of the authoritative preacher / writer's position is located not in a category which can be defined as state authority nor a rival dissenting minister but in a figure which exceeds and disrupts those categories, that of woman.

My reading of Bunyan's writings focuses both on the contradictions within the range of meanings and positions allotted to women within the texts and on a number of figures of female resistance. Raising the possibility of voicing or writing contra-dictions, these figures of resistance interrogate the imaginary universality and transcendence of the texts' logocentric framework and counter the force of exclusion with powerful evidence of a difference which cannot be effaced.

The figures I propose to examine – Sister Witt, Elizabeth Bunyan and Agnes Beaumont – operate in different ways, yet all connect with other figures of female resistance both of the seventeenth century and of the twentieth century. As textual figures, Sister Witt and Elizabeth Bunyan both reveal and contest the subjugation of women so vehemently demanded, and needed, by their 'author', John Bunyan. A literally marginal figure in annotated editions of Bunyan's writings, Agnes Beaumont has been effectively denied the position of author within traditional criticism of the period, yet her narrative may be read as a text from the margins which challenges the patriarchal values of the seventeenth century and of the discursive framework of literary studies which has continued to marginalize her writing. There is, of course, a fourth, and multiple, figure of resistance, assumed in my argument, that of the feminist reader for whom margins and silences may offer the material for textual and cultural resistances today.

The threatening female voice which Bunyan's texts attempt to silence may be read as an echo of the unruly female speech and writing of the revolutionary period. Female prophets such as Eleanor Davies, Mary Cary and Anna Trapnel intervened in political and religious debates, often through a form of conspicuously irrational speech and writing which, as Christine Berg and Philippa Berry have suggested, challenged conventional notions of order and subjectivity.[1] Claims by women to be transmitting the Word, even to embody the Logos, could be seen as threatening the apparently secure masculine identity of God. These women can be seen to have claimed a position from which to speak, but although their utterances challenged a patriarchal symbolic and social order, their position as prophets made them vulnerable to marginalization. Their potent irrationality could be categorized as hysteria, their apocalyptic pronouncements could be read as ravings when they no longer suited short-term political aims. Attempts to contain this unruly female speech and writing were made throughout the period leading up to the Restoration, as the Commonwealth establishment became a target for its criticism. After 1660 the defeat and failure of much revolutionary activity saw a further reduction in prophetic activity, but the threat implicit in unruly female speech remained. Women continued to play an active role in a number of different religious movements, forming the majority in many nonconformist congregations. The Quaker Margaret Fell's most famous text, *Womens Speaking Justified*, stands as evidence of attempts by women to adopt active positions within church affairs, to claim a position from which to speak.[2] Published in 1667, Fell's text mobilizes scriptural references more frequently employed to legitimate the silencing of women in order to legitimate the female voice. Fell's career, her claim to a public position, her subsequent imprisonment and the ability of her texts to exceed the constraints imposed on the body and voice of the author are, ironically, paralleled by the career and textual history of John Bunyan.

Grace Abounding to the Chief of Sinners, published in 1666, six years before Bunyan's release from his imprisonment for unlicensed preaching and one year before *Womens Speaking Justified*, is conventionally read as a conversion narrative, required by most dissenting churches before admission. It may also be read, however, as a powerful claim to a position of authority within a framework of pastoral power. The text is addressed to the Bedford congregation of which Bunyan officially became minister three months before his release. Bunyan addresses this readership as his *'children'*, whilst himself occupying a series of discontinuous positions which point to the conflicting discourses within which the text may be read. As dutiful subject of divine authority Bunyan is both Chief of Sinners, servant of Christ, and a text in which divine grace may be read. As a claimant of pastoral authority he is shepherd to his flock, minister and, perhaps most insistently, father. He sums up his ultimate aim in ensuring the salvation of his readers with the following words: *'my Soul hath fatherly care and desire after your spiritual and everlasting welfare'.*[3]

In the main body of the text as first published scant reference is made to women. His first wife, who is unnamed, is referred to only in relation to her father who was 'counted godly' and whose godly books she brought to her husband as a dowry (*Grace Abounding*, p. 8). The position of Bunyan as pastoral father is thus seen to be supported by an implied connection with his wife's 'real' father, his wife standing only as a channel for material and spiritual goods between the two father figures. As a woman she occupies no position other than that of a link.

Three years before the publication of *Grace Abounding*, Bunyan had published a treatise on works which offered a succinct formulation of the place and duties of women within the domestic space, in terms which echo many of the conduct manuals of the period. The godly wife must regard her husband as 'her head and lord' and 'ought in every thing to be in subjection to him, and do all she doth, as having her warrant, licence and authority from him'.[4] Afforded a position analogous to that of the church, subject to the absolute authority of Christ, the woman must beware of an *'idle, talking,* or *brangling tongue'*, of a 'wandring and gossoping spirit'; *'immodest apparel'* or *'wanton gate'* (*Christian Behaviour*, p. 33). Despite a qualification that he does not 'intend women should be their husbands slaves', the ordained subjection of women under their husbands is offered as absolute, reinforced by reference to traditional scriptural oppositions which privilege the male as divine and the divine as male over woman as worldly (*Christian Behaviour*, p. 34). Patriarchal and Christian imperatives thus reinforce one another in the development of a model family in which 'Wives should be about their own husbands business at home' (*Christian Behaviour*, p. 33). This text may be read as an attempt to secure the fragile authority of the unlicensed minister by associating him with a project of promoting good order within a domestic space. Earlier charged with antinomianism and associated with the Ranter threat to social order,

Bunyan offers here a text which identifies '*disorder in Families and Places*' and attempts to secure his own position as speaker and writer by prescribing fixed positions for men and women, which hold the latter in a subservient relation which mirrors the textual position of his first wife in the later text (*Christian Behaviour*, p. 10).

Twenty years later Bunyan, now official minister of the Bedford congregation he had addressed in *Grace Abounding*, already acclaimed as author of *The Pilgrim's Progress*, published a combative treatise called *A Case of Conscience Resolved*. Published in the year of Margaret Fell's second imprisonment, this text is ostensibly addressed to a Mr K., but the threat which the text attempts to counter is clearly identified as the female voice. *A Case of Conscience Resolved* is a response to the challenge posed to Bunyan's authority, and to the hierarchical structure of authority, by women holding separate meetings or services. Bunyan's initial address differentiates between the 'Godly Women' and 'Honoured Sisters' of his congregation who are 'subject to the Word', and a 'leader' whose gender is unspecified but who is swiftly identified as Mr K.[5] Bunyan's insistence that it is Mr K.'s intervention in the affair which has prompted him to respond for the '*Honour and good Order*' of the women in question sets up an opposition between an aggressive male outsider and an ordered community of believers (*Conscience Resolved*, p. 296). In this way the opinions of women involved in the argument can be exiled from the text, although the assertion that '*I dare not make your selves the Authors of your own miscarriage in this*' attests to the perceived threat of female authorship or agency in the affair (*Conscience Resolved*, p. 295). Opposing female reactions are anticipated in advance and defined in terms which echo the unacceptable and ungodly behaviour outlined in *Christian Behaviour*: '*I am like enough to run the* Gantlet *among you and to partake most smartly of the scourge of the Tongues of some, and to be soundly Brow-beaten for it by others*' (*Conscience Resolved*, p. 296). The text continues to emphasize Bunyan's paternal authority over his congregation and to efface gendered difference within that congregation. Repetition of phrases such as 'our question' and 'among us' suggest a consensus within Bunyan's congregation, tellingly identified as 'my Brethren', a consensus, an identity produced in contrast to Mr K., the rival father-figure and 'his' women (*Conscience Resolved*, p. 300). The text argues not only that separate women's meetings are unlawful, but that the female voice in mixed assemblies is not to compete with the male: 'they [women] should also not be the mouth of the assembly, but in heart, desires, grones, and Tears, they should go along with the Men' (*Conscience Resolved*, p. 324).

The one legitimate space offered to women, a space which recalls the safe domestic space of *Christian Behaviour* is, not surprisingly, 'the closet': 'Be as often in your closets as you will; the oftener there, the better. This is your Duty, this is your Priviledge' (*Conscience Resolved*, p. 329). The necessity of women staying in this 'sanctified' place or space is offered as a matter of the utmost importance, for 'when women keep their places, and Men manage their Worshipping of God as they should, we shall have better days for the Church of God, in the world' (*Conscience Resolved*, p. 329). Women are offered only a glimpse of freedom from their ordained position of inferiority, a freedom available only in the dissolution of gender distinctions which will accompany the day of salvation. In the moment of reincorporation in divine being 'these distinctions of Sexes shall be laid a side' and 'with a *notwithstanding* you shall be saved' (*Conscience Resolved*, pp. 323–4). The trace of hierarchically-defined difference, implied in 'notwithstanding', is a necessary component in a discursive strategy which demands the association of maleness with order and divinity and femaleness with disorder or unruliness and transgressive humanity.

This association of femaleness with unruliness, figured in the female voice, is strikingly evident in the first textual figure of contra-diction I wish to examine. In the absence of any conclusive evidence of the attitudes and actions of the female members of Bunyan's congregation who, by 1683, had clearly sought a different role in church affairs and had attempted to negotiate for separate meetings, this figure may have a particular significance. Sister Witt appears in a series of entries in the Bedford Church Book in 1673.[6] Written in Bunyan's handwriting, a feature which has guaranteed this text the double-edged position of authentic background to the 'canonical' texts, these entries indicate Bunyan's direct involvement in the expulsion of a female member accused of 'railing'. The first entry records that 'an accusation was brought against our sister Witt, otherwise Worrin, for railing'. It is noted that 'the sister to be dealt with should first be heard (because she pretends she can make her defence)'. No record is offered of Sister Witt's own defence and the final entry records that 'was cast out of the church the wife of Bro. Witt, for railing and other wicked practices'. In the same entry a period of fasting and prayer is decreed 'because of som disorders among som in the congregation'. 'Railing' Sister Witt, once known, before marriage, as Sister Worrin, who dared to raise her voice not only to rail but to present her own defence is first denied autonomous status, being referred to now as 'wife of Bro. Witt', and then expelled. Here textual strategies of exclusion (the denial of a name of her own and the omission of her defence) seem initially to perform the silencing of woman demanded in Bunyan's treatises. The railing woman's textual position in a non-canonical, archive text has subsequently remained a marginal or background one, yet her railing connects with other female voices within and around Bunyan's writings.

The first voice is presented in an addition to *Grace Abounding*,

published only after the death of the author. One of Bunyan's supporting arguments in *A Case of Conscience Resolved* had been that 'if
those most fond of Womens Meetings for Prayer, were to petition
the King for their lives, they would not set Women to be their
Advocates to him' (*Conscience Resolved*, p. 308). Women it seems are
unfit to occupy such a position in public engagements of an overtly
political nature. Yet, in Bunyan's account of his imprisonment and
trial in 1661, it is related that Bunyan's wife (his second) petitioned
the justices at the Midsummer Assizes for her husband's release. The
wife has no name, her reported actions and words are circumscribed
by assurances that it is Bunyan who is acting 'by' her and that her
feelings in anticipation of such unaccustomed public endeavour are
appropriately 'feminine'. She thus approaches the justices' chamber
'with a bashed face, and a trembling heart', both characteristics recommended to women in the act of worship in *A Case of Conscience
Resolved*.[7] Her address to the justices, however, betrays no such hesit-
ancy or anxiety. Her speech as presented is direct and accusatory, as
she challenges the justices to release her husband on the grounds of
wrongful imprisonment, concluding that 'he is a Tinker, and a poor
man; therefore he is despised, and cannot have justice' (*My Imprisonment*, p. 128). Whilst this text cannot be treated as a verbatim account,
it is presented as such, representing a woman adopting a public,
adversarial role. As such it acts as a textual contradiction of Bunyan's
own argument, pointing to the limits of authorial control over texts and
to the possibility of female resistance within the most overtly patriarchal frameworks.

Bunyan's second wife is unnamed in his writings. His contemporary
biographer names her Elizabeth, but the absence of any texts in her
name have restricted her position within criticism of seventeenth-
century writings to that of a shadowy figure in her husband's
supposedly extra-textual life. As a figure of contra-diction within a text,
she may occupy a more powerful position, empowering interrogations
of exclusion and resistance within texts bearing more authoritative
names.

The final textual figure of contra-diction I wish to examine is Agnes
Beaumont. Agnes Beaumont figures in three texts: two bear the name
'John Bunyan', one her own. In 1680, three years before the publication
of *A Case of Conscience Resolved*, Bunyan made a number of additions to
Grace Abounding, including an extensive and vehement denial of charges
of womanizing. The accusations are summarized as: 'that I had my
Misses, my *Whores*, my *Bastards*, yea, *two wives at once*, and the like'
(*Grace Abounding*, p. 93). The passage moves from the refutation of
such charges to an assertion of his difficulty in maintaining even polite
relations with women:

Those know, and can also bear me witness, with whom I have been most intimately concerned, that it is a rare thing to see me carry it pleasant towards a Woman; the common Salutation of a woman I abhor, 'tis odious to me in whosoever I see it. Their Company alone, I cannot away with. (*Grace Abounding*, p. 94)

No woman is named in this section; it is Woman who figures in this declaration. Bunyan's attempt to protect his pastoral position of authority from readings which suggest that his position poses a threat to the social and sexual order demands that he relocate that threat within a dangerous female sexuality. The pastoral father, it seems, may be all too easily viewed as a seducer and the meaning of pastoral relations, apparently purged of sexual implications in a discourse which privileges spiritual relations to God over material relations with family members, is open to question. As a pastoral father figure, Bunyan may be read by his contemporaries as transgressing the bounds of legitimate pastoral authority, exploiting the power relations of his ministry in order to seduce female members of the congregation. The fragility of the minister's authority, and the possibility of radically divergent interpretations of his status, is reinforced in the same section by reported accusations that he was 'a Witch, a Jesuit, a Highway-man, and the like' (*Grace Abounding*, p. 93). Editions of *Grace Abounding* conventionally connect this passage with a narrative written by my final figure of contra-diction, although her story is always presented as an adjunct to Bunyan's.

Agnes Beaumont's name occurs in the Bedford Church Book as a new member of the congregation in 1672, one year before the record of the expulsion of Sister Witt. Hers is the first name to be entered in Bunyan's own handwriting in the only direct reference to her by the minister; Bunyan's writings make no other reference to Agnes Beaumont by name. In a text first published a century later, bearing the name 'Agnes Beaumont' as the author, a narrative is presented which foregrounds the unstable relations of power, authority and gender-difference within the conflicting discursive formations, in which Bunyan, as minister and father figure, and Beaumont, as member of the congregation and daughter, were positioned.[8]

This is the story of a daughter attempting to negotiate a position of dutiful obedience to two rival father figures – her own father, and her pastoral father, Bunyan. Her mother is dead, her father refuses to allow her to attend a meeting at which Bunyan is to preach – she has work to do, looking after her father. To obey her father would be to deny her duty to the ultimate father figure, God, figured to her in Bunyan. Eventually her father agrees that she may attend the meeting, but as a young woman she cannot travel alone. Her brother, a parish officer, who appears to have been sympathetic to the nonconformist cause but not a member of the Bedford congregation, attempts to provide her with transport, first with a friend who fails to arrive and then with Bunyan himself, who called by chance at her brother's house on the way to the meeting. Bunyan is described as reluctant to take Agnes, anticipating her father's anger, but as eventually giving in to her brother's entreaties. Beaumont recounts that her father, on hearing that she has travelled with Bunyan, 'fell into a pastion' and intended to pull her 'off of the horse backe' if he caught up with them.[9] She acknowledges a sense of pleasure and pride which she felt on riding with 'such A man as he was', but recalls that 'my pride had a fall' when a local priest sees Bunyan and Beaumont together and later 'did scandalise us after a base maner, and did raise a very wicked report of us, which was altogether false, blessed be god' (*Persecution*, pp. 16, 17). It is this report which seems to connect with the refutations of womanizing in *Grace Abounding* and with the later description of her father's mistrust of Bunyan's use of his pastoral authority.

Left alone after the meeting, at which she received 'new manifestations' of divine 'love' which she early in the text suggests always preceded some trial or misfortune, she returns home to find herself locked out by her father and threatened with disinheritance if she does not promise not to attend a meeting again (*Persecution*, p. 18). The conflicting demands upon her of the rival fathers cannot be reconciled. Her choice is between two sacrifices, of social position, a place in society, or of salvation, a place in heaven.

Beaumont's description of her attempt to negotiate her conflicting duties to God and father emphasizes both the force and 'reality' of her spiritual and mental struggle and the terrifying consequences of disobedience to either father. Her physical exclusion from her father's house is seen as mirroring the exclusion from heaven should she fail to obey her divine father's commands. The description of her father's repeated questions and of his holding 'the key out to mee' similarly locates her situation within a tradition of scriptural trials, whilst emphasizing the particularity of the dilemma of an excluded woman (*Persecution*, p. 41). She is offered protection by her brother, which she reluctantly accepts, yet his attempts to intervene with their father on her behalf are rebuffed by her on the grounds that the father 'was more provoked with what he said than he was with mee' (*Persecution*, p. 28). Whilst herself challenging paternal authority when it conflicts with her duty to God, Beaumont resists association with her brother's threat to her father's authority, which might not be read as similarly motivated or justified, and refuses to be relocated within her brother's household. It is clear that, whilst the consequences of exclusion from her father's house were terrifying on several levels, Beaumont refused to evade them by appealing to an alternative figure of male protection. The struggle is presented as that of father and daughter, and emphasis is repeatedly placed on the closeness of that relationship and its complex network of relations of power and desire. It is implied towards the end of the text that Beaumont had been allotted a larger part of her father's property in his will. The father is thus seen to afford his daughter a degree of material independence after his death, which contrasts sharply with his response to her actions during his lifetime. John Beaumont is presented as an irascible and, at times, physically threatening character, but he is not demonized or presented as ungodly. His behaviour towards his daughter cannot be interpreted as stemming from any individual malice, but is offered as the result of the conflicting pressures brought to bear upon him in the collision of different models of authority.

Beaumont tries to gain entry to the house by various means, after spending a night of torment in the barn, but eventually, despite her resolve to 'begg my bread from doore to doore', she succumbs to her father's demand and promises not to attend any more meetings during his lifetime (*Persecution*, p. 38). Beaumont describes her behaviour at this point as 'peeter like' and having been admitted to her father's house is assailed by scriptural texts which reinforce her conviction that by not forsaking her father she has forsaken Christ who will, in turn, deny her before God the father (*Persecution*, p. 38). Her 'terrour and gillt and rendings of Contience' are barely assuaged by her 'poore father' who was then 'very loveing to mee, And bid me gitt him some Supper' (*Persecution*, pp. 42, 43). On the following night her father tells of his anxiety about his daughter's behaviour when first converted in terms which echo other writings on female prophets: Beaumont, it appears, did not eat, drink or sleep, and was assumed by her father to be 'distracted'. The father acknowledges that her conversion had, however, led him to 'Crye to the Lord in Secret' and to 'goe to meetings', but that an 'evill minded man in the towne would set him against the meetings' (*Persecution*, p. 48).[10] Another day passes and while the daughter is still in 'a sorrowfull frame', her father 'did eate as good A dinner as ever I saw him eate' (*Persecution*, p. 50). After supper and 'A pipe of Tobacco' her father retires to a bed which his daughter has warmed with 'Coales'. As she is 'Covering of him' the words 'runn through' her mind: 'The End is Come, The End is Come, the time drayeth neere' (*Persecution*, pp. 51, 52). She is later awoken by her father who complains of 'A paine at my heart' (*Persecution*, p. 54). There follows a detailed account of what appears to be a fatal coronary, as the father finally collapses after retiring to his chamber to 'have A stoole' (*Persecution*, p. 58). Beaumont tries to lift him and in her description of this she refers to the subsequent interpretation by others of a dream mentioned earlier in the text, in which she had tried and failed to lift a fallen apple tree in her father's garden, as 'signifying' this scene. As

Vera J. Camden has suggested, this prophetic dream may bear a trace of wish-fulfilment, acting as a vehicle for the daughter's desire which cannot be reconciled with the law of the father.[11] Her recollection of this dream, and her acceptance of the interpretation of it as prophetic, also act as a counterbalance to her apparent guilt that her father's collapse was occasioned by her neglect of her daughterly duties.

Finally she runs to her brother's house for help, through 'deepe' snow and wearing 'noe Stockins' (*Persecution*, p. 59). When she returns with her brother, their father dies and funeral arrangements are made the next day. Before the funeral can take place, Beaumont is accused of murdering her father on Bunyan's counsel, with 'stuffe' given to her by Bunyan (*Persecution*, p. 72). Her accusor is the aptly named Mr ffeery, a rejected suitor. An inquest is held to determine whether or not there is sufficient evidence to try Agnes Beaumont for petty treason, for which the penalty would be burning at the stake. No evidence can be found and the daughter survives her ordeal not only to attain a secure social position, eventually marrying two husbands in later life, the second called Stor(e)y, but to write her own story. In so doing she begins to chart a different space – a space of writing.

In her writing, Agnes Beaumont is presented as a female character whose actions are seen to threaten the precarious balance of patriarchal power relations within which Bunyan's position of authority and her position of subjection are constructed. Claiming the position of writer, she presents a text which both exposes the tensions and contradictions within such power relations and stands as a contra-diction, a woman's text which tests the limits of textual and discursive strategies of exclusion. By the end of the text both fathers have been effectively silenced; it is the daughter's, the woman's turn.

The text generally conforms to the model of nonconformist spiritual narrative and is offered as evidence of the double action of God upon his subject: subjecting her to 'tryalls and temptations' whilst granting her 'his teaching and comfortable presence' (*Persecution*, p. 3). On the first page God is thus presented as having 'often given me cause to say it was good for me that I have been afflicted' (*Persecution*, p. 3). But the narrative invites conflicting interpretations of the cause of her character's suffering. Although divine judgment is offered as paramount and human interpretation offered as flawed, the text both includes alternative readings of events and their significance, as in Beaumont's dream of the apple tree, and invites the reader to make judgments about Beaumont's situation on the basis of her textual evidence, as the coroner does at the inquest. As Agnes Beaumont, the character, requested that her father's body be 'opened' to reveal the cause of death, so Agnes Beaumont, the writer, presents a version of her self which the reader is invited to examine. The narrative ends with an account of Beaumont's triumphant self-display in the market as she deliberately shows herself in public to those who had spread rumours that 'now I had Confest that I had poysoned my father, and yt i was quite distracted' (*Persecution*, p. 87). The mis-reading of her condition, by those who confuse spiritual abjection or ecstasy with clinical distraction or abnormality, including her father and her neighbours, is countered by the presentation of textual evidence which both contradicts that reading and has contra-dictory effects. At the end of the text God the father ostensibly remains in place as source and guarantee of truth and meaning. The implicit connection between divinity and patriarchy has, however, been inter-rogated and Beaumont's text may be read as a contra-diction within a discursive framework which its author could not evade.

Agnes Beaumont's text was not published until 1760. In editions and criticism of Bunyan's writings, her narrative has been recuperated as a marginal note. In a move which perhaps suggests the recognition in her narrative of a trace of earlier, syntactically and culturally unruly female writing, the editor of one modern edition of her text, confronted with what he termed 'a reckless prodigality of commas', has corrected her 'hopeless' punctuation (*Persecution*, p. vi). The insertion of a hyphen between 'contra' and 'diction' in this essay may also be defined as an example of 'hopeless' punctuation, but as a reader of Agnes Beaumont's text and as writer of this text, that is a definition which I would hope to contra-dict.

Notes

1. Christine Berg and Philippa Berry, '"Spiritual whoredom": an essay on female prophets in the seventeenth century', in F. Barker *et al.* (eds), *1642: Literature and Power in the Seventeenth Century* (Colchester: University of Essex, 1981), pp. 37–53.

2. Margaret Fell, *Womens Speaking Justified, Proved and Allowed of by the Scriptures, All such as speak by the Spirit and Power of the Lord Jesus, and how Women were the first that preached the Tidings of the Resurrection of Jesus, and were sent by Christ's Own Command, before He ascended to the Father. John 20.17* (Los Angeles: The Augustan Reprint Society, 1979). For a thorough analysis of Margaret Fell's involvement in the Quaker movement and of other, more disruptive female figures, see Christine Trevett, *Women and Quakerism in the Seventeenth Century* (York: The Ebor Press, 1991).

3. John Bunyan, *Grace Abounding to the Chief of Sinners* (Oxford: Clarendon Press, 1962), p. 1.

4. John Bunyan, *Christian Behaviour*, in *Miscellaneous Works* (Oxford: Clarendon Press 1987), III, pp. 32, 33.

5. John Bunyan, *A Case of Conscience Resolved*, in *Miscellaneous Works* (Oxford: Clarendon Press, 1989), IV, pp. 295, 297.

6. These entries in the Bedford church records are reproduced in G. B. Harrison's introduction to *The Narrative of the Persecution of Agnes Beaumont in 1674* (London: Constable and Co. Limited, 1930), pp. xi–xii.

7. John Bunyan, *A Relation of My Imprisonment*, in *Grace Abounding*, p. 126; *Conscience Resolved*, p. 326.

8. First published in 1760 with other stories as *An Abstract of the Gracious Dealings of GOD. With several Eminent Christians, their conversions and sufferings. Taken from Authentic Manuscripts, And published, For the comfort and Establishment of Serious Minds, by Samuel James.*

9. Harrison (ed.), *Narrative of the Persecution of Agnes Beaumont*, pp. 15, 16.

10. The 'evill minded man' is Mr Lane, the local vicar who spread the rumours about Beaumont and Bunyan.

11. Vera J. Camden (ed.), *The Narrative of the Persecutions of Agnes Beaumont* (East Lansing: Colleagues Press, 1992), pp. 24–5. Camden's introduction to this most recent edition of Beaumont's text is excellent and the publication of a new edition is to be welcomed. I have, however, chosen not to employ her edition in quoting the text in this essay because of her decision to update the spelling and punctuation.

Seditious Sisterhood: Women Publishers of Opposition Literature at the Restoration

Maureen Bell

One day in April 1664, a woman of about fifty called Elizabeth Calvert was let out of the Gatehouse prison in London. She had been in prison, without trial, for two months. Before her arrest, she had spent at least three months on the run with her maid, Elizabeth Evans, who was never caught. During her imprisonment she was interrogated in connection with a series of 'show trials' of printers and publishers which took place in February. Presumably she refused to give information, since she was not called as a witness. But although the trials were all over by the end of February, she was not released. No charges were made against her and she faced an indefinite period of imprisonment.[1]

During this period in the Gatehouse prison, she petitioned several times for release to look after her elder son, Nathaniel, then in his early twenties and seriously ill. Nathaniel had been in prison too, but was now free on bail, and he may have been suffering from a form of fever contracted during his imprisonment. Elizabeth's husband, Giles, had died the previous summer, probably also as a result of prison fever contracted in Newgate prison. Some of Elizabeth's petitions from prison survive, referring to Nathaniel 'all the tyme of her said imprisonment being dangerously sick', and enclosing a physician's testimony to the seriousness of Nathaniel's condition, to substantiate her appeal for compassionate treatment. She asked to be allowed bail to visit him, describing him as 'the comfort and staffe of her life and age', but her request had no effect. Her last petition from prison shows that her release, when it did come, was too late. Nathaniel was, it says, 'ever since fryday morning dead and is yett unburied and that small livelihood shee hath left is now like to bee lost and your petitioner utterly ruined'. At last, on 8 April, after six months of running, hiding and imprisonment, she was released to bury her son.[2]

The purpose of this paper is first, briefly, to explain why Elizabeth Calvert's fortunes had reached this low point; secondly, to demonstrate that in 1664 a number of women in the book trade found themselves in the same position, hounded by the authorities, with husbands dead, children to support and debts accumulating; and thirdly, to look at their response to a defeat both political and personal, and to suggest why women in particular were important in the survival of the opposition press.

Before 1664

Elizabeth and Giles Calvert had run a bookshop at the sign of the Black Spread Eagle at the west end of St Paul's. For more then twenty years, since 1641, they had been among the leading publishers and sellers of radical Puritan books and pamphlets: they published works by Seekers, Ranters, Quakers, Levellers, Diggers, republicans and continental radicals like Boehme and Niclaes. Their shop was a meeting place for such groups and was used as a forwarding address by participants. Theirs was a flourishing business in the years of the Interregnum, and they worked alongside and in co-operation with other radical publishing families like Thomas and Martha Simmons (Martha was Giles Calvert's sister), Thomas and Anna Brewster, Hannah Allen and her second husband Livewell Chapman and, among the younger generation, the printer Simon Dover and his wife Joan.

For all of them, the restoration of Charles II to the throne was both a blow to their political and religious positions and, obviously enough, a threat to their livelihoods. They did not, however, discontinue the line in publishing which, in the changed political climate of the Restoration, was now regarded by the authorities as 'seditious'. In the years immediately following the Restoration, books upholding republicanism, anti-monarchist pamphlets, and compilations of prophecies designed to point out God's disapproval of the King, continued to circulate. It was not difficult for those concerned with the control of the press to guess who was behind these publications, but preventing their continued publication and circulation proved to be a problem. Throughout 1661 and 1662 a series of warrants was issued naming Giles and Elizabeth Calvert, Thomas Brewster, Hannah Allen, Livewell Chapman, Francis Smith and Elizabeth Evans.[3] Some of the booksellers (the Calverts included) were found and arrested; others (like Chapman and Brewster) fled, only to be arrested later on. But still the offensive and provocative pamphlets were being printed and distributed. For example, in 1661 Giles Calvert was imprisoned for publishing a 'libel' called *Mirabilis annus* ..., one of a series of pamphlets which, in the view of the authorities, was:

a forgery of false and feigned prodigies, prognosticating mischievous events to the King, and instilling into the hearts of subjects a superstitious belief thereof, and a dislike and hatred of His Majesty's person and government, and preparing them to effect a damnable design for his destruction, and the change of government.[4]

Yet despite the arrest of Giles and the flight of the other stationers involved, this offensive pamphlet was immediately reprinted, while Giles was still in prison, and was distributed quickly and widely – by Elizabeth Calvert. She was, of course, arrested eventually; but by that time the damage had been done and the pamphlet had reached its audience.

The difficulty for the controlling authorities – and in particular for Roger L'Estrange, Surveyor of the Press – was that while the culprits were well known and were frequently arrested and questioned, the law as it stood made conviction almost impossible. A new law to control the press, known as the Licensing Act, was brought in the following year, in 1662. Even this proved ineffective. In 1663 Roger L'Estrange published his *Considerations and proposals in order to the regulation of the press* to demonstrate what he saw as the danger of such publications, and to detail the grounds on which, in his view, certain books should be suppressed. His frustration with the inadequacy of the Licensing Act is clear: 'not One Person has been Fin'd, and but one Prosecuted, (as is credibly Affirm'd) since the Late Act, notwithstanding so much Treason and Sedition Printed and disperst since That time'.[5]

L'Estrange knew who was responsible for this 'Treason and Sedition' and in his pamphlet he names the Calverts, Brewsters, Chapmans and Dovers as the chief offenders, labelling them 'The Confederates'. As the official in charge of the regulation of the press, and anxious to rehabilitate his own tarnished reputation as an ardent royalist, L'Estrange undertook a personal crusade to pursue the 'Confederate' printers and publishers, and to put an end to their activities.

By the time that Elizabeth Calvert emerged from prison in 1664 (only a year after the publication of L'Estrange's *Considerations and proposals*), it seemed that L'Estrange's crusade had succeeded. A wave of arrests and a dawn raid of a secret press furnished L'Estrange with enough evidence to mount trials in February 1664. By April, when Elizabeth Calvert was released, not only had her husband died from his imprisonment, but the printer John Twyn had been executed for treason, and in the same month that she was released the printer Simon Dover and the bookseller Thomas Brewster, both convicted on a lesser charge, died in Newgate prison. Hannah Allen and Livewell Chapman went out of business, and a junior 'Confederate', Francis Smith, lost his shop.[6] L'Estrange could fairly have claimed to have smashed the 'Confederate Knot' of printers and publishers once and for all.

The widows

What L'Estrange had perhaps overlooked, however, was that the *women* had survived. None of them, of course, was in a very strong position. Elizabeth Calvert was in sole charge of a business which, formerly prosperous, was now financially insecure. More than a year of intermittent arrests and flight involving herself, Giles, Nathaniel, their maid Elizabeth Evans and their apprentice Matthew Stevenson had proved costly, and she was now in debt. The only other surviving member of the family was her younger son Giles, then about ten years old. The following year was the year of the plague, which emptied London and ruined trade; and in the following year, 1666, her premises and stock were destroyed by the Great Fire. Anna Brewster, the widow of Thomas, was also in debt and had dependent children to support. She eventually appealed to her creditors to accept eight shillings in the pound, explaining that 'She has sustained considerable losses by the long Imprisonment of her late Husband, and otherwise, whereby shee is reduced into a low Condicion'.[7] Joan Dover, whose husband Simon had also died in prison, was a younger woman with a baby son. For all three of these women, it must have been a daunting prospect to discharge debts, support their children, resume trading and rebuild their respective businesses. To continue, moreover, to publish and distribute 'sedition' would add serious risks to lives already precarious. Yet that is precisely what these women did.

The evidence for the women's continued involvement in opposition publishing is patchy. Some information can be gleaned from statements by informers, which in themselves need to be treated with caution; but taken together with notes of interrogations, prison records and other notes preserved in the Public Record Office, a partial reconstruction is possible. It was usual for stationers' widows to remarry within the trade, thereby retaining the privileges, equipment and rights in copies owned by their first husbands.[8] Joan Dover, the younger woman left with a baby son, quickly married another printer, John Darby, and both as 'widow Dover' and as 'wife of Darby' her perseverance in opposition publishing is apparent in the following years. Both Elizabeth Calvert and Anna Brewster, however, remained single, and their names occur in the records for the next ten years in connection with illegal printing and publishing. Elizabeth Calvert seems not only to have rebuilt her bookselling business, finding new premises after the Great Fire and trading in books entirely acceptable to the authorities, but also to have sustained an 'under-the-counter' trade in seditious pamphlets.[9]

Opposition goes underground

At the time of the Restoration, the older women were already well-experienced members of the London book trade. In the first four years of the Restoration, they were forced to develop a new expertise in running clandestine publishing. In the Interregnum years, and indeed throughout their married lives, they had participated in the day-to-day running of the business, taking over sole responsibility during the absences of their husbands. Since the Restoration they had been left in sole charge of bookshops and printing houses during their husbands' frequent spells in prison or on the run. They had acted as their husbands' agents, and had worked for their husbands' release from prison, obtaining legal advice, organizing bail, negotiating loans to cover expenses and repeatedly submitting petitions of appeal. When, by the summer of 1664, L'Estrange had apparently smashed the male 'Confederates', the women were well adapted to the changed circumstances of their particular branch of the book trade. Joan Dover was herself in trouble for seditious printing almost as soon as Simon was dead: 'Widow Dover' appears in a list of printers of Fifth Monarchist and Quaker books supplied by an informer. She was alleged to have printed *The jury-man charged* and *England's warning* as well as books by the Quaker Rebeccah Travers. Joan and her new husband, John Darby, had warrants issued for their arrest in the summer of 1664.[10]

The plague year of 1665 and the Great Fire of 1666 disrupted every aspect of the book trade, centred as it was on the city and in particular the area around St Paul's Cathedral which was devastated by the fire. But in 1668, when L'Estrange began another onslaught on seditious printers, this same group of women was in his sights. He had suspicions that a secret press was at work in London, and surviving documents relating to his investigation show that Joan Darby, Anna Brewster and Elizabeth Calvert were at the heart of the underground trade. In fact there were two secret presses. One was in Blue Anchor Alley and was run by the Darbys, and the other was in Southwark, run by Elizabeth Calvert.[11] L'Estrange questioned the hawkers who were caught selling the illegal pamphlets in the streets, and learnt that they had been supplied by a carpenter in Blue Anchor Alley. The carpenter said that he had got the papers from Anna Brewster. Anna Brewster refused to say who had been her source of supply. Her son admitted that *he* had received papers from Joan Darby, but without an admission from Anna Brewster herself, L'Estrange could not prove the link. His own notes point to the hopelessness of pinning down the women:

I do not heare that Darbys wife has been examind, & beyond doubt she'll confesse nothing, for shee and Brewster, are taken to be a

couple of ye Craftyest & most obstinate ... of ye trade. Ag[ains]t
Darby himselfe, I see nothing as yet. So that only Brewster stands
answerable, & Printing does not concern her.[12]

The women had set up an effective system of pyramid distribution, with
Anna Brewster acting as intermediary between the Darbys who were the
printers and the carpenter who supplied the hawkers. There were
enough links in the chain of distribution for L'Estrange to find it
impossible – provided the women themselves refused to co-operate –
to convict anyone. John Darby was arrested, but as L'Estrange ruefully
admitted, 'Mr. Derby ye Printer is in Custody, but no witness appears
directly ag[ains]t him'.[13] So, while knowing full well how the pyramid
worked, L'Estrange could not assemble enough direct evidence to stop
its operation. It was difficult to prosecute a married woman in any case,
a fact which worked in favour of Joan Darby as the head of the
pyramid.[14] While it might be possible for L'Estrange to implicate her
in the distribution network, there was only the circumstantial evidence
of her marriage to John Darby to suggest that he was the printer of
the pamphlets, and no indictment could be obtained on such circumstantial evidence. As long as Joan Darby refused to talk, her husband
(unless caught red-handed) would be beyond the reach of prosecution
since she was the only link between him and the distributors. John
Darby was released on bail and Anna Brewster, who had been committed to the Gatehouse, was freed.

At the same time as L'Estrange was pursuing the Blue Anchor Alley
press, Elizabeth Calvert's secret press in Southwark was being raided
by the Stationers' Company. The owner of the house where the press
was found, Elizabeth Poole, was arrested, and on the following day a
warrant was issued for the arrest of Elizabeth Calvert. The story of
the Southwark raid is somewhat complicated by the possibility that the
officials of the Stationers' Company who siezed the pamphlets stored
there may have been acting not (as was L'Estrange) to suppress
seditious printing but rather in their own interests, to get their hands
on the 'libels' which they could then sell for themselves.[15] Precisely
what the 'libels' were is not clear, but there is evidence that Elizabeth
Calbert may have been printing political verse satires now attributed
to Andrew Marvell, including his 'Directions to a Painter' and 'Clarendon's Housewarming', which mocked Clarendon's ostentatious new
mansion built partly out of the remains of St Paul's Cathedral.[16]

After 1668 the same women surface sporadically in the records,
sometimes in association with investigations into 'seditious' printing
and publishing. Joan Darby continued in the book trade at least until
1683, and Anna Brewster was associated with opposition publishing for
many years.[17] Ten years after the Blue Anchor Alley press was detected,

Anna Brewster was still being pursued by L'Estrange. She was in hiding in 1678 and was found three months after the warrant for her arrest had been issued. L'Estrange again could not satisfactorily prove her involvement but was convinced that she was responsible for dispersing several 'libels' including *The Letter About the Test*, *Two Speeches of the Duke of Buckingham and Lord Shaftesbury*, *Jenks' Speech*, *The Growth of Popery* and *A List of the Members of Parliament*. The following year, 1679, she was imprisoned with Mary Thompson and two letter office clerks for dispersing another 'seditious' pamphlet, and in 1680 she was associated with Francis Smith, the only one of the male 'Confederates' to survive and eventually rebuild his business.[18]

It is indicative of Elizabeth Calvert's extraordinary persistence that, despite the raid on her Southwark press in 1668, by the autumn of the same year she was again involved in seditious publishing, this time John Wilson's *Nehushtan*, an attack on the Church of England. Wilson's text combines justification of nonconformity with hostility to Catholicism and a blatant attack on the Stuarts through biblical analogy. The implied identification of Ahaz, the wicked father, with Charles I, and the contrast between Ahaz's reforming son Hezekiah and the indolent Charles II, were presumably the features of the pamphlet which drew official action:

An illustrious *example* hereof we have in this place in King *Hezekiah*, who no sooner came to the *Throne*, but he falls upon the work of *Reformation*, with all zeal and diligence. He does not only purge his Royal *Palace*, most lamentably defiled with his Fathers impurities, but he also cleanses the *Nation*, which was in like manner over-spread therewith, abolishes *strange* worship, destroys the *Instruments* and *Monuments* of Idolatry, and roots out whatever he finds contrary to the *Law*.[19]

For publishing this, Elizabeth Calvert was imprisoned in the King's Bench, from where she petitioned for pardon.[20] There are many more examples of her implication in opposition printing and publishing in the 1660s, but she was not successfully brought to trial until 1671. Tried in March of that year, having jumped bail to avoid appearing at the previous Sessions, she was convicted and fined twenty marks. Thomas Palmer, a bookseller tried on the same day, was fined 40 marks and pilloried for his part in dispersing libels. Elizabeth Calvert was probably unable to pay the fine and was committed to Newgate. On her release she was to appear at the next Sessions to answer for her fine, but defaulted; she was then bound over to appear in a year's time, but defaulted again despite being bound to the amount of £100 and with two sureties each of £50.[21] After this she published few works and her accumulated debts, the trial itself, and the renewed persecution of dissenters seem to have combined to prevent her pursuing her 'usual practices'. Nonetheless, she carried on the bookshop and the legal side of her trade, selling less outspoken – but still nonconformist – works, old stock saved from the Fire, and a few popular secular books. In October 1674 she made her will, and died shortly after.[22]

Women's voices?

Why offer this narrative at a conference about voicing women and women's voices? These women's voices cannot speak directly to us, they wrote no books themselves, and except for Elizabeth Calvert none has left surviving notes or letters. True, they published among other things some works *by* women (particularly by women Quakers and Baptists),[23] but for the most part the voices preserved in the texts they took risks to print and circulate are men's voices, voicing opposition to monarchy in general and the Stuarts in particular, to Catholicism, to the Church of England, and to the denial of toleration for nonconformity. When we read these oppositional voices – as, for example, in Marvell's satirical 'Painter' poems – we attend to the male satirical voice, without being aware of the ways in which those who took part in the material production and circulation of such texts attracted greater risks to themselves than did the safely anonymous author.

It is precisely because of the perseverance of these women that L'Estrange's attempt to silence the opposition press in the 1660s did not succeed. There were easier – and legal – ways to make a living for stationers' widows with children to support, and on the deaths of their husbands they could, presumably, have decided to 'go straight' as orthodox stationers' wives carrying on existing businesses in their own right. That they did not make that choice, instead facing repeated harrassment, imprisonment and arrest for at least the next ten years suggests either that the illegal trade was too lucrative to ignore, or that they actually cared about the causes for which, indirectly, their families and livelihoods had been devastated. Perhaps there was a coincidence of economic and political interests. Whatever their reasons, they kept the opposition press going under the most difficult of circumstances, and developed an expertise in frustrating the authorities from which the next generation of opposition stationers could learn. The flourishing of the opposition press is usually seen as a phenomenon of the late 1670s and 1680s and indeed there is a second generation of women booksellers involved then: women like Jane Curtis and Eleanor Smith, Francis Smith's daughter, who were both brought to trial in the 1680s. The strategies and excuses, arguments and evasions used by the women of the 1680s were inherited from the earlier generation, and transmitted by those who, like Joan Darby and Eleanor Smith senior, were at the beginning of their careers in 1664.

Prosecuting women, and especially wives, was difficult under common law, and the women of the early Restoration period not only became familiar with legal loopholes but also knew when their silence could protect themselves and their associates.[24] They recognized, too, the way in which sharing responsibility could provide some protection and frustrate detection. They endured the cat-and-mouse arrests, which very rarely resulted in prosecution, numerous fines, interrogations and indefinite periods of imprisonment as part of the process, and when they were cornered used their legal position as 'innocent, silly women', claiming ignorance, promising not to reoffend – and then doing just that. Not only did they maintain the means of opposition publishing in the earliest years of the Restoration, but they established ways of frustrating the authorities which had become more or less traditional in the trade twenty years later.

I began with 8 April 1664, when Elizabeth Calvert went home to bury her son and to embark on what would prove to be ten years of underground 'seditious' publishing. In the 1990s we are a long distance from that moment: in time, in ideas, in our conceptions of what words like 'woman' and 'censorship' might mean. The temptation to draw false analogies and to sentimentalize history is strong, but must be resisted. Some of the principles – religious toleration, republicanism – which found a voice through these women's work may be noble ideals, but the virulent anti-Catholicism, incitement to hatred (especially of the French) and gloating at physical misfortune which were their favourite tactics should warn us against simple admiration. Nonetheless, after a fourth Conservative general election victory, this seems an appropriate time to honour these women: women who in the midst of not just political and religious defeat, but also bereavement, facing an uncertain future with dependent children and a host of pressing financial and practical problems, opted for persistence rather than paralysis. In printing, publishing and distributing the books and pamphlets officially labelled 'seditious', they refused by their actions to let the voice of opposition be silenced.

Notes

1. For the trials of the printer Twyn (who was executed for treason for printing *A Treatise of the Execution of Justice*, the copy of which he got from Elizabeth Calvert's maid, Elizabeth Evans), and the trials of the other stationers, see T. B. Howell, *A Complete Collection of State Trials*, 34 vols

(1816–28), VI. For a full account of the events leading up to the trials, see Maureen Bell, 'Elizabeth Calvert and the "Confederates"', *Publishing History* 32 (1992), pp. 5–49.

2. Petitions are in the Public Record Office: PRO SP29 / 95:98; SP29 / 96:64.
3. Warrants, interrogations and releases from prison are recorded in Public Record Office, *Calendar of State Papers: Domestic Series* (1856–1972) [hereafter cited as *CSPD*] for the appropriate years. The career of Hannah Allen is dealt with at length in Maureen Bell, 'Hannah Allen and the development of a Puritan publishing business', *Publishing History* 8 (1989), pp. 5–66.
4. Quotation taken from the warrant issued for Elizabeth Calvert's arrest on 4 October 1661, *CSPD* 1661 / 2, p. 106.
5. Roger L'Estrange, *Considerations and proposals in order to the regulation of the press* (London: A. C., 1663), p. 25.
6. See Bell, 'Elizabeth Calvert and the "Confederates"', for a fuller narrative of these events.
7. Stationers' Company, Court Book D, 109v–110, 5 June 1665. Elizabeth Calvert was also in debt to the Stationers' Company. In February 1667 she was ordered to repay £10 within a month, and in July 1670 she was still in debt to the Company: Stationers' Company, Court Book D, 128v (13 February 1667) and 173 (4 July 1670).
8. The privileges accorded to stationers' widows, and their patterns of re-marriage and independent trading, are discussed in Maureen Bell, 'Women in the English book trade 1557–1700', *Leipziger Jahrbuch zur Buchgeschichte* (forthcoming, 1996).
9. Since the conference, I have published a more detailed reconstruction of their activities, '"Her usual practices": the later career of Elizabeth Calvert, 1664–75', *Publishing History* 35 (1994), pp. 5–64.
10. *CSPD* 1663 / 4, p. 577; 1664 / 5, p. 148; 1667 / 8, pp. 360, 361.
11. See Bell, '"Her usual practices"'.
12. PRO SP29 / 239:5, letter from L'Estrange to Secretary of State Williamson, 26 April 1668. For other documents relating to the investigation see *CSPD* 1667 / 8, pp. 282, 294, 318–19, 350, 353–4, 357–8, 378.
13. PRO SP29 / 239:6.
14. On the difficulties of prosecuting married women, legally 'femes coverts', see D. Rosenberg, 'Coverture in criminal law: ancient "defender" of married women', *UCD Law Review* 6 (1973), pp. 83–101, and Sir Matthew Hale, *Historia placitorum coronae* (1736), p. 45.
15. Documents relating to the Southwark press are Stationers' Company Court Book D, 139v (5 May 1668); *CSPD* 1667 / 8, pp. 363, 380, 409; PRO SP29 / 239:93 and 239:156. The possibility of the duplicity of the raiders is discussed in Bell, '"Her usual practices"'.
16. Elizabeth Calvert was indicted for the publication of these satires: City of London Record Office, Sessions File SF205.
17. Joan Darby and her husband were being investigated in September 1683: see *CSPD* 1683 July–Sept., p. 432.
18. *CSPD* 1667 / 8, pp. 360, 378; 1678, pp. 188, 372–3. See also Maureen Bell, 'Elizabeth Calvert and the "Confederates"', pp. 30–1.

19. John Wilson, *Nehushtan: or, A Sober and Peaceable Discourse, Concerning the Abolishing of Things Abused to Superstition and Idolatry* (1668), p. 2.

20. PRO SP29/113:128 (misdated: probably written October 1668, not 1665 as calendared).

21. The progress of her prosecution can be tracked through the Sessions Files and Minute Books in the CLRO, beginning with the indictment (SM 36, G. D., 7 December 1670). I am currently working on a more detailed account of the trial than is offered in '"Her usual practices"'.

22. Samuel Petto's *The Difference Between the Old and New Covenant Stated* (1674) and William Rabisha's *The Whole Body of Cookery Dissected* (1675) both contain lists of books printed for and sold by Elizabeth Calvert (see '"Her usual practices"' for transcripts of the lists). In fact, Elizabeth Calvert may have died before the Rabisha book was finished: she made her will on 19 October 1674, and it was proved on 5 February the following year. For a transcript of the will, see A. E. Terry, 'Giles Calvert, mid-seventeenth century English bookseller and publisher', unpublished Columbia University MSc thesis (1937), pp. 67–8 and Appendix.

23. For example, Hannah Allen published Henry Jessey's account of the fasting Sarah Wight, including much of her reported speech, in *The Exceeding Riches of Grace Advanced by the Spirit of Grace* (1647, 1648); the Quaker women's tithing petition, *These Several Papers was Sent to the Parliament the Twentieth Day of the Fifth Moneth, 1659*, was sold at the Calverts' shop, and Elizabeth Calvert was advertised as selling conversion narratives by women (Sarah Davy's *Heaven realiz'd* [1670], and the anonymous *Conversion exemplified*); and Joan Darby, as noted above, was reputedly the printer of work by the Quaker Rebeccah Travers.

24. See note 14 above; and for discussion of women's exploitation of their legal status as inferior to men, see Bell, 'Elizabeth Calvert and the "Confederates"' and 'Women and the opposition press after the Restoration', in John Lucas (ed.), *Writing and Radicalism* (forthcoming, 1996).

Index